Alastair Sawday's
Special Places to Stay

French

Hotels, Inns
& Other Places

1st Edition

Edited by Susan Luraschi

Typesetting, Conversion & Reprographics:	Avonset, Bath
Maps:	Bartholomew Mapping Service, a division of HarperCollins Publishers, Glasgow
Printing:	Midas Book Printers, UK
Design:	Caroline King & Springboard Design, Bristol
UK Distribution:	Portfolio, London
US Distribution:	The Globe Pequot Press, Guilford, Connecticut

First published in April 2000
Alastair Sawday Publishing Co. Ltd
44 Ambra Vale East, Bristol BS8 4RE, UK.

The Globe Pequot Press
P.O. Box 480
Guilford, Connecticut 06437
USA

First edition 2000

ISBN 1-901970-08-6 in the UK

ISBN 0-7627-0725-9 in the US

Printed in Slovenia

Alastair Sawday's
Special Places to Stay

French Hotels, Inns & Other Places

"All the affection I have for the French is for the whole
nation, and it seems to be a little honey spread over all
the bread I eat in their land."

Mary Wollstonecraft

The
Globe
Pequot
Press

Guilford
Connecticut, USA

Alastair Sawday Publishing
Bristol, UK

Acknowledgements

We flung Susan Luraschi in at the deep end, and - true to her American 'can do' tradition - she swam.

'Deep' because she knew nothing about the work, and dangerously little about us. But she has worked miracles. In the best traditions of struggling writers in garrets, she has been cooped up in a minute office at the top of her building, wrestling with a hostile database, not quite 'looking down the throats of gargoyles' (to quote our description of a Paris hotel) but certainly peering into an oft-unfriendly screen. I apologise to her for failing to deliver the buttressing she needed. But, at least, she has had a delightful young helper, Mathias Fournier, whose calm presence has been balm to her soul.

None of our books on France is yet possible without Ann Cooke-Yarborough. She has achieved wonders of support with the unseen hand of Brendan Flanagan on her shoulder. All hail, too, to all the people mentioned below for so calmly helping to bring the complex bits and pieces together to make the book.

Alastair Sawday

Series Editor:.................... Alastair Sawday
Editor:.............................. Susan Luraschi
Managing Editor:............. Annie Shillito
Production Manager:........ Julia Richardson
Editorial Assistant:........... Russell Wilkinson
Administration:................. Sally George, Kate Harris
Inspections:...................... Douglas Arestegui, Richard & Linda Armspach, Lillian Bell, Alyson & Colin Browne, Sue Capstick, Meredith Dickinson, John Edwards, Valerie Foix, Georgina Gabriel, Michèle Goëmon, Diana Harris, Ursula Kotthaus-Gissinger, Carol Lenthal, Jo-Bell Moore, Johanna Morris, Amanda & Louis Peck, Caroline Portway, Eve Puddy, Elizabeth Yates
Additional Writing:........... Jo Boissevain, Gina Boughton, Lindsay Butler, Ann Cooke-Yarborough, Sue Dammann, Brendan Flanagan
Accounts:......................... Sheila Clifton, Sandra Hasell, Maureen Humphries, Jenny Purdy
Cover Design:................... Caroline King

And our essential support team in Bristol: Jackie King and the staff of Alastair Sawday's Tours.

Introduction

Are you one of those who, catatonic with tiredness, will surreptitiously pull off an autoroute and slip wordlessly into a banal chain hotel? You are a bit embarrassed, of course, aware that you might bump into some friends from home doing the same. Or you may be one of those who are nervous of having your French tested out round the dinner table in a very intimate little *chambre d'hôtes*. (Not surprising if, like me, you are prone to such errors as: "Ah, Madame, quel plaisir de boire du vin sans préservatif!")

This book is for you! Many who have enjoyed using our French B&B book have said that, much as they relish being 'at home' with the French, it is occasionally a relief to collapse into a hotel bed and come down to dinner without having to speak to anyone. Here, then are some of the nicest and most beguiling hotels and other places to sleep in France. You now have no excuse for popping into those out-of-town sleeping centres that litter France. If you are the sort of person who likes to support your village shop at home you can now support that local French hotel too.

The places in this new book, by no means all hotels, are not, however, as anonymous as you may fear. They are owned by some remarkable characters, often passionate about what they do and about the area in which they live. You will be hard-pressed to find that tired old French cynicism. Ugliness and appalling taste are, too, rare within these pages - though we occasionally let a glimpse of them through when there is a special reason for doing so, such as a stunning view or irresistible owners.

We hope we have not been dull. There is a railway station with an old Pullman train in here; there are castles, ancient dwellings of rare beauty, a few eccentricities. There will be people who become your friends for life, others who are irresistible caricatures. Your love for France will be reinforced and deepened, and perhaps you will even come to value the cantankerousness of the French on the international political stage. The mixture is, I hope, what makes our books so special. If you don't have fun in France with this book then hats will be eaten!

Alastair Sawday

Introduction

Who is this book for?

It is for the butcher, the baker, the candlestick-maker, but not for the 'consumer', the mini-bar seeker, the palate-destroyer. It is for those who appreciate the non-conformist efforts of our owners who have refused to yield to pressures from all sides and who have followed their own passions.

It is for anyone who wants to dip in and out of a whole gamut of interesting places to stay in France. You may be someone who usually books unpretentious family-run inns but who likes the occasional 'splurge' in a Loire château or a smart Provençal hotel. Or, you may be tired of large chain hotels and be yearning for something more characterful, less formal.

We just hope that you won't 'do' 10 places in 10 days. Stay a few days at least and get under the skin of the place.

Is this book different?

Other Places

The Other Places are diverse and individual and range from manor houses to châteaux, from farmhouses to an entire village. Some of them are private homes. Many of their owners were reticent about joining because they are not set up to provide the same services as a fully-fledged hotel, and fear the arrival of guests with grand hotel expectations. We told them that our readers know the difference. So please read the descriptions carefully and pick out the places comfortable for you. These Other Places offer a real insight into things French - the owners love sharing their knowledge of their regions - and are definitely special.

Hotels

We have always admired the variety, professionalism and value of French hotels. Some of our favourites here have been in the same families for years, with the younger generation now coming on board with new skills and ideas; many have made monumental efforts to restore their beautiful buildings and to create the kind of hotel we look for, with character and a genuinely personal touch. More and more are offering 'extras' such as vineyard tours, guides to walking paths, ballooning, musical evenings, visits to the landing beaches, cookery and wine tasting courses. Ask them, well in advance, to organise a mushroom hunt or a morning at the market and they will make every effort to help. There are treasures in these pages.

Inns

Nothing is better, after a grim journey, than to open the door of one of our *Auberges* (Inns) and be greeted by the smell of freshly-baked bread, the tinkle of knife against plate and to join the bustle of other diners. Food is the object here and sometimes the rooms take second place. We have not judged these rooms using the same criteria we use for hotels with restaurants but they will always be good value, clean and comfortable.

How we choose our special places

At times we have overlooked the plain bedroom for a breathtaking spot; or the lack of a restaurant because of particularly caring owners. However, there's hardly a place in the book where dinner can't be had within a few minutes walk or a five minute drive. Whatever the price, these places are marvellous value: there are more than 190 where you can book a double room for under £60, and half of them provide a great meal for around £10.

Whatever the caveats, all the places in this book are here because WE LIKE THEM. We hope you will quickly learn to read between our lines and pick up the subtleties of 'Sawday-speak'. If, for example, we love the people but find the décor odd, we try to avoid describing the latter!

If you are unhappy about anything, be it the welcome, the room, the bathroom or the food, I do urge you to talk first to the manager or owner. They need your feedback. We do too; your comments - both good and bad - are the lifeblood of our books.

One last, but important, point: owners pay a fee to help us cover the heavy production costs of a full-colour book. But payment is a fee, not a bribe! Once we include the wrong people and places for the wrong reasons, we will cease to be special.

How to use this book

Finding the houses

The ENTRY NUMBER is at the bottom of each entry; we use it in the indexes and on the maps. Please use it when writing to us, with the edition number.

Each entry also has the 1/200,000 Michelin Regional Map reference as 'MMap' followed by the relevant map and fold numbers, e.g. 'MMap 245-31' is Regional Map No 245, fold No 31.

Our maps

Our maps are to give you a rough idea of where these places are and must be used in tandem with a good road map such as the Michelin Atlas (with its invaluable index of place names at the back).

Directions

Apart from motorway exits, our directions take you to each place from one direction only. They have been checked by the owners but you may

Introduction

occasionally find that '3 kilometres' turns out to be '5 kilometres'. It's worth going the extra distance before turning around. We give cardinal indications - N S E W - where appropriate and name the French roads with the letters they carry on French maps and road signs:

A = Autoroute. Toll motorways with junctions that usually have the same name/number on both sides.

N = Route Nationale. The old trunk roads that are still fast, don't charge tolls, but often go through towns.

D = Route Départementale. Smaller country roads with relatively little traffic, except the locals who may surprise you with their speed.

1 mile = 1.6 km (Tip for the mathematically challenged: take the kms, divide by 8 and multiply by 5. Hey presto, you've got miles.)

Ask for a brochure when booking ahead - they usually include maps. Even better, ask them to send you their map (*plan d'accès*). Or, you can have it faxed to the place you're staying before your visit. If our directions are poor, please tell us; you may save people a big row over map-reading!

Rooms

In general our range of prices is for a room for two, the lowest price being the bottom of the slow season to the highest at the height of demand (High season is winter for the Alps, summer for the Riviera.)

The abbreviation 'p.p.' means 'per person'.

You may assume that single rooms cost less than doubles, if they exist. A discount may be given for a single person in a double room; ask.

In Europe, a double means 1 room with 1 double bed, a twin room means 1 room with 2 single beds. Some hotels now have rooms with Velcro beds that magically become one or the other so this problem is avoided.

Half-board (*demi-pension*) includes breakfast and dinner. Full-board (*pension complète*) includes all three meals. Prices given are generally per person and include the room. Some would prickle at the idea of being locked into this formula, perhaps with memories of deadly dining rooms filled with holidaymakers and puréed vegetable soup night after night. You really wouldn't want to miss out on the food at one of our half-board places. Do ask about reduced rates when booking longer stays.

Our full board places are rare birds, mostly in secluded areas where the alternative might be a long drive to a mediocre meal. Why traipse around a tourist-filled Annecy when you could relax, gaze at the lake from the dining terrace and quietly retire to your room after dinner?

Menus

The expression *prix fixe* (one price) has gone out of fashion, perhaps because of its blue-collar origins. Those three (or even four) course meals are now referred to as 'menus'. Don't turn your nose up at the limited menus; they usually offer the best local ingredients, straight from that morning's market, prepared with the greatest care. Many of our places provide childrens' menus, too.

Dinner with your host - Table d'hôtes

Another treat is the home cooking in the many small places in this book - from sublime dining with delicate porcelain, starched cloths, moulded 18th-century ceilings and elegant conversation to a simple farmhouse meal at a wooden table with most of the produce being plucked, shucked or skinned that morning. Why not try both?

How to call

Our telephone numbers give the ten-digit number every French subscriber now has, e.g. (0)1 23 45 67 89

- when dialling **from inside** France dial all ten digits including the bracketed zero, i.e. 01 23 45 67 89;

- when dialling France **from outside** the country, use your international access code then the country code for France - 33 - followed by the last 9 digits omitting the bracketed zero i.e. 00 33 1 23 45 67 89;

- to telephone Great Britain (and USA) from France dial, 00 44 (00 1 for USA) and the number without its initial zero.

- numbers beginning (0)6 are mobile phones and will cost you accordingly.

- To be connected with an English-speaking operator in the USA dial: 0800990011 for AT&T; 0800990087 for Sprint; 0800990019 for MCI.

Children

We do not use the child-friendly symbol in this book as most of our places welcome them. However, our descriptions usually let you know if the place is really only suitable for older, well-behaved children.

Closed

When given in months, this means the whole of both months. The closed dates for hotel and restaurant are not necessarily the same.

Introduction

Prices

We give Euro equivalents for room prices as the French Franc will disappear by July 2002, and will become rarer as that date approaches.

Tips for travel in France

Reservations and deposits

It is essential to book ahead in the high season and always adviseable. It is not necessary to use the owner/manager's names given when making your booking. Most places require a credit card number or a personal cheque to confirm a reservation. The personal cheque will be returned to you on arrival. If you are arriving late, a polite phone call is necessary if you want your room to be kept for you. Many places will not hold a room after 5 pm unless they have been warned of a late arrival.

Plumbing and bathrooms

US plumbing is still magnificent compared to much of ours. Europeans have grown up with smaller spaces, exposed pipes and other oddities. If you are wary of such things, then go for the places which are obviously modernised and probably more expensive. Most baths will have a shower attachment but not necessarily a curtain. We indicate those few places where toilets and/or bathrooms are shared with other guests.

Telephones

Experienced travellers know that using hotel phones can be prohibitively expensive except for local calls. The easiest way to make calls is to buy a pre-paid phone card (*télécarte*), available from tobacco counters, post offices, train stations, airports and hypermarkets. (50 or 100 Frs). There are plenty of phone boxes, even in the countryside.

Post offices

Post offices are open from 8am to 7pm and from 8am to midday on Saturdays. *La Poste* is well signposted. Here you can cash or send international postal cheques and money orders. Some also have fax and coin and card-operated telephone services. In the larger cities, most have exchange facilities and they give good rates with no commission.

Tourist offices

The Tourist offices (*Syndicat d'Initiatives*) will tell you about the three-day antique fair the next day, or the string quartet performing that night. Local volunteers may provide interesting, inexpensive outings. Most offices have English speakers. (Opening hours vary).

Introduction

Electrical Appliances

There is usually a hair dryer in your bathroom or at reception. You need a
plug adaptor for the 220-volt 50-cycle AC current. Americans also need a
voltage transformer (heavy and expensive). This goes for computers as well,
unless they have been manufactured with bi-voltage capabilities.

Money - How to pay

We have marked the few places which do not accept credit cards. There is a
hefty charge for cashing a cheque, be it personal, Travellers or Eurocheque,
so owners are not keen on them. It is easy today to withdraw foreign
currencies from an ATM machine. Virtually all ATMs in France take Visa
and Mastercard and some are linked to Cirrus and to Plus systems. This
method has the added bonus of better exchange rates than banks. France
is by far the best-equipped European country for ATMs. American Express
and Diner's credit cards are not as welcome as others and may be refused
(except at the most expensive places) as they involve higher commissions.

Taxe de Séjour

This is a small tax that local councils (mostly on the seaside) are allowed
to levy on all visitors paying for accommodation. Some councils do, some
don't. So you may find your bill increased by 4, 5 or 9 Francs per head
and per day. Owners don't like this at all, but their hands are tied.

Tipping

Almost all restaurants include tax and a 15% percent service charge; the
words *service compris* indicate this on this bill. If a meal or service has been
particularly good, leaving another 10-20 Frs is customary as is
leaving the small change from your bill if you paid in cash.

At larger hotels 10 Frs for a piece of luggage taken to your room is normal,
as is 5-10 Frs a day for the chambermaid.

Taxis traditionally receive 10 to 15% of the metered fare. There will be an
additional charge for each piece of luggage and a pick-up at train stations.

The Net

We now have over 600 *Special Places* from Britain, France, Ireland, Spain,
Portugal and Italy on our site, constantly being updated and expanded.
There is also a section covering our walking tours. We hope you will visit
and send your comments.

Our email: **specialplaces@sawdays.co.uk**

Our website: **www.sawdays.co.uk**

Symbols

Treat each one as a guide rather than a statement of fact:

 Pets welcome. There may be a supplement to pay. Discuss when booking.

 Vegetarians catered for with advance warning.

 Indicates basic ground-floor access for people of limited mobility and at least one bedroom accessible without steps, but not full facilities for wheelchair-bound guests.

 Indicates full and approved wheelchair facilities in at least one bedrooms and access to all ground-floor common areas.

 Swimming is possible on the premises or nearby in a public pool, lake, river or the sea. Please check the Quick Reference index at the back of the book for a complete listing of places with private pools.

A tennis court is available for guests on, or near, the premises.

You can either borrow or hire bikes here.

This establishment has pets of its own: dog, cat, duck, parrot.

Air conditioning in bedrooms and/or restaurant or both.

Parking on premises or in a public car park. Most of these are secure.

Only cash or cheques accepted, no credit or debit cards.

An evening meal is available. Some of the smaller places need advance booking.

Lift installed. It may stop short of the top floor or start on the first floor.

Disclaimer

We make no claims to pure objectivity in judging our *special places to stay*. They are here because we like them. Our opinions and tastes are ours alone and this book is a statement of them; we cross our fingers and hope that you will share them.

We have done our utmost to get our facts right but apologise unreservedly for any mistakes that may have crept in. Sometimes, too, prices shift, usually upward, and 'things' change. We would be grateful to be told of any errors or changes, however small.

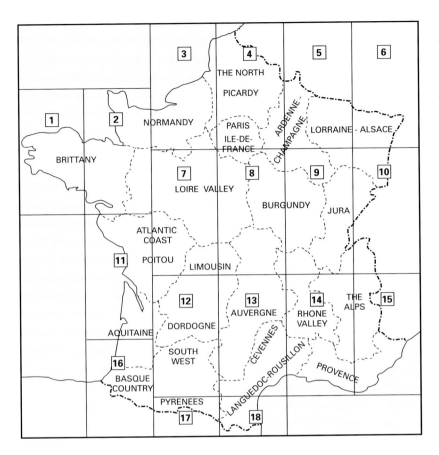

General Map

Contents

Contents

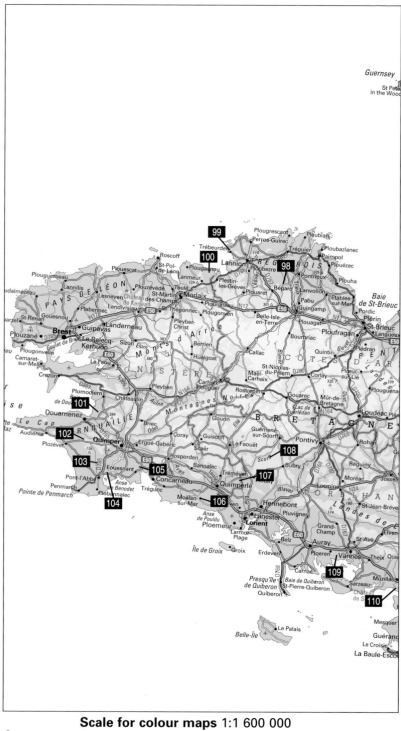

Scale for colour maps 1:1 600 000
(1cm:16km or 1 inch:25.25 miles)

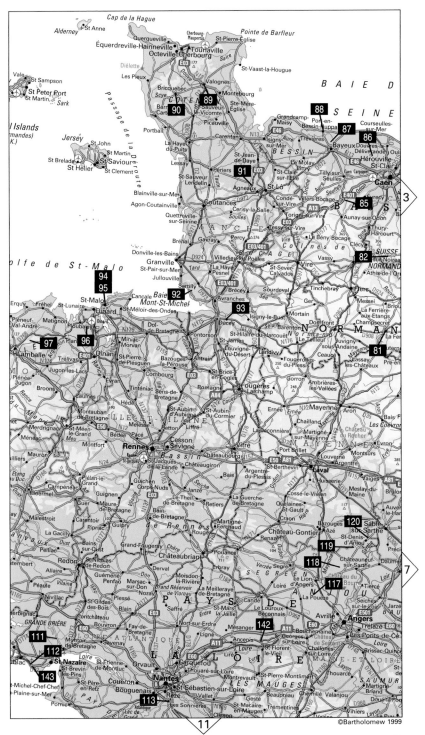

©Bartholomew 1999

2

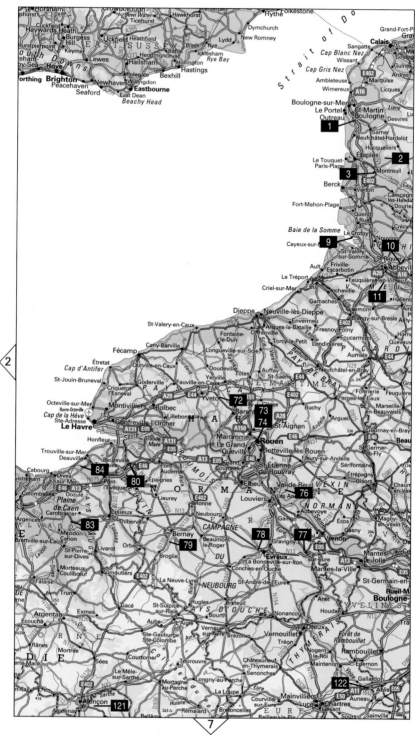

3

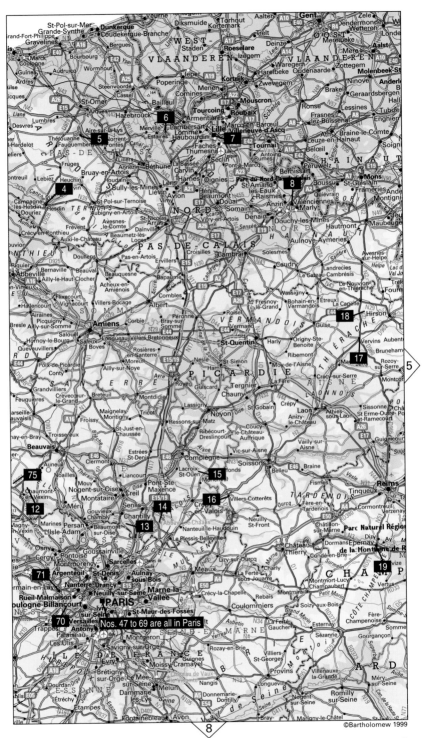

4

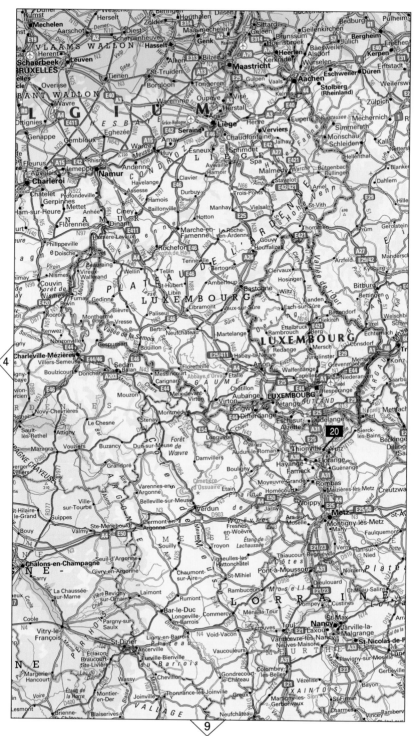

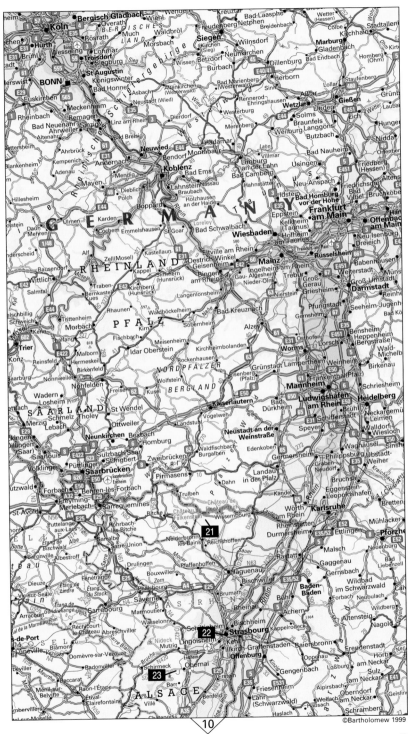

6

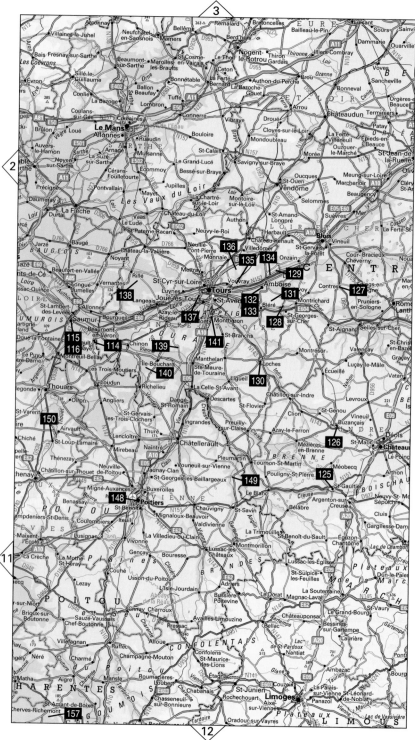

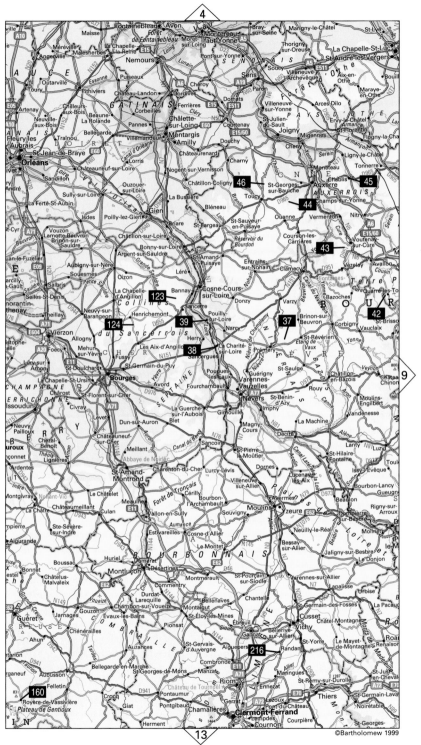

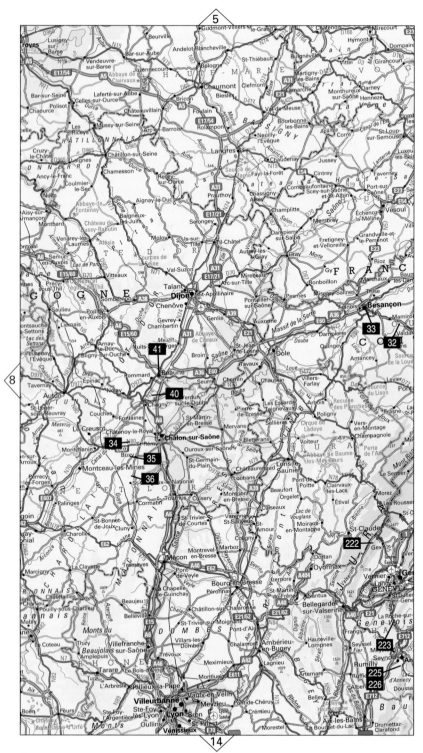

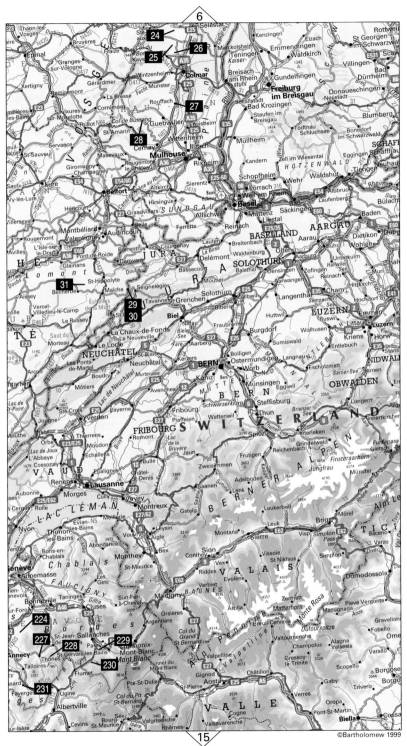

©Bartholomew 1999

10

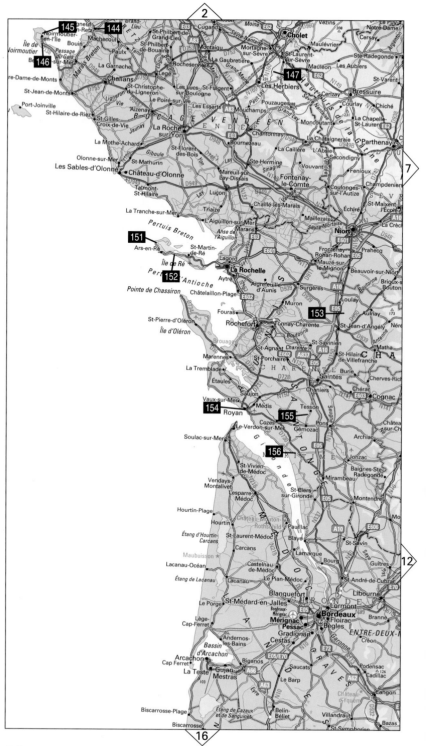

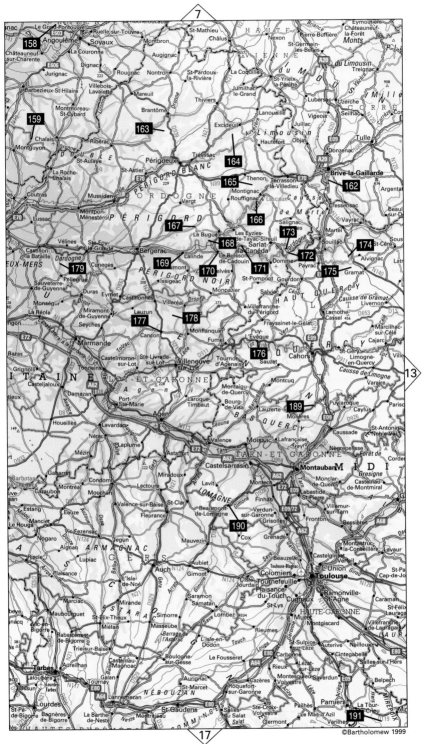

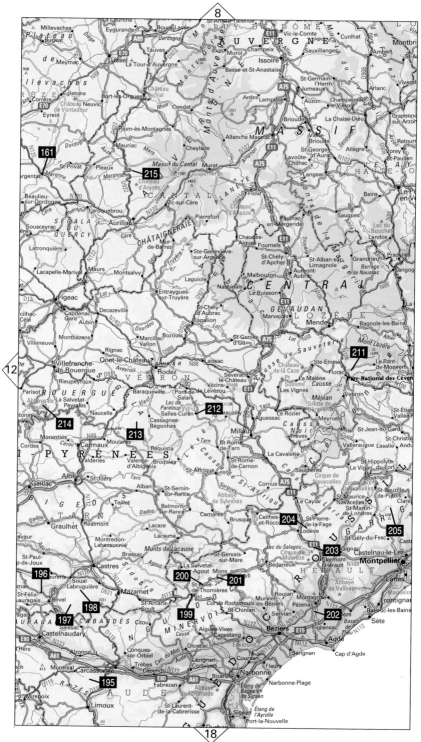

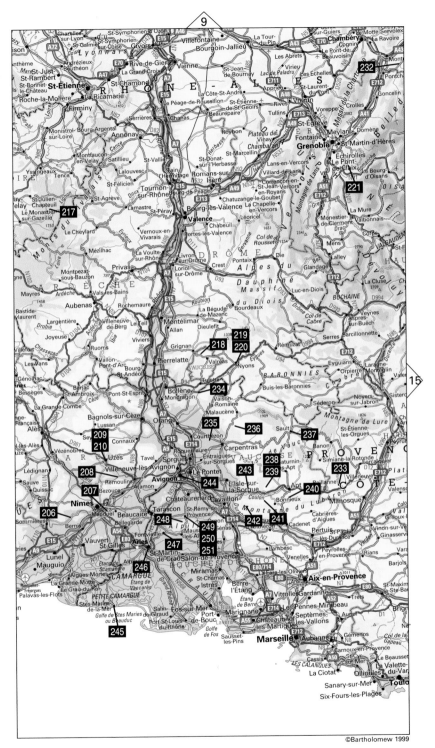

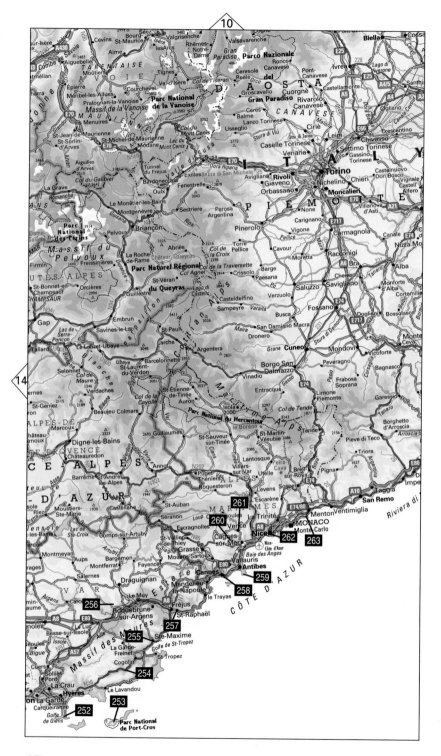

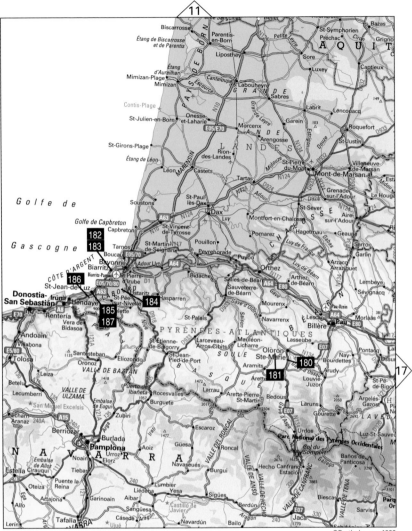

©Bartholomew 1999

16

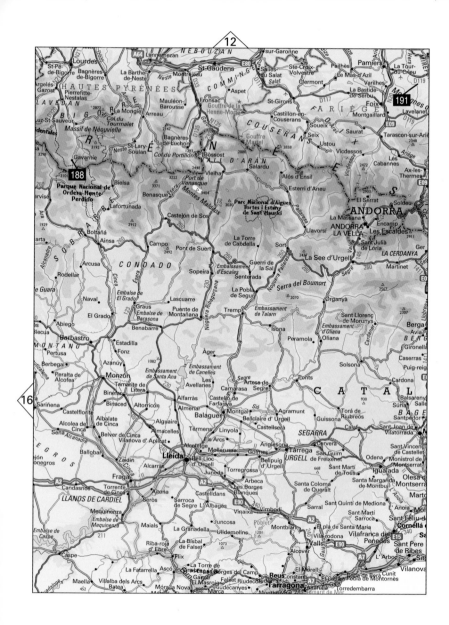

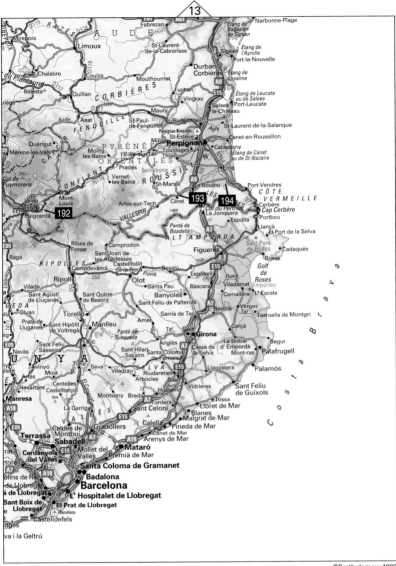

©Bartholomew 1999

18

The North
Picardy
The Ardennes
Champagne

CDT Aube, P. Praliaud

It is a strange, mongrel, merry place
this town of Boulogne.
W M Thackeray

Hôtel Cléry

Château d'Hesdin l'Abbé
62360 Hesdin l'Abbé
Pas-de-Calais

Tel: (0)3 21 83 19 83
Fax: (0)3 21 87 52 59

M Lard

What is it that brings a sense of peace and tranquility to a place? Even the guests seemed to have been touched by it. It must be the low-keyed attentiveness of the owner and his staff, plus the five-hectare garden. It has wonderfully ancient trees. There are great swathes of green, too, and the kitchen garden is encircled with flowers and rows of boxwood. The two sitting rooms have moulded ceilings and are places to read or dream in. The intricate swirls of a delicate wrought-iron balustrade draw you up the stairs to an afternoon siesta. Your room might be mansard-roofed with a bay window overlooking the park. Or a luxury suite in the 'cottage' on the ground floor. Both are clothed in Monet pastels and have good bathrooms. Less expensive rooms come with a shower. After your walk around the park or a game of tennis, aperitifs are taken in front of a fire in the evening. A small restaurant, mostly for guests, is open every weeknight. It is very formal, very 'floral' — the sort of place where diners speak in hushed voices — but that's part of the fun. All this awaits you only 35 minutes from Calais.

Rooms: 22 including 9 junior suites.
Price: Doubles 330-650 Frs
(€ 50.31-99.09); suites 620-850 Frs.
Extra bed 100 Frs.
Breakfast: 60 Frs.
Meals: Dinner 145-265 Frs.
Closed: Mid-December-end January.
Restaurant closed Sunday evenings.

A16 exit 28 dir. Samer. Between Samer and Boulogne N1 to Hesdin l'Abbé. In Hesdin l'Abbé left at traffic lights. Hotel 200m on right. Signposted.

Auberge d'Inxent

Vallée de la Course
62170 Inxent
Pas-de-Calais

Tel: (0)3 21 90 71 19
Fax: (0)3 21 86 31 67

Laurence & Jean-Marc Six

And, the lucky winner is... believe it or not, some people who collect bottle caps do win prizes. As *sommelier* in a large restaurant in Lille, Jean Marc won the Perrier financial aid prize on the luck of a draw. Off he tripped with his young wife and two children to a most emerald green valley and claimed a whitewashed, geranium-boxed dream of an 18th-century country inn. Order a trout on their vine-covered terrace and back comes a live one in a bucket from their superb trout farm across the road on the banks of the river Course. Needless to say Jean Marc's exceptional, reasonably priced wine list and creative use of local produce should lead to a prolonged stay. Inside all is wood beams askew, low ceilings, a battery of copper pans behind the original zinc countertop, red-checked tablecloths and the warmth and cosiness of a country kitchen with burning fireplaces on chilly days. The beamed-ceiling bedrooms have been recently furnished with cherry wood copies of antiques and the walls papered to look ragged. Some of the nicest people win the nicest prizes.

Rooms: 6 doubles.
Price: 295-370 Frs (€ 44.97-56.41).
Breakfast: 40 Frs.
Meals: Lunch & dinner 85-225 Frs.
Closed: December 20-January 20.

From Montreuil sur Mer N1 dir. Boulogne for approx. 4km; right on D127 dir. Inxent, Vallée de la Course. Signposted.

Hôtel de France

Rue Petit Coquempot
62170 Montreuil sur Mer
Pas-de-Calais

Tel: (0)3 21 06 05 36
Fax: (0)3 21 06 05 36
E-mail: janie@janie-hoteldefrance.com
web: www.janie-hoteldefrance.com

Janie & Patrick Harpur

Once you're through the archway and into the magical 9th-century courtyard, the entrance to the hotel disappears behind a multi-colored canopy of flower baskets. The yellow-ragged walls of the reception area hold court to antique velvet chairs, a collection of memorabilia on the mantlepiece and a convivial horseshoe bar. You will be among honoured guests; here Victor Hugo wrote part of *Les Misérables*, here slept, apparently, kings of England and France as well as General Haig and Lawrence Stern. Janie, also a frequent guest, gradually fell under the spell of the place and convinced the aging owner that she could do a more dynamic job of it. It was rebuilt in the 14th and 16th centuries as a religious centre, the corridors are slightly tilted with time. Bright yellow doors lead to simply furnished spaces with antique beds and *armoires*. A surprisingly large and airy breakfast room sometimes doubles as a stage for a band and a party. Telephones and TVs would only distract from the atmosphere. There are fine restaurants to be found within the ramparts of Montreuil sur Mer. *Check bathroom arrangements when booking.*

Rooms: 14: 3 doubles; 10 doubles/twins; 1 family suite with 2 doubles & 1 single.
Price: 350-600 Frs (€ 53.36-91.47).
Breakfast: 45 Frs.
Meals: Separate restaurant in courtyard also serving crêpes & snacks in season.
Closed: January-end March

From A16 exit 26 dir. Montreuil for 4km. Continue through central square straight ahead. Up a steep hill to the right. First right. Parking behind hotel.

Les Trois Fontaines

16 rue d'Abbeville
62140 Marconne Hesdin
Pas-de-Calais

Tel: (0)3 21 86 81 65
Fax: (0)3 21 86 33 34

Arnaud Descamps

Here is a long, low, plain modern building dressed up to look like a typical French inn — and succeeding. With its half-length nets and flower boxes, it fits into the little market town (wonderful market on Thursday mornings) as if it had always been there and the pavement tables are well used by locals. So, of course, is the restaurant. Arnaud Descamps is friendly and anxious to please. He took over in 1999 and is concentrating on the quality of the food he serves in his panelled, chequer-floored dining room: menus change every day and there's a special one for children. Bedrooms are in a separate building overlooking the very fine garden. This building has its own pleasant lobby and a long terrace that runs in front of the French windows: each room has its own table and chairs for summer breakfasts. The rooms are in traditional French style with quiet wallpapers and candlewick bedcovers. It is, indeed, a very typical small French hotel; it's quiet, good value and well placed for cross-Channel vistors and the great beaches of Le Touquet and Berck.

Rooms: 10 doubles/twins.
Price: 300-350 Frs (€ 45.73-53.36).
Breakfast: 40 Frs.
Meals: Lunch & dinner 95-180 Frs. Picnic lunch available.
Closed: Never.

From Calais dir. Arras. After Montreuil N39 dir. Hesdin. Follow signs to Marconne centre. Hotel opposite Mairie.

4

ASP Map No: 4

Hostellerie Trois Mousquetaires

Château du Fort de la Redoute
62120 Aire sur la Lys
Pas-de-Calais

Tel: (0)3 21 39 01 11
Fax: (0)3 21 39 50 10

Philippe Venet

The ghost of d'Artagnan lingers here. The little town of Air de Lys has a former barrack room built in 1600 which was once run by the fourth musketeer; an incredibly delicate example of the Flemish Renaissance style. Things have not changed that much either in this 19th-century château built upon the ruins of a Vauban fort. Sitting rooms with open fires, high backed blue velvet chairs, wooden cabinets, bedrooms with half (*demi-lune*) and full canopies, slightly frozen in time with flowery bedspreads and curtains. The building is in the middle of a well groomed 3 hectare garden, the weeping willow and ornamental trees reflecting side by side with the ducks and swans. Have a game of *pétanque* or a go on the putting green. Jolly Monsieur Venet has created a bit of a sensation by opening up his sparkling kitchen so now it can be seen from parts of the dining room; something rarely done in France. He is rightly proud of his staff and of his creative menus, too. More modern rooms (and fitness facilites) in the annexe attached to the hotel. A good address between the Artois hills and the Flander plains.

Rooms: 33: 2 suites, 8 twins & 20 doubles in château; 2 doubles & 1 triple in annexe.
Price: Doubles 285-620 Frs (€ 43.45-94.52); suites 880 Frs. Extra bed 100 Frs.
Breakfast: 58 Frs.
Meals: Dinner 120-350 Frs.
Closed: Mid-December-mid-January.

From Calais A36 exit 4 Thérouanne to Aire sur la Lys.

Station Bac Saint-Maur

77 rue de la Gare
62840 Sailly sur la Lys
Pas-de-Calais

Tel: (0)3 21 02 68 20
Fax: (0)3 21 02 74 37
E-mail: chefdegare@wanadoo.fr

Vincent & Valérie Laruelle

Vincent, *Chef de Gare*, and his young crew of conductors man this 1921 bistro-converted red-bricked train station filled with vintage suitcases and trunks spewing ancient tourist brochures. There are miniature tin trains, a wind-up wooden telephone, hand-held lanterns, sepia etchings on the walls, antique wall clocks and a paraphernalia of reminders of the golden era of train travel. You may dine in the station and then retire to your rooms in the carriage of an authentic 'PLM' that travelled the Paris, Lyon, Mediterranean lines. Let Valérie know in advance and you will be served in the elegant restaurant compartment with its warm mahogany walls inlaid with mother of pearl. Retire to your 1st class *couchettes* and to dreams of the Orient Express. As if on cue, a real train passes by every now and again adding its clanking to the authenticity. A full playground just outside, a children's menu, antique high-chairs and Socrates the parrot make this a super place for kids. The next day take a tour along the Lys aboard a barge; the lock is only 400 metres from the station.

Rooms: 6 pullman compartments with 2 singles each.
Price: 180-360 Frs (€ 27.44-54.88).
Breakfast: 40 Frs.
Meals: Lunch & dinner 50-95 Frs. Served in train 180-330 Frs.
Closed: January 2-16.

From A25, exit 9 dir. Erquinghem, then Sailly sur la Lys. At Bac St Maur, take second left immediately after Havet factory. 20 mins from Lille.

Hôtel Brueghel

5 Parvis Saint Maurice
59000 Lille
Nord

Tel: (0)3 20 06 06 69
Fax: (0)3 20 63 25 27

Danièle Lhernie

A quick stroll from the train station along lively pedestrian streets, keeping your eye out for the spires of the Saint Maurice church, will get you there in no time. How Danièle Lhernie achieves such a homely feel in such a big city hotel is a bit of a mystery. But you feel it as soon as you walk in the door. Could it be the restored 19th-century elevator with its clanking wrought-iron doors, the warm wooden panelling of the reception desk or the cheery young staff? The Flemish grandmother in one painting is no relation but all the other objects in the lobby and breakfast rooms belong to Daniele; she confesses her obsession with, and joy in, haunting the many local antique markets. There is even an annual three-day orgy when all of Lille empty their attics and survive on chips and beer. The rooms are small and tastefully done; antique rattan chairs, 'distressed' desks, splashes of sea-blue in the bathrooms. Try 204, a pale yellow wall and a view of the church. If you come by car, public parking is no problem but call ahead to avoid getting lost in the one-way streets.

Rooms: 66: 62 doubles & 4 apartments.
Price: Doubles 385-570 Frs
(€ 58.69-86.9); apartments 480-570 Frs.
Breakfast: 40 Frs.
Meals: Many fine restaurants in town.
Closed: Never.

In centre of town on pedestrian street. Best to call for directions to city car park.

Auberge du Bon Fermier

64-66 rue de Famars
59300 Valenciennes
Nord

Tel: (0)3 27 46 68 25
Fax: (0)3 27 33 75 01

M Beine

Forget your high heels, for the cobblestones in the flowered courtyard penetrate into the bar, reception and restaurant of this 16th-century *auberge*. It is a maze of passageways, burnished beams and tiny staircases. A bright copper-bellied *lavabo* greets you at the top of the stairs leading to the rooms. Looking down from a glassed-in corridor, you can almost hear the clatter of hooves arriving in the courtyard, now a quiet terrace for afternoon tea and snacks. The rooms are delightful, one with tapestried curtains and walls, another with red bricks and wooden struts, all with baths and bathrobes. There are also two larger, lighter ground-floor rooms with post-modern lamps and tables. Downstairs a suit of armour guards a wooden reception dais and comes to life in the evenings when the main restaurant is lit only by candles. The passengers jostling between Paris and Brussels were probably delighted to have been delayed in this cosy staging inn. Monsieur Beine, who also runs the wine shop up the street, takes enormous trouble to create new menus with his chef.

Rooms: 16 doubles/twins.
Price: 480-850 Frs (€ 73.18-129.58).
Breakfast: 45 Frs.
Meals: Lunch & dinner 128-285 Frs.
Closed: Never.

From Cambrai A2 dir. Brussels, exit Valenciennes Centre. Do not get off the autoroute before. Keep heading for Valenciennes Centre. Signposted.

Les Tourelles

2-5 rue Pierre Guerlain
80550 Le Crotoy
Somme

Tel: (0)3 22 27 16 33
Fax: (0)3 22 27 11 45

Dominique & Gilles Ferrerra da Silva

This bizarre 1850's structure was faithfully refurbished in 1994 by a group of young Belgian couples besotted with the view overlooking the vast Bay of the Somme. The white crenellated flourishes are set off by a warm lobster blush topped with a widow's walk and two turrets with pointy blue hats (rooms inside). The sitting room, like the rest of the hotel and staff, has such a welcoming feel (games piled in the corner, tables for writing, real armchairs, seven different teas at the bar) that even a day of two of drizzle won't matter. A deceptively simple blue and white marine scheme has been used throughout. The rooms are pristine; crisp white bedspreads and blue trim. The glassed-in dining room is presided over by a large papier mâché shark hanging from the ceiling and there may be an exhibition of lively artwork on the walls. Children under 14 can sleep in the bunk-bedded, snappy sailor's room with a below-decks feel. An early dinner for the young ones is served, then it's off to the enclosed back garden, or a huge sand playing area across from the hotel porch where deck chairs wait in the dusk.

Rooms: 23: 15 en suite, 8 with sink, sharing baths & wc & dormitory for children age 5-12 (12 bunkbeds).
Price: 215-330 Frs (€ 32.78-50.31).
Breakfast: 35 Frs.
Meals: Lunch & dinner 120-160 Frs.
Closed: 3-4 weeks in January.

From Calais, A16 dir. Paris exit Baie de Somme/Le Crotoy/St Valéry on D940 to Le Crotoy. Just outside village of Le Crotoy on a bluff overlooking the bay.

Hôtel Jean de Bruges

18 place de l'Eglise
80135 Saint Riquier
Somme

Tel: (0)3 22 28 30 30
Fax: (0)3 22 28 00 69
E-mail: jeandebruges@wanadoo.fr
web: www.somme-tourisme.com/jdb.htm

Bernadette Stubbe

Starting from scratch can be a blessing. Being bang next to a flamboyant gothic 15th-century abbey can be another. Both these and a popular classical music festival in July led Bernadette Stubbe and her husband to take a deep breath and redesign a magnificent white-stone 17th-century mansion on the main square. An astute architect brought in light from above to diffuse a soft glow on beige rattan chairs and white linen curtains. A cluster of decanters sparkle on a perfect honey-coloured country-style table top. Here is a minimum of decoration but each piece exquisite, like the tall glass-door bookcase in the breakfast room. Continuing the monastic theme into the bedrooms it becomes simple luxury with textured wallpaper, white *piqué* bedspreads, beige in the thick muslin drapes and carpeting. A desk and an antique *armoire* complete the picture. Soft robes and white tiled bathrooms follow suit. Snacks and drinks are served on the terrace overlooking the square which now houses a rural museum and the town hall. 5 minutes off the Calais auto route and you are back in the centre of Medieval France.

Rooms: 9: 8 doubles/twins & 1 suite.
Price: 550-700 Frs (€ 83.85-106.71).
Extra bed 75 Frs.
Breakfast: 60 Frs.
Meals: Sandwiches & snacks on terrace 50-80 Frs.
Closed: January. Restaurant closed Sunday nights.

From Calais A16 dir. Paris, exit 22 St Riquier, then 8km on D925. Right on main square next to Cathedral.

Manoir de la Renardière

80580 Erondelle
Somme

Tel: (0)3 22 27 13 00
Fax: (0)3 22 27 13 12

Hélène Thaon d'Arnoldi

It really is the most extraordinary house, perched in Victorian splendour on its wooded hill with a view that plunges down past the trees, across the bird-filled wetlands of the Baie de Somme to the Channel. And Hélène is the most remarkable woman, packing the energy and creativity of five into a small frame. Her house is in her image, full of precious things from her colourful and romantic past: grandfather in Hussar's pointed helmet and epaulettes, porcelain jugs and silver teapots, books galore, quantities of fine furniture — no room for bulls or children here. Rooms are different sizes, all very individual, all cosy. She receives her guests with refined enthusiasm and her candlelit dinners in the perfect little white dining room are famous, as are her musical evenings in the big *salon*. She also has a 'cottage pub', the Blue Rabbit, in an outbuilding where the atmosphere is less formal, wine is served by the glass and homely meals can be had twice a week. The quiet is almost tangible, the garden a triumph of imaginative eye and sheer hard work, the experience incomparable.

Rooms: 4: 3 doubles & 1 suite for 2/4.
Price: 650 Frs (€ 99.09).
Breakfast: Included.
Meals: Dinner, inc. wine, 250-300 Frs.
Closed: December-January; open on request.

Manoir is on D13 between Huppy N28 and Liercourt D901.

Château de Reilly

60240 Reilly
Oise

Tel: (0)3 44 49 03 05
Fax: (0)3 44 49 23 39

Hilary Pearson & David Gauthier

They are young, enthusiastic and bright... and they love their old family house. David, who's French, has converted the mill-house into a French country 'pub': Toby jugs and a pianist on Fridays. You breakfast there or in your room. Hilary, who's English, has unleashed her decorating flair on the big château bedrooms, using just enough fabric and furniture, tassels and prints then leaving the space to reveal itself. Her colour schemes have character but don't intrude (rich green with pale pink, deep raspberry with royal blue and white or eau-de-nil and ivory) and the new bathrooms are very stylish, the one shower a smart, glass, quarter-circle. Vast *Victor Hugo* is the most château-esque room in its double-draped windows and tasselled wallpaper. Modern comfort in well-respected old surroundings, lots of space, heart-stoppingly peaceful views, a great sloping lawn that beckons, the listed medieval village across the valley calling out to be painted. The reception rooms may be full of wedding guests but residents go straight through the panelled hall to their first-floor hideaways.

Rooms: 4 rooms, including a suite for four.
Price: 390-490 Frs (€ 59.46-74.7);
suite 650 Frs.
Breakfast: Included.
Meals: Lunch 65-90 Frs; dinner à la carte
(average 170 Frs).
Closed: Christmas & New Year.

A16 exit Beauvais Nord. In Beauvais dir.
Mantes la Jolie for about 30km. After
Chaumont en Vexin, right on D153 to
Reilly. Château entrance on right entering village.

Relais d'Aumale

37 place des Fêtes
Montgrésin
60560 Orry La Ville
Oise

Tel: (0)3 44 54 61 31
Fax: (0)3 44 54 69 15
E-mail: relaisd.aumale@wanadoo.fr
web: www.pageszoom.com/relais-aumale

M & Mme Hofheinz

In a little village, the great forest of Chantilly on its doorstep, this multi-faceted hunting lodge has character and a dazzling Armagnac collection on the carved stone mantelpiece. The lounge is deliciously tempting in its rich red garb with beams above and more bottles on the side. In contrast, the 1990s dining room is all glass, air, and light, opening onto the terrace for long summer dinners; breakfast is usually in the cosy, panelled room next to the bar. There's a garden, too. Bedrooms are comfortable without being exciting: a good size, with excellent custom-made furniture and the occasional antique, warm, soft colours and fabrics, good bathrooms and double-glazing (the road through the village passes the gate but we gather there is very little traffic at night). The two big suites in the 'Little House' by the road are light, pale and very smart. And of course the Noble Horse, star of Chantilly, is everywhere — in ancient and modern style, arranged on walls and shelves, mounted in frames and cabinets by the relaxed and naturally friendly Hofheinz couple.

Rooms: 24: 22 doubles/twins & 2 suites for 4.
Price: Doubles 600-800 Frs (€ 91.47-121.96); suites 800-1100 Frs. Extra bed 60 Frs.
Breakfast: 60 Frs.
Meals: Lunch 210 Frs; dinner 220 Frs.
Closed: Christmas & New Year.

A1 exit 7 dir. Chantilly on N17 for 4km; fork left after La Chapelle en Serval on D9240 dir. Montgrésin; signposted in village.

Château d'Ermenonville

Rue René Girardin
60950 Ermenonville
Oise

Tel: (0)3 44 54 00 26
Fax: (0)3 44 54 01 00
E-mail: chato.ermenonville@wanadoo.com
web: www.chateauxandcountry.com/chateaux/ermenonville

Christophe Claireau

Walking up to this pure French château you can almost feel the history of the princes who have lived, visited, died here — it has also belonged to Signor Bugatti and the Hare Krishna movement. It is genuine old elegance on a human scale. No wonder Rousseau came to think great thoughts in the 'Baroque' garden (his tomb still attracts literati). The blond building stands like a sculpture in the velvet of fine lawns, tall trees and water; the peace of the place is tangible. There's splendour in the iron-balustraded stone staircase, the vast drawing room's double-aspect onto informal parkland and symmetrical courtyard, the dining room with its fine white linen and its stylish but friendly waiters. Rooms all have style. Be extravagant and take a suite for the full château experience: round, panelled tower bedroom, pure French *salon*, marble fireplace, views over moat and park. The smaller rooms are excellent value, especially on the second floor where lower ceilings make them so cosy: on the deep wooden window seat over the lake you could be in the bows of a boat.

Rooms: 49: 47 doubles/twins & 2 suites for 2/3.
Price: Doubles 390-1650 Frs (€ 59.46-251.54); suites 1340-1650 Frs.
Breakfast: 80 Frs.
Meals: Lunch & dinner 195-450 Frs.
Closed: Never.

*From A1 exit dir. Chantilly &
Ermenonville. Follow signs to Ermenonville
through Plailly, Mortefontaine and forest.
Turn left into village, then right. Hotel on left after bridge. Ring at gate.*

A La Bonne Idée

3 rue des Meuniers
60350 Saint Jean aux Bois
Oise

Tel: (0)3 44 42 84 09
Fax: (0)3 44 42 80 45
E-mail: a-la-bonne-idee-
auberge@wanadoo.fr
web: www.a-la-bonne-idee.fr

Michel & Huguette Royer

Deep in the forest, the walled village is worth a visit and the Bonne Idée (*extra-muros*) is where sophisticates from Paris and Brussels come to escape the excitement, knowing they will find a genuine welcome, country peace and superb food cooked by the *patron*. The inn, once a woodcutters' dive, still has masses of old timber and tiling in what could be called romantic-rustic style. Start with a drink by the fire in the bar, move to an elegant table in the dining room where bread warms by the great fireplace, and enjoy a fine meal served by stylish yet easy-going waiters. A tour of the pretty garden will tell you that vegetables and poultry are home-grown, though the deer and wild sow are purely decorative reminders of the house's hunting-lodge past. Here are the summer terrace and space for children to play. Bedrooms, four in the main house, the rest in the converted stables, are rustic oak or attractive Louis XVI and perfectly comfortable. Ideal for walking, cycling, riding and relaxing; Compiègne and the great castle of Pierrefonds are very close.

Rooms: 24: 22 doubles/twins & 2 apartments.
Price: 380-450 Frs (€ 57.93-68.60); apartments 480 Frs.
Breakfast: Buffet 55 Frs.
Meals: Lunch & dinner from 130 Frs.
Closed: January-February.

From A1 exit 9 dir. Verberie/Compiègne. Through Verberie, left on D332 dir. Compiègne for approx. 5km; right on D85 dir. St Jean aux Bois.

Hôtel Le Régent

26 rue du Général Mangin
02600 Villers Cotterêts
Aisne

Tel: (0)3 23 96 01 46
Fax: (0)3 23 96 37 57

Mme Thiébault

This is a gracious old 18th-century hotel, built around a spacious cobbled courtyard with a flowering cherry beside a stone well. You wouldn't be surprised to see a carriage come through the archway, with galloping horses anxious for their stable and their cargo ready for supper and bed. No supper now, unfortunately, but there are several restaurants a short stroll away in this attractive, though busy, little town. The only time you might have a problem is on Sunday night. Breakfast is in a somewhat gloomy room with green wallpaper, brightened by pale pink tablecloths. The building actually goes back to the 16th century and is full of atmosphere. The rooms are being carefully renovated and some open onto a covered wooden balcony behind a thick hedge of flowers. A 30-minute drive away is the railway carriage where Marshal Foch signed the armistice at the end of the First World War, while in nearby Pierrefonds is an amazing château with more turrets than Sleeping Beauty's castle. Speaking of which, the (reputedly) real thing is less than an hour away, which could be of great interest to your children. *No smoking in some rooms.*

Rooms: 18 doubles/twins, some with Jacuzzis.
Price: 175-420 Frs (€ 26.68-64.03).
Breakfast: 50 Frs.
Meals: Restaurants in town.
Closed: Sundays November-end March.

From Pierrefonds on D973 dir. Villers Cotterêts town centre. Hotel 100m from post office on Rue Général Mangin.

La Tour du Roy
45 rue du Général Leclerc
02140 Vervins
Aisne

Tel: (0)3 23 98 00 11
Fax: (0)3 23 98 00 11

M & Mme Devignes

Madame, with references from all over the world, wears the chef's hat here: food is centre-stage, and resoundingly applauded. Monsieur, a delightful character, is wedded to his hotel, which he bought roofless 30 years ago and has renovated quite beautifully. You arrive in the attractive courtyard with its flower beds and stone fountain. The building has nooks, crannies and corners; swathes of original brickwork; restored stone details. The dining room is, of course, seriously inviting, dressed in wood and marble, pretty antiques and unusual windows and alcoves. The turrets, all that remain of the 11th-century town fortifications where the original building stood, have amazing semi-circular bedrooms, stained-glass windows, hand-painted basins, tapestries. Beds are old carved pieces and every room contains a framed menu from a different restaurant — the corridors are lined with framed menus, too! A place to spoil yourself with two or three days of luxurious living and eating. They can arrange canal trips and champagne tastings, château visits and steam-train journeys. *Five non-smoking rooms.*

Rooms: 22: 14 doubles/twins & 8 suites.
Price: Doubles 350-600 Frs
(€ 53.36-91.47); suites 600-1000 Frs.
Breakfast: 80 Frs.
Meals: Lunch/dinner 180-500 Frs (550 Frs menu includes ½ bottle champagne). Picnic lunch 100 Frs.
Closed: Never.

A26 exit 13 dir. Vervins on N2. Follow centre ville signs. Hotel directly on right. Parking off street through gate, past main building.

Hôtel Clos de Montvinage

RN2
02580 Etréaupont
Aisne

Tel: (0)3 23 97 91 10
Fax: (0)3 23 97 48 92

Jane Lise & Nathalie Trokay

Such a pretty house, so totally French! That decorative brickwork is typical of northern France in the 1870s. Built as a private mansion, Montvinage still has the warm atmosphere of a family house with some lovely furniture, oriental rugs and a grand piano. You can play table-tennis or French billiards or lounge in leather armchairs — the English club comes to mind. Bedrooms, all large, comfortable and clean, are Louis-Philippe French with quilted covers, mild floral wallpapers and 'candle' lights. The new restaurant in the old stables leads off the cosy bar where chess and darts beckon; the larger restaurant still has its collection of paintings; both give onto the garden. There's croquet, tennis, wonderful walking in the gentle hills and the great Gothic cathedral of Laon with its curious oxen-decked tower to be visited. But, above all, the welcome you will receive from the Trokays (Nathalie speaks excellent English) is memorable. They will organise visits to champagne cellars, advise on canoeing and fishing trips, provide itineraries — superbly helpful.

Rooms: 20: 19 doubles/twins &
1 apartment for 4.
Price: 360-460 Frs (€ 54.88-70.13).
Special full-board rates for 2 days.
Breakfast: 41 Frs.
Meals: Lunch & dinner 92-195 Frs. Picnic
lunch approx. 50 Frs.
Closed: One week in August & one in
February. Restaurant closed Sunday night
& Monday lunchtime.

A26 exit 13. On N2 towards Vervins/
Etréaupont. Hotel on road out of town on
right.

Le Clos Raymi

3 rue Joseph de Venoge
51200 Epernay
Marne

Tel: (0)3 26 51 00 58
Fax: (0)3 26 51 18 98
E-mail: closraymi@wanadoo.fr

Mme Woda

What more seductive combination than champagne and culture? Easy to get to from both the Reims cathedral and the champagne vineyards, this cosy hotel has the added attraction of Madame Woda herself. Ever attentive to the comfort of her guests, she purrs with pride in her recent renovation of the Chandon (the other half of Moet) family house. The intricate, pale blue mosaic covering the entrance hall and the hardwood staircase were left alone but her artistic touch is everywhere in the good beds dressed in vintage linens, the attractive bathrooms with scented lotions and bath salts, fresh flowers in every room, etchings and paintings from the 1930s, even books of poetry on a shelf. Take a peek at the downstairs bathroom with its cubist paintings and an interesting replacement for the usual sink. A champagne apéritif can be organised in a splendid little sitting room with a fireplace and, if weather permits, the buffet breakfast can be taken in the parasoled garden behind the house. Madame Woda will help you organise champagne tastings and has her favourite people to recommend.

Rooms: 7: 6 doubles & 1 twin.
Price: Doubles 750-840 Frs (€ 114.34-128.06);
twin 570 Frs. Extra bed 100 Frs.
Breakfast: 75 Frs.
Meals: Available locally.
Closed: Three weeks in February.

From Paris A4 exit Château Thierry. N3 to Epernay.

Lorraine
Alsace
Franche-Comté

France has neither winter, summer, nor morals —
apart from these drawbacks it is a fine country
Mark Twain

L'Horizon

50 route du Crève-Cœur
57100 Thionville
Moselle

Tel: (0)3 82 88 53 65
Fax: (0)3 82 34 55 84
E-mail: info@lhorizon.com
web: www.lhorizon.com

Jean-Paul & Anne-Marie Speck

The house is only 50 years old but its arcading anchors it and Virginia has crept all over it, clothing its façade in lively warm character. Here is comfortable living in graceful surroundings, as in an elegant private house. A huge terrace envelops the ground floor — from here and from the smart restaurant you have plunging views over Thionville with an astounding, glittering cityscape at night. Some first-floor rooms give onto a balcony over the same view. Despite the surprising hall with its marbled flooring and glamorous tented ceiling, the bedrooms are classic French chic (though carpets may be a little worn here and there and some rooms are smaller than others) and bathrooms border on the luxurious. But above all, you will warm to your utterly charming hosts. Monsieur Speck is passionate about Second World War history: the Maginot Line is all around, Thionville is on the Liberty Road that is marked every kilometre from Cherbourg, in Normandy, to Bastogne in Lorraine. He is fascinating on the subject.

Rooms: 10 double/twins.
Price: 480-820 Frs (€ 73.18-125.01).
Breakfast: 60 Frs.
Meals: Lunch & dinner 215-325 Frs.
Closed: January-February. Restaurant closed Saturdays & Monday lunchtimes.

From A31 exit 40 dir. Thionville. Follow signs for Bel Air Hospital north of town. At hospital bear left up hill leaving town. Hotel is 400m up on left opposite woodland.

Hôtel Anthon
Obersteinbach
67510 Lembach
Bas-Rhin

Tel: (0)3 88 09 55 01
Fax: (0)3 88 09 50 52

Danielle Flaig

Less than mountains, more than hills, the lushly-wooded slopes are pure Vosges Forest, the clear Steinbach snakes its way through pastures, red rocky outcrops emerge in forbidding contrast to such bucolic enchantment. This little hotel, in the same deep pinky-orange colour as the rocks, is in typical Vosges style. Inside, more warm wood, including a fine carved staircase, echoes the living forest. It is sweetly simple — not basic in any way, just pretty and uncluttered, with carved wardrobes and typical Vosges dining chairs, peachy beige or dull turquoise green paintwork, coir floors. Bedrooms are not big but, again, prettily done with gingham duvets, starched cloths on round tables, windows onto the quiet night. The first-floor breakfast room is delightful — immaculate white cloths and regional pottery — but the restaurant, definitely in a different class, is the heart of this place. In the big, embracing room with its refined table settings and service, delicious dishes await you after your days of discovering the area — and Madame's huge collection of soup tureens is dazzling.

Rooms: 9 doubles/twins.
Price: 350 Frs (€ 53.36).
Breakfast: 60 Frs.
Meals: Lunch & dinner 135-275 Frs; gourmet menu 380 Frs.
Closed: January. Restaurant closed Tuesdays & Wednesdays.

From Haguenau D3 & D27 through Woerth to Lembach (25km); there, D3 through Tannenbrück and Niedersteinbach to Obersteinbach. Hotel in village centre.

Hôtel du Dragon

2 rue de l'Ecarlate
67000 Strasbourg
Bas-Rhin

Tel: (0)3 88 35 79 80
Fax: (0)3 88 25 78 95
E-mail: hotel@dragon.fr
web: www.dragon.fr

Jean Zimmer

In the heart of old Strasbourg, looking over river and cathedral, the Dragon is grandly, solidly 17th-century on the outside, sleekly, refreshingly 20th-century on the inside. Built as a private mansion — where Louis XIV stayed on his way to visit Marie-Antoinette in Austria — it became an hotel ten years ago. The little courtyard received a classically pedimented porch and potted shrubs: a pretty place for an evening drink. Inside, they took a deeply contemporary approach: it is sober, infinitely stylish and extraordinarily restful. Variegated grey and white are the basics: grey curtains on white walls, superb grey pinstripe carpeting, interestingly-laid grey and white tiles in the bathrooms, blue and green bedcovers for a dash of colour. And some good abstract paintings hang here and there, to great advantage. After 20 years as a mountain guide, Monsieur Zimmer has returned to his native Strasbourg and intends to make the Dragon as welcoming as it is elegant. He is quiet and gentle and has a predilection for English-speaking guests. *Not all rooms have river views.*

Rooms: 32: 30 doubles/twins & 2 apartments for three.
Price: Doubles 495-705 Frs (€ 75.46-107.48); apartments 950 Frs.
Breakfast: 60 Frs.
Meals: Many fine restaurants in town.
Closed: Never.

Across the river from Petite France, off quai St Nicolas.

Le Beau Site

Place de l'Eglise
67530 Ottrott le Haut
Bas-Rhin

Tel: (0)3 88 95 80 61
Fax: (0)3 88 95 86 41

Sabine & Ernest Schaetzel

Spirituality flows down from Mont Sainte Odile, an ancient pilgrimage centre that looms behind Ottrott, but the lobby of this engaging old building — it was built as a restaurant in the 19th century — brings instant earthly comfort to the visitor with its warm colours, wood panelling, subtle lighting and oriental rugs on tiled floors; and when you go through to the pretty, inviting *salon* you are greeted by a fine collection of old coffee grinders. Monsieur Schaetzel is a pleasure to meet too. He may look stern and imposing but his tones are dulcet and measured and he's a heavenly host. He is also the chef, a happy cook who mixes lots of fine local specialities with more mainstream French cuisine and serves good red wine from his brother's vineyard to accompany them. There are other wines, of course, there's even a cosy wine bar (*winstub*), and the Sunday lunch buffet is a most convivial affair. Bedrooms, varying from small to large, are excellent in modernised Romantic Alsace style and have almost flashily luxurious bathrooms.

Rooms: 18 some with terraces.
Price: 320-900 Frs (€ 48.78-137.2).
Extra bed 110 Frs.
Breakfast: 60 Frs.
Meals: Lunch & dinner 100-250 Frs.
Excellent wine cellar.
Closed: February. Restaurant closed Sunday night, Monday & Tuesday lunchtime.

From A35 exit Molsheim dir. Obernai to Ottrott on D426. Hotel top of town left towards foothills of Vosges.

Auberge La Meunière

30 rue Sainte-Anne
68590 Thannenkirch
Haut-Rhin

Tel: (0)3 89 73 10 47
Fax: (0)3 89 73 12 31
E-mail:
info@aubergelameuniere.com
web: www.aubergelameuniere.com

M & Mme Dumoulin

A feeling of warmth and hospitality pervades this Alsatian auberge. Madame runs the place like clockwork, and is charming; Monsieur, engaging and easy-going, is head chef. Behind the pink-washed walls of this old inn lies a vastly comfortable interior — wooden panelling and decorative open brickwork on the walls, beamed ceilings and gleaming terracotta tiled floors. Wooden framed windows, attractively arched in the traditional style, are beautifully renovated. Bedrooms, sized from small to large, are cosy yet uncluttered with lovely views — this is cherry tree country and there are orchard-studded hills wherever you look. One bedroom has three walls, a bay window and a balcony — like being in a square lighthouse! Bed linen is of the crispest, even in the traditionally carved baby's rocker. Bathrooms, white-tiled with wooden slatted blinds and the latest fittings, are luxurious. No garden, but a large terrace, and a fitness area with Jacuzzi and sauna. Delicious Alsatian food and wines in the wood-panelled restaurant, where children dine well too.

Rooms: 23: 17 doubles/twins & 6 apartments for 4.
Price: Doubles 380-510 Frs (€ 57.93-77.75); apartments 740 Frs including breakfast. Extra bed 80 Frs.
Breakfast: 40 Frs.
Meals: Lunch & dinner à la carte. Menu 100-135 Frs. Children 40 Frs.
Closed: December 20-March 25.

From Ribeauvillé N on D1b; left to Thannenkirch on D42. On right in village.

Hostellerie des Seigneurs de Ribeaupierre

11 rue du Château
68150 Ribeauvillé
Haut-Rhin

Tel: (0)3 89 73 70 31
Fax: (0)3 89 73 71 21

Marie-Cécile Barth

In 1730, under the Ancien Régime, when lords of manors (*seigneurs*) made their living by taxing their inferiors, those of Ribeaupierre had this building put up as their tax office, and it certainly has a solid, determined look. Nowadays, the atmosphere behind that fine timbered façade is warm, dark, hushed, almost ecclesiastical: this is a place for quiet, serious people who appreciate good things properly done. Downstairs is the small lobby with the open fireplace and the old well interestingly side by side, then the enfolding vault of the breakfast room which welcomes you every morning. It is all cosy and perfectly decorated with pretty curtains and cloths to set off beams, timbers and old stones. There are occasional antiques and the bedrooms, which vary in size, are showcases for beautifully-tailored soft furnishings and duvet covers in Pierre Frey fabrics. Bathrooms are very nice indeed, too. In fact, not a mistake has been made, the ladies of the manor are most agreeable with their guests and the little town is a delightful place to visit.

Rooms: 10: 7 doubles & 3 suites.
Price: 650-950 Frs (€ 99.09-144.83).
Extra child's bed 150 Frs.
Breakfast: Included.
Meals: Available locally.
Closed: January-February.

Grand'Rue dir. Place de la Sinne; there, bear right. Hotel near St Grégoire church on corner of 2 streets.

MMap 242-31   **ASP Map No: 10**

Au Riesling

5 route du Vin
68340 Zellenberg
Haut-Rhin

Tel: (0)3 89 47 85 85
Fax: (0)3 89 47 92 08

Famille Rentz

There are storks over there, the emblematic storks of Alsace. And the famous grape grows in the vineyards that sweep west to the little medieval town on the hill and east to the distant Black Forest and the breakfast sunrise — a timeless setting for a new hotel. The Rentz family has grown wine for generations — vines lick the foundations of the inn — but the Rentz ladies have been hoteliers for only 20 years. And they excell at it. The two sisters are all smiles and discreet attentiveness — not gushing, just seriously good hostesses. The décor is astonishingly 1970s, coolly-tiled but solidly, warmly wood-panelled, coffer-ceilinged and bronze-trimmed. There are some fairly busy wallpapers, curly chairs and custom-made headboard-cum-shelf units but bedrooms are not too small, have embroidered tablecloths and views. The dining room, where lots of Alsace specialities are served, is magnificently panoramic; the even more panoramic terrace is ideal in fine weather. There is wine-tasting next door and all those quaint villages to be explored, under the eagle eye of mother stork.

Rooms: 36 doubles/twins.
Price: 310-450 Frs (€ 47.26-68.6).
Breakfast: 50 Frs.
Meals: Lunch & dinner 120-280 Frs.
Picnic lunch 50 Frs.
Closed: January-end February. Restaurant closed Sunday evenings & Mondays.

D1B between Mittelwihr and Ribeauvillé, north of Riquewihr. Town centre of Zellenberg is off this road but hotel is ON road, on right when leaving village N towards Ribeauvillé (2km).

Château d'Isenbourg
68250 Rouffach
Haut-Rhin

Tel: (0)3 89 78 58 50
Fax: (0)3 89 78 53 70
web: www.chateaux-hotels.com
E-mail: isenbourg@wanadoo.fr

Inge Meitinger

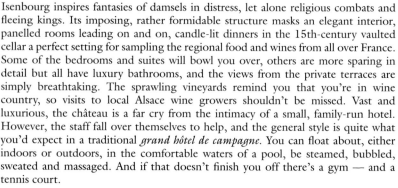

Isenbourg inspires fantasies of damsels in distress, let alone religious combats and fleeing kings. Its imposing, rather formidable structure masks an elegant interior, panelled rooms leading on and on, candle-lit dinners in the 15th-century vaulted cellar a perfect setting for sampling the regional food and wines from all over France. Some of the bedrooms and suites will bowl you over, others are more sparing in detail but all have luxury bathrooms, and the views from the private terraces are simply breathtaking. The sprawling vineyards remind you that you're in wine country, so visits to local Alsace wine growers shouldn't be missed. Vast and luxurious, the château is a far cry from the intimacy of a small, family-run hotel. However, the staff fall over themselves to help, and the general style is quite what you'd expect in a traditional *grand hôtel de campagne*. You can float about, either indoors or outdoors, in the comfortable waters of a pool, be steamed, bubbled, sweated and massaged. And if that doesn't finish you off there's a gym — and a tennis court.

Rooms: 40: 37 doubles/twins & 3 apartment.
Price: Doubles 720-1600 Frs (€ 109.76-243.92); apartment 1650-2100 Frs.
Breakfast: 30 Frs.
Meals: Lunch & dinner 280-380 Frs; Gourmet menu, including champagne & wine, 700 Frs.
Closed: Mid-January-March 10.

From A35 exit 28 onto D1 W for 7km; left on N83 to Rouffach (10km).

Hostellerie Saint Barnabé

68530 Murbach Buhl
Haut-Rhin

Tel: (0)3 89 62 14 14
Fax: (0)3 89 62 14 15

M & Mme Orban

The young owners of this angular, 100-year-old, flower-decked hotel are spontaneously smiley, chatty and attentive. He is the chef — trained with France's best and chef at Château d'Isenbourg for some years, so food is important here, and good. She is the perfect adviser on what to do between the Vosges hills and the Alsace plain: there are typical Alsatian villages and wine-growers to visit, bike-rides and good fishing places (they also have mini-golf on the spot). The ferny woods are full of paths and burbling brooks and there's skiing in the snow season. There are two sorts of guestrooms: in the main house they are big, decorated with care and individuality (the yellow and white room has an iron-frame canopied bed, the red and white one twin head cushions and super-soft quilts), have smashing bathrooms and occasionally balconies; in the separate building behind, they are smaller and more old-fashioned (and cheaper!) but are gradually being renovated; bedroom doors will soon all have typically Alsatian hand-painted, floral decoration. A great place for both nature-lovers and gourmets.

Rooms: 22 doubles/twins, 2 triples & 1 apartment. Some in annexe.
Price: Doubles 400-480 Frs (€ 60.98-73.18); triples 850 Frs; apartment 1200.
Breakfast: Buffet 65 Frs.
Meals: Lunch & dinner 350-385 Frs; gourmet 650 Frs. Picnic lunch 80 Frs.
Closed: Mid-January-February. Restaurant closed Mondays & Wednesdays lunchtime.

From N83 (betwen Belfort & Colmar)
D430 dir. Guebwiller/Lautenbach; D429 dir. Buhl then Murbach. Hotel on left.

Hôtel Taillard
25470 Goumois
Doubs

Tel: (0)3 81 44 20 75
Fax: (0)3 81 44 26 15
web: www.hoteltaillard.com

M Taillard

Stand on the terrace and let your eye plunge and soar over the thick forests, across the border and into Switzerland — it is gasp-worthy. The building, an 18th-century farmhouse, was turned into a hotel by the Taillard family in 1875; the current Taillard, as well as being a thoroughly charming host, is a very competent painter; his works decorate some rooms. His wife does all the upholstery; her skills are evident too. Using good furniture, some antiques, quiltings and pretty lamps, she has made the bedrooms soft and comforting. But let's start in the warm and inviting lobby where wood panelling, rush matting and a fine old grandfather clock greet you. Thence to the dining room, which grabs those magnificent views with its great bay windows and seats you by them in splendour — elegant tables and pretty, splendid food. Outside, the swimming pool seems to float in that sea of woods and mountain pastures that spreads beyond the tame/wild garden. Back indoors, there are temptations such as log fires and billiards, fitness and Jacuzzi, and just such a welcoming atmosphere.

Rooms: 22: 14 doubles/twins, 7 triples & 1 quadruple.
Price: 275-530 Frs (€ 41.92-80.8); quadruple 720 Frs.
Breakfast: Buffet 55 Frs.
Meals: Lunch & dinner 115-350 Frs.
Closed: Mid-November-end March. Restaurant closed Weds lunchtimes (except July & Aug). Wed evenings March, Oct-Nov.

From A36 exit 7 dir. Montbéliard Sud then D437 dir. Maîche/Bern. After St Hippolyte D437 left dir. Goumois. Hotel on right looking over Goumois before arriving in town.

Auberge Le Moulin du Plain

25470 Goumois
Doubs

Tel: (0)3 81 44 41 99
Fax: (0)3 81 44 45 70
web: www.moulinduplain.com

M & Mme Choulet

Across the River Doubs, which ripples over its little rapids below the terrace, are the steep, wooded Swiss hillsides: the frontier guards are 30m down the road and here, at the bottom of the deep valley, after wondering if you've gone the right way, you reach a glorious haven of trees and water, a paradise for fishing enthusiasts (1st-category fly-fishing). So much so that they have a room for hanging thigh-boots and another for preparing tackle and talking fishing. The views are striking, there's great walking for non-fishers and the restaurant naturally specialises in trout, local morel mushrooms and other regional delights. The elder Choulets left farming in 1960 to transform their derelict mill into a comfortable country inn and their son, the friendly, engaging chef, and his wife are now gradually taking over — a lovely family who take good care of their guests and provide all the licences you need for fishing. The interior is still fairly 1960s, there's a cosy panelled bar, a very big dining room overlooking the river and fairly banal, but comfortable, bedrooms and bathrooms.

Rooms: 22: 13 doubles/twins, 7 triples
& 2 quadruples.
Price: Doubles 295-340 Frs
(€ 44.97-51.83); triples 375 Frs;
quadruples 445 Frs.
Breakfast: 35 Frs in room; buffet 42 Frs.
Meals: Lunch & dinner 95-190 Frs. À la
carte menu also available.
Closed: November-Easter.

From A36 (between Besançon & Montbeliard)
N437 dir. Maîche. 8 km after St Hippolyte left
D437. In Gourmois left just before frontier
guard. 4 km alongside river Doubs.

Le Moulin
25380 Vaucluse
Doubs

Tel: (0)3 81 44 35 18
Fax: (0)3 81 44 35 18

Claire & Camille Malavaux

Lucky guests get one of the balcony rooms, but the whole house oozes personality. It was built in 1930 by an Italian architect for the manager of the sawmill powered by the crystal-clear River Dessoubre that flows at the bottom of the garden. There are private fishing rights for enthusiasts, fabulous countryside for nature-lovers and a beautifully kept walled kitchen garden with raised beds for fresh ingredients on the table each day. Inside, the house is still deliciously 1930s and the charming elderly Malavaux couple have decorated it simply and fittingly, in keeping with original features such as floor tiles — those extravagant patterns they loved so much — and fireplaces — wiggly marbles from an Art Deco catalogue. Walls are white, the décor is fairly minimalist with an occasional fling into ruched curtains, and the open stairwell with rooms leading off the landings reminds you that this was a family house. We felt it was just as old-fashioned as it needed to be and the neat, clean rooms were perfect for a very quiet night's sleep. People come back year after year.

Rooms: 6 doubles/twins.
Price: 260-380 Frs (€ 39.64-57.93).
Extra bed 70 Frs.
Breakfast: 40 Frs.
Meals: Lunch & dinner 105-135 Frs.
Closed: January 5-mid-February & first
week October. Restaurant closed
Wednesday lunchtime.

*A36 exit Baumes les Dames dir. Pontarlier
on D50. Left D464 dir. Sancey Le
Long/Cours St. Maurice for 2km to Pont
Neuf. Right dir. Consolation for 0.5km.
Hotel on left.*

Le Moulin du Prieuré

25620 Mamirolle
Bonnevaux Le Prieuré
Doubs

Tel: (0)3 81 59 21 47
Fax: (0)3 81 59 28 79

M & Mme Migot

Country-lovers flock here, so do foodies. In dramatically beautiful countryside, at the bottom of the deep Muning valley, it was built as a water-mill for an abbey. Less obvious is that it was first built in the 13th century. The mill-wheel still turns but instead of flour the Moulin produces gourmet cooking: Monsieur Migot worked with world-famous Michel Guérard and after only a year here his talent is widely hailed. There is a lot of dark, rather austere rusticity in the main building where the dining and sitting rooms are — beams and antlers, high-backed Louis XIV chairs and bits of pewter — but the veranda is full of light and there are attractive riverside terraces and gardens. Bedrooms are in chalets in the grounds and are not rustic. Colours are contemporary pastels, furniture is new, traditional bentwood style: simple and perfectly comfortable. Fish to your heart's content, relax into freedom and wonderful walks, visit the Courbet museum, discover lovely Besançon and come back to seriously good food with no sound but the birds and the winds and the stream chattering to each other.

Rooms: 8 doubles/twins.
Price: 380-450 Frs (€ 57.93-68.6).
Breakfast: 55 Frs.
Meals: Lunch & dinner 195-345 Frs.
Closed: January 10- February 10.
Restaurant closed Tuesdays & Wednesdays
from September-end March.

From Besançon N57 towards Lausanne/
Pontarlier. Right D67 dir. Ornans; 5km
after Tarcenay, left dir. Bonnevaux Le
Prieuré 3km. Hotel on right deep down in
valley.

Hôtel Castan
6 square Castan
25000 Besançon
Doubs

Tel: (0)3 81 65 02 00
Fax: (0)3 81 83 01 02

Gérard Dintroz

Besançon is a place where French history ripples from Julius Caesar down to us. In the heart of the lovely old city, this hotel is a marriage of classical French elegance and sophisticated modern comforts. It is brokered by the enthusiastic, hard-working Dintroz couple who fell in love with the dilapidated mansion, did some serious renovation and made it a perfect place to stay. First, the exquisite courtyard where a riot of fronds, flowers and trumpet vines splatters the old stones and cobbles with vibrant life. Three wings enclose this peaceful space, sheltering the house from the city. Inside, reception and breakfast areas are panelled and inviting, bedrooms are all refined creativity and beautiful finishes — chandeliers, canopies, mouldings and French antiques — and bathrooms are modern, luxurious, with period fittings. The emphasis is on quality and elegance. Your hosts are delightful and like guests who share their pleasure in fine things: he is friendly and engaging, she is bright and communicative and makes the delicious jams served in lovely china at their very special breakfasts.

Rooms: 10 doubles/twins.
Price: 580-980 Frs (€ 88.42-149.4).
Breakfast: 60 Frs.
Meals: Many fine restaurants in town.
Closed: Dec. 24-Jan. 4 & August 1-20.

In Besançon dir. Centre Ville/ Vieille Ville & La Citadelle. Hotel signposted; on small Castan Square. Enter interior courtyard and through coach gate.

Burgundy

H. Nègre

Beaune, a small French town surrounded only by
Burgundy. Wine is so important in Beaune
that they keep it in a museum
Art Buchwald

Le Monestier

Le Bourg
71640 Saint Denis de Vaux
Saône-et-Loire

Tel: (0)3 85 44 50 68
Fax: (0)3 85 44 50 68
E-mail: lemonastier@wanadoo.fr
web: www.lemonastier.com

Margrit & Peter Koller

We almost got lost here, but the valley is a very pretty place to get lost in and Peter was "working on" the signposting. You drive into the large grounds through wrought-iron gates, past attractive outbuildings and a swimming pool set in the grass, with huge old trees nearby. It looks a little bit like a Home Counties golf club! But no. Margrit and Peter are Swiss and bought Le Monestier in 1999. Peter can be seen walking round in an apron. He is in charge of the cooking and you can expect some serious eating. Not to say that your host is serious; you will find he has a most un-Swiss sense of humour. The reception rooms are comfortable though they may not be to everyone's taste. One bedroom has its own loo and a bathroom down the corridor, but this is made up for by a private terrace on top of one of the towers. You will be very well looked after here and tennis, fishing, riding and golf are close at hand. More importantly for many: you will be in the very centre of the Côte Chalonnaise region and may not even need the car to visit the vineyards of Mercurey, Givry and Rully.

Rooms: 6 doubles.
Price: 450-600 Frs (€ 68.6-91.47).
Breakfast: Included.
Meals: Dinner 120 Frs; wine 60 Frs.
Closed: Never.

A6 exit Chalon Nord; D978 to Châtenoy le Royal then Mellecey. Then D48 dir St Denis de Vaux. In village follow signposts — just keep going up.

L'Orangerie
Lieu dit Vingelles
71390 Moroges
Saône-et-Loire

Tel: (0)3 85 47 91 94
Fax: (0)3 85 47 98 49

David Eades & Niels Lierow

Ring the bell on the wooden gate and then wander up through neat gardens. They are alive with colour. Light spills into the sitting room entrance through vine-clad arched windows, cream walls and Indian rugs adding to the simple elegance of this gracious *maison de maître*. Antiques and travel are David's passion, his gentle Irish brogue enchanting. He not only makes excellent tea imported from Ceylon but his breakfasts are fit for a king (hardly surprising, since he also interviews European royalty for a 'prestigious' magazine). Evening meals should be reserved in advance. The grand staircase in the centre of the house could have come straight off a 1930's luxury cruise liner, interesting paintings and stylish oriental fabrics contributing to a mix of styles that somehow go well together. The bedrooms, with their seersucker linen and antique prints, are lovely, and the bathrooms classically tasteful. Being in the heart of Burgundy vineyard country, you are also in the heart of silence. Terraced lawns lead down to the swimming pool, the trees and meadows. Sybaritic, but in the best possible taste.

Rooms: 5 doubles/twins.
Price: 400-550 Frs (€ 60.98-83.85).
Breakfast: Copious breakfast inc.
Meals: Dinner 170 Frs, on reservation.
Closed: November-Easter.

From A6 exit Chalon Sud on N80 dir. Le Creusot; exit Moroges. Signposted from centre of village.

Auberge du Cheval Blanc

71390 Saint Boil
Saône-et-Loire

Tel: (0)3 85 44 03 16
Fax: (0)3 85 44 07 25

M & Mme Jany Cantin

A tonic if you are tired of the standardisation of all things. Everything about it — from the formal furniture, the striped wallpaper, the parquet floors, the great curtains gathered at the waist, to the gravelled courtyard with trumpet vines, wrought-iron white garden furniture, shuttered and dormer windows — is what the French do with such aplomb. Yet, having said all that, Martine and Jany make the place. He is a well-built Burgundian, a fitting descendant of generations of *bons viveurs* and creator of some spectacular dishes in the restaurant — across the road from the hotel. Martine's generosity and kindness add something very special to the hotel. It is a trifle functional upstairs, perhaps, as is often the case, but very much a *maison de maitre* and up the most lovely wooden staircase. On the top floor the beams are exposed, and varnished. The two front rooms up there have charming *oeil de boeuf* windows. Bathrooms are all fine, with nothing outstanding to report. Dine outside under the lime trees in summer and appreciate the survival of such places, and such people.

Rooms: 10 doubles/twins.
Price: 380-490 Frs (€ 57.93-74.7).
Breakfast: 58 Frs.
Meals: Lunch & dinner 140 Frs.
Closed: February 10-March 10.

A6 exit Chalon sur Saône Sud on D80 dir. Le Creusot, then D981 dir. Cluny for 10km to St Boil. Hotel on right in village.

Ferme Auberge du Vieux Château
58700 Oulon
Nièvre

Tel: (0)3 86 68 06 77

Famille Fayolle-Tilliot

In deepest undulating Burgundy, you enter the old farm courtyard to massive barns — huge doors to match — and perfect creeper-covered turret. Parts of it are 13th-century; it has a fairytale atmosphere and is a paradise for families with children: apart from the fenced swimming pool (covered in cooler weather), there are kittens and lambs (in the season), berries to harvest, lots of space. The delightful Fayolle family are renowned for their welcome and their food. Fresh veg from the kitchen garden, meat, milk and cheese from the farm, poultry and *foie gras* from the farmyard and Madame weaving it magically together in the kitchen with the odd grandchild helper. When the weather forbids outside eating, retreat to the beamed restaurant, with a large open fireplace and dried flowers. And there's a brilliant vaulted cellar where brandy and singing take place some evenings. Bedrooms are unexciting in their small-flower get-up, their ceiling tiles and small bathrooms but they do have the most stupendous view south over meadows and the village church: an image of rural paradise.

Rooms: 10: some sleep four (some bathrooms shared); & 1 self-catering cottage.
Price: Doubles 250-300 Frs (€ 38.11-45.73); quadruples 450-500 Frs; cottage 1500-2500 Frs per week.
Breakfast: Included.
Meals: Lunch & dinner 110 Frs.
Closed: Never.

From Nevers, D977 through Guérigny to Prémery. Just past Prémery, right on D977 dir. Corbigny; signposted.

Le Grand Monarque

33 quai Clémenceau
58400 La Charité sur Loire
Nièvre

Tel: (0)3 86 70 21 73
Fax: (0)3 86 69 62 32
E-mail: le.grand.monarque@wanadoo.fr

M Grennerat

A feast for the senses awaits you here: the great Loire flows at the feet of the Grand Monarque, her shimmering limpidity enveloping the old bridge and the little medieval town; Monsieur Grennerat's cooking is a treat for eyes, nose and tongue. Passionate about food and wine, he actively encourages better taste and smell education among French and foreign, old and young — another warrior against junk food. An historical gold-mine, he will tell the tale of his 17th-century hotel as it shadowed the march of French history. The suspended staircase, an architectural marvel, leads to totally French, flocked rooms on the first floor and brighter, more recent rooms on the second. Here, huge old stuctural timbers, recycled 300 years ago from disused transport boats, jut into bathrooms, embrace beds, frame roof windows. There are some four-posters, one mezzanine bathroom, embossed tiling and floral wallpapers — variety galore. Later, enjoy the 1930's atmosphere of the restaurant, the view of river and bridge, the intense subtlety of the table. France at her cultural best.

Rooms: 15: 12 doubles/twins, 1 triple, 1 suite & 1 family room.
Price: 350-600 Frs (€ 53.36-91.47). Family room price depends upon number of occupants.
Breakfast: 50 Frs.
Meals: Lunch & dinner 98-238 Frs. À la carte menu also available.
Closed: Never.

From the bridge of La Charité direction Nevers. Hotel is 100m on right.

Le Relais Fleuri/Le Coq Hardi

42 avenue du la Tuilerie
58150 Pouilly sur Loire
Nièvre

Tel: (0)3 86 39 12 99
Fax: (0)3 86 39 14 15

Philippe & Dominique Martin

Ideal for a quick stop, perhaps, rather than a long stay — though a pool is planned — but if you like your French food you'll love it. Monsieur and Madame Martin bought the Coq Hardi, and its reputation for its restaurant, three years ago and are gradually doing it up. Monsieur gained his experience at the Espérance at St. Père-sous-Vézelay — one of France's top restaurants — and judging by the smiles of the customers staggering away at 4 p.m. it is probably worth staying here just for the food. In summer, meals are served on a vine-covered terrace overlooking the Loire. The hotel's original rooms upstairs are a bit gloomy, though some have terraces over the garden, but will soon be redone. One bathroom is high kitsch: with black and yellow tiles and green basin and fittings — not for much longer! The newly decorated rooms are in what appears to be a boat shed. They are all pleasantly done in blue or yellow but the best thing is the windows: some are arched, others have elegant stained glass. Ineffably, properly, French.

Rooms: 10: 9 doubles & 1 suite.
Price: 290-450 Frs (€ 44.21-68.6).
Breakfast: 50 Frs.
Meals: Lunch & dinner 110-260 Frs.
Closed: Mid-December-mid-January.
Restaurant closed Tuesday evenings &
Wednesdays from October-end May.

From N7 south of Cosne sur Loire, north of
Nevers, turn off at Pouilly. Signposted
opposite Pouilly wine co-op building.

Château d'Ecutigny

21360 Bligny sur Ouche
Côte-d'Or

Tel: (0)3 80 20 19 14
Fax: (0)3 80 20 19 15
E-mail: Chateau.Ecutigny@wanadoo.fr
web: perso.wanadoo.fr/chateau.ecutigny/

Françoise & Patrick Rochet

This is a real castle. It was built in the 12th century to station soldiers guarding the Duke of Burgundy's land from marauding French. Bits were added over the years but it was abandoned at the end of the 18th century and fell to ruin, until it was rescued by Françoise and Patrick. The château is an Historic Monument, with the secret passages and Rapunzel towers to prove it, but has been made light, airy and really beautiful inside, without a trace of having been 'done up'. The room is in the palest muted colours — not quite pastels — and sparsely furnished with a subtle mix of country pieces and elegant antiques. Bathrooms are large, with cast-iron baths on feet and some with warm terracotta tiles. The floors throughout the château are either mellow terracotta or wood — you won't be walking barefoot on icy stone. Children will love exploring the cellars, stables and farm and Françoise will not be fazed by them: she used to run a crèche! This may be why the place runs so smoothly. Comfortable and relaxed despite the grandeur.

Rooms: 6: 5 doubles & 1 suite.
Price: Doubles/twins 500-700 Frs
(€ 76.22-106.71); suite 1000 Frs.
Breakfast: Included.
Meals: Dinner, including aperitif & wine,
250 Frs; picnic lunch with wine available.
Closed: Never.

*From A6 exit Pouilly en Auxois. Follow signs
to Bligny sur Ouche, then Ecutigny. Take last
turning on right on leaving village.*

Hôtel Le Cep

27 rue Maufoux
21200 Beaune
Côte-d'Or

Tel: (0)3 80 22 35 48
Fax: (0)3 80 22 76 80
E-mail: hotel-le-cep@wanadoo.fr
web: www.slh.com/hotelcep/

Jean-Claude Bernard

This listed building in the prettiest part of Beaune dates partly from the 14th century and more largely from the Renaissance; the architecture alone is compelling — including, as it does, a wonderful stone staircase and a tower with an unrivalled view over Beaune. But what will make your stay is the warm, friendly *family* atmosphere M. Bernard has managed to maintain. This is clear not only in his relationship with his guests but also with his staff who follow his lead and give a really exceptional level of friendly, smiling service. Each bedroom — furnished with carefully chosen antiques — is named after one of the *grands crus* of the Côte-D'Or and the bathrooms come with monogrammed bathrobes. You breakfast in the old vaulted cellars of the house in winter (very cosy) or in a Renaissance courtyard in summer; afterwards you can set off to explore *routes de vin* in the Beaune countryside. Louis IX slept in this building and you will approve his choice. One might wish for more light, but the fine darkly-panelled rooms were designed to impress.

Rooms: 46: 36 doubles/twins & 10 suites.
Price: Doubles 700-1350 Frs
(€ 106.71-205.81); suites 1500-1800 Frs.
Breakfast: 80 Frs.
Meals: Dinner from 180 Frs.
Closed: Never.

From A24 S exit 24 dir. Centre Ville. Straight over roundabout and left after BP petrol station onto Rue des Vignes Rouges; straight over 2 roundabouts, then right at lights on Rue Maufoux. Hotel is on right after second set of lights.

ASP Map No: 9   MMap 243-27   **41**

L'Auberge de l'Atre

Les Lavaults
89630 Quarré les Tombes
Yonne

Tel: (0)3 86 32 20 79
Fax: (0)3 86 32 28 25

Francis Salamolard

The Auberge de l'Atre is known around here for one of the best small restaurants in the area. We watched the chefs in their white hats and full regalia carefully inspecting the day's mushroom harvest, brought in by various pickers from the village. Francis, the charming head chef, who also runs the hotel with his wife Odile, has an impressive wine cellar. In the winter he can often be found digging down there to make more space to store his newest vintages. The auberge forms part of a tiny hamlet in the Morvan National Park. Surrounded by woods and farmland, it started out as a farm, with newer bits being added to house bedrooms. The garden is pretty and has swings for children — they may spot a gnome or two lurking in the bushes. The reception rooms and dining room are in the old farmhouse: fairly dark with heavy beams but attractively arranged with round tables set with crisp white cloths and flowers. A broad tower staircase leads up to some bedrooms and down to the cellar and a room for tastings. Bedrooms are fairly modern-looking, though some furniture is antique and some have the old beams. A very pleasant stop.

Rooms: 9: 5 doubles & 4 triples.
Price: 450-550 Frs (€ 68.6-83.85).
Breakfast: 50 Frs.
Meals: Lunch & dinner à la carte.
Closed: February. Restaurant closed Tuesday nights & Wednesdays.

From Avallon D10 to Quarré les Tombes. Continue through town to Les Lavaults. Signposted.

Château de Vault de Lugny

11 rue du Château
89200 Avallon
Yonne

Tel: (0)3 86 34 07 86
Fax: (0)3 86 34 16 36
E-mail: hotel@lugny.com
web: www.lugny.com

Elisabeth Matherat Audan

It might seem a bit daunting. When you drive up to the imposing electronically-controlled wrought-iron gates of Vault de Lugny, they swing open in reply to your name. You are then greeted at the door by a smiling Elisabeth Matherat Audan and staff, all eager to relieve you of your baggage. This is definitely not cheap and cheerful, but neither is it stuffy. Elisabeth, who has run the château since the death of her father, is friendly and very much a hands-on, charming hostess. Mostly built in the 16th century, but with bits going back to the 13th, Lugny is a château of great elegance with white shutters and high Burgundian roofs. The rooms are huge and imposing: the King's chamber has 18-foot ceilings and a sprawling canopied bed. You can have a four-course dinner at a long table before a crackling fire in the stone-vaulted old kitchen, or in the garden in the summer. You can play tennis or fish — rackets and rods are provided — or wander round the still, green moat through the huge grounds. The only odd touch is a wildly expensive gift shop beside the reception desk, but apparently this was set up by popular demand.

Rooms: 12: 3 doubles, 7 junior suites, 1 suite & 1 triple.
Price: Doubles 950-2500 Frs
(€ 144.83-381.12); triple 1900 Frs; junior suites 1700-2500 Frs; suite 2300 Frs.
Breakfast: Included.
Meals: Dinner 290-480 Frs; lunch & picnics on request.
Closed: Mid-November-mid-March.

Autoroute A6 exit Avallon to Avallon then
D957 dir. Vézelay for 4km. In Pontaubert right after church.

Château de Ribourdin

89240 Chevannes
Yonne

Tel: (0)3 86 41 23 16
Fax: (0)3 86 41 23 16

Claude & Mairie-Claude Brodard

The gravel is raked and hedges trimmed around a fantastic collection of 16th-century fortified farm buildings complete with towered château, pigeon house and arrow slits. Guest rooms are in the converted barn, which has a separate entrance from the Brodard's own home (the château). M Brodard has done a fine job of the renovation; you can see the 'before' photographs. His latest project is a games room leading on to the swimming pool — so you'll be happy in all weathers. The ground floor room is to full handicapped spec. — and the upstairs ones are a good size too — nicely, if a little impersonally, decorated. There are some interesting pieces of old furniture and sparklingly clean, tiled bathrooms. Your host, who's something of a jam expert — ever heard of carrot jam? — prepares breakfast in the salon/breakfast room with its tea-room style round tables, open fire and courtyard view. Great countryside, only ten minutes walk from the pretty village with gourmet restaurant, and ten minutes by car from Auxerre, slightly longer if you take one of the bicycles for hire.

Rooms: 5 doubles/twins.
Price: Doubles 350-400 Frs
(€ 53.36-60.98). Extra bed 70 Frs.
Breakfast: Included.
Meals: Available locally.
Closed: Never.

From A6 exit Auxerre Nord onto N6 dir. Auxerre, then right dir. St Georges. Straight across all roundabouts to traffic lights. In village of Chevannes, first left, last house on leaving village.

Hostellerie des Clos
Rue Jules Rathier
89800 Chablis
Yonne

Tel: (0)3 86 42 10 63
Fax: (0)3 86 42 17 11
E-mail: host.clos@wanadoo.fr
web: www.hostellerie-des-clos.fr

Michel Vignaud

Not for the faint-hearted; you have to eat dinner. But you may well have come here to do that very thing, in which case you may be close to Heaven. (The nuns who lived here until the 1980s presumably were). Monsieur — handsome, moustachioed, chef-hatted — is an aesthete and a foodie through and through. Eating is a serious business, done with charm, intelligence, taste and, above all, professionalism. Some of our readers will shy away from the discreet formality, even opulence, but those who stay here are usually thrilled with it. The food upstages the rooms and their bathrooms, but that is no criticism. The dining room is a place of great, orange curtains held open with tassels, flowers on tables, white columns and delicate glassware. The sitting room is where you recover from the gargantuan gastronomic marathons, in formal, striped armchairs and at low mahogany round tables, perhaps before a log fire. It is a 12th-century building of classic beauty with a lovely garden, surrounded by vineyards. Words like 'refined' spring to mind.

Rooms: 26: 24 doubles, 1 triple & 1 quadruple.
Price: Doubles 310-550 Frs (€ 47.26-83.85); triple & quadruple 650 Frs.
Breakfast: 58 Frs.
Meals: Dinner 200-450 Frs, mandatory half-board.
Closed: December 20-mid-January.

A6 exit at Auxerre Sud. Hotel well signposted in Chablis.

Petit Manoir des Bruyères

89240 Villefargeau
Yonne

Tel: (0)3 86 41 32 82
Fax: (0)3 86 41 32 82

Pierre & Monique Joullié

A Rococo place unlike anything you've ever seen. Behind the creeper-clothed façade with only the Burgundian roof as a clue, is eye-boggling glamour. A vast beamed living room, an endless polished dining table, rows of tapestried chairs, shiny ornaments. Upstairs, stagger out of the loo, once you've found the door in the *trompe-l'œil* walls, to cupids, carvings, gildings, satyrs, velvet walls and clouds on the ceilings. There's a many-mirrored bathroom reflecting multiple magical images of you, marble pillars and gold-cushioned bath; a Louis XIV room with red/gold bathroom with gold/ivory taps; an antique wooden throne with bell-chime flush. *Madame de Maintenon* has a coronet canopy, a long thin *œuil de bœuf* window and a shower that whooshes between basin and loo. The 'biscuit' is taken by the deeply, heavily pink suite with its carved fireplace, painted ceilings and corner columns — wild! But such are the enthusiasm of the owners, the peace of house and garden, the quality of comfort, food and wine, that we feel it's perfect for lovers of French extravaganzas. *No smoking in some rooms.*

Rooms: 4: 2 doubles/twins and 2 suites.
Price: 600-900 Frs (€ 91.47-137.2).
Breakfast: Included.
Meals: Dinner 200 Frs.
Closed: Never.

From Auxerre D965 to Villefargeau; there, right on C5 to Bruyères.

Paris
Ile de France

Peter the great said of Paris that if he possessed such a
town he would be tempted to burn it down, for
fear it should absorb the rest of his Empire.
Augustus Hare

Hôtel des Tuileries
10 rue Saint Hyacinthe
75001
Paris

Tel: (0)1 42 61 04 17
Fax: (0)1 49 27 91 26
E-mail: htuileri@aol.com
web: hometown.aol.com/htuileri/

Jean-Jacques Vidal

The charming Tuileries has a friendly, family atmosphere. The many oriental rugs — most of them on walls — sit well in the quiet old building as its listed façade moves skywards to the rhythm of balconies, arches and mouldings. Great doors give onto a white hall with rugs, mirrors, pictures old and new, then the elegant little *salons* and the basement breakfast room, while a generous curving staircase leads upwards. A mildly oriental element reigns: one room is like a soft Persian tent, another has a clever draping of yellow cloth over white bed, there are Chinese-vase lamps, Chinese-inspired wallpaper, paisley fabrics. Colours are skilfull — a white room has dark blue carpet, pale blue damask curtains and bedcover, a richly-coloured rug behind the delightful cane bedhead — lighting is good, there are pretty antiques, country pieces, modern elements and good marble bathrooms. One room has a long narrow dressing table in carved painted wood and Empire bed and armchairs (Empress Josephine lived here). Family apartments are possible and the deluxe rooms excellent.

Rooms: 26: 18 doubles/twins & 8 apartments.
Price: Singles & doubles 690-1400 Frs (€ 105.19-213.43); apartments 1200-1600 Frs.
Breakfast: Buffet 70 Frs.
Meals: Available locally.
Closed: Never.

Metro: *Tuileries, Pyramides,* **RER** *Opéra-Auber.* **Car Park:** *Place Vendôme, Marché St. Honoré.*

Le Pavillon Bastille
65 rue de Lyon
75012
Paris

Tel: (0)1 43 43 65 65
Fax: (0)1 43 43 96 52
E-mail:
hotel-pavillon@akamail.com
web: www.france-paris.com/
pavillon-us.html

Fabienne Fournier

Around the new Opera House are the trendy bars and clubs; the arty crowd are in the old Marais nearby: the Pavillon's mix of old townhouse façade and high-modern interior is fitting. Its leitmotivs are blue and yellow, music score (*opéra oblige*) and circle segment — a sophisticated designer triumph. And service is paramount: cross the front court and ring the bell: attentive staff come and carry your luggage. There are wine-tastings in the Post Modernist lobby among the columns and 16th-century masks. Small rooms, all alike, have custom-made elements, mirrors and superb beds; the minibar unit carries a curved mirror and a vase of flowers under an ultra-mod fragment of light; bedside lighting is perfect; bathrooms have marble and fluffy towels. Breakfast is in the vaulted cellar or, in good weather, in the pretty but noisy courtyard. Then cross the road to visit the fascinating array of artisans' studios beneath the arches of the disused railway line or walk on top along the leafy Green Stream. *The higher price is for extra services e.g. opera bookings — do enquire.*

Rooms: 24 including 1 suite.
Price: Singles & doubles 840-955 Frs
(€ 128.06-145.59); suite 1375 Frs.
Breakfast: Buffet 70 Frs.
Meals: Light meals 50-100 Frs.
Closed: Never.
Metro: *Bastille;* **RER** *Gare de Lyon.*

Le Relais du Louvre

19 rue des Prêtres St Germain l'Auxerrois
75001
Paris

Tel: (0)1 40 41 96 42
Fax: (0)1 40 41 96 44
E-mail: au-relais-du-louvre@dial.oleane.com

Sophie Aulnette

Look down the throats of gargoyles. Soak up the history. Revolutionaries printed their newspaper in the cellar here; it was Puccini's Café Momus in *La Bohême* and still rings with the famous carillon next door. It's an utterly delightful place with a charming young manageress. Antiques and oriental rugs complement the modernity of firm beds and perfect bathrooms. Front rooms look onto Gothic windows and flying buttresses ("flying buttocks" one child innocently called them) and the austerely neo-Classical Louvre; others give onto a light-filled patio. The top-floor junior suites have twin beds and a sofa, pastel walls, exuberant-print upholstery, good storage and heaps of light from their mansard windows. The apartment is big and beautiful with fireplace, books, music, old engravings and a superb veranda kitchen. Other, smaller rooms are luminous, fresh and restful. You feel softly secluded and coddled, the sense of service is highly developed and, as there is no breakfast room, breakfast comes to you! *On each floor, two rooms can become a family suite.*

Rooms: 21: 18 doubles, 2 junior suites & 1 apartment.
Price: Doubles 650-1000 Frs (€ 99.09-152.45); suites 1300-1500 Frs; apartment 2400 Frs.
Breakfast: 60 Frs (in bedroom).
Meals: Light meals 30-100 Frs.
Closed: Never.

Metro: *Louvre-Rivoli, Pont Neuf*; RER *Châtelet-Les Halles.*

ASP Map No: 4

Hôtel Britannique

20 avenue Victoria
75001
Paris

Tel: (0)1 42 33 74 59
Fax: (0)1 42 33 12 65
E-mail: mailbox@hotel-britannique.fr
web: www.hotel-britannique.fr

J-F Danjou

On a quietish street by the Châtelet and originally run by the Baxters, it is now owned by an ex-naval man with a passion for Turner whose *Jessica* greets you in the lobby, whose oils and watercolours adorn the bedroom walls while the *Fighting Temeraire* dominates the 'saloon', alongside a model galleon and an HMV gramophone horn. There is a lush feel to the hallways but do try the staircase: elegantly pink and grey, it has handsome old oak chests on each landing. Average-small rooms with custom-made elements, pastel walls, heavy muted green and red fabrics, boxes of pot-pourri for extra florality and perfectly adequate bathrooms. Nice modern double-framed mirrors too. Higher floors have views over roofs and treetops. On the avenue below, plants, furniture and birds are still sold — it's fun in the daytime. The semi-basement breakfast room, lit by a glass roof, has a wall cabinet housing a silver teapot presented to the Baxters "at Whitsuntide 1861 by their Scarborough friends". It is simply comfortable with no ancient flourishes and a generally friendly reception.

Rooms: 40 doubles/twins.
Price: 790-1080 Frs (€ 120.43-164.64).
Extra bed 126 Frs.
Breakfast: 65 Frs for a copious buffet.
Meals: Available locally.
Closed: Never.

Metro: *Châtelet; RER Châtelet-Les Halles.*

Hôtel Saint Merry

78 rue de la Verrerie
75004
Paris

Tel: (0)1 42 78 14 15
Fax: (0)1 40 29 06 82
web: www.ibrguide.com

Christian Crabbe

Lovers of the Gothic, seekers of the unusual, come hither! It snuggles so closely up to St Merry that, in the suite, a cornice thrusts its way into the *salon* and elsewhere flying buttresses provide the most original of bed canopies. Monsieur Crabbe, who greets you with attention and enthusiasm, has laboured 35 years to make the old house worthy of its origins, reworking old neo-Gothic pieces and creating an astounding environment. It starts in reception: high-backed chairs, an elaborate pew, linen-fold cupboard doors, telephone in a confessional. Décor is sober, to set off the festival of dark carving: original beams, terracotta tiles, plain velvet or 'medieval-stripe' fabrics, cast-iron light fittings — and surprisingly colourful bathrooms. Some rooms have views up to the Sorbonne; the cheaper ones are small and basic; the suite with private staircase, timbered *salon* (Paris's only Gothic *salon*?), cosy bedroom and fascinating low-beamed bathroom, is a masterpiece of style and adaptation. *Difficult motor access in this pedestrian street and no lift in hotel.*

Rooms: 12: 11 doubles/twins & 1 suite.
Price: 480-1200 Frs (€ 73.18-182.94);
suite 1800 Frs. Extra bed 250 Frs.
Breakfast: 55 Frs (in bedroom).
Meals: Wide choice at your doorstep.
Closed: Never.

Metro: *Hôtel de Ville, Châtelet;* **RER**
Châtelet-Les Halles.

ASP Map No: 4

Hôtel de Notre Dame

19 rue Maître Albert
75005
Paris

Tel: (0)1 43 26 79 00
Fax: (0)1 46 33 50 11

Jean-Pierre Fouhety

A stone's throw from Notre Dame but hidden from the tourist tides in a select little area of unusual shops and smart residences, this fine old frontage opens onto a large lobby adorned with tapestry, bits of antiquity and deep armchairs. Openness reigns — these people genuinely like people and greet you with smiles and humour. If the age of the building (1600s) is evident in its convoluted corridors, contemporary style dictates their smart black dados with tan or sea-green uppers. Bedrooms also mix old and new. There are beams and exposed stones, some enormous, and cathedral views from the higher floors (through smaller windows). Like the 'porch' over each door, the custom-made desk units are nicely curvy and cupboards often have a useful suitcase space at floor level. The new padded upholstery is warm and colourful with contemporary mixes of yellow, red and blue and the translucent Japanese screen doors to bathrooms are an excellent idea for small layouts; not all baths are full size. The black eunuch officially portrayed as Marie-Antoinette's feathered fan bearer lived here...

Rooms: 34 doubles/twins.
Price: 750-850 Frs (€ 114.34-129.58).
Breakfast: 40 Frs.
Meals: Available locally.
Closed: Never.

Metro: *Maubert Mutualité;* **RER** *St Michel-Notre Dame.*

Le Notre-Dame Hôtel

1 quai Saint Michel
75005
Paris

Tel: (0)1 43 54 20 43
Fax: (0)1 43 26 61 75

Jean-Pierre Fouhety

If you want to be at the hub of Latin Quarter life, students jostling on the pavements, cars pouring across the Seine, Notre Dame serenely unmoved, then climb up from the noisy embankment. The hotel has been magnificently refurbished, public areas brightly decked in red checks, the *salon*-breakfast room, with its plunging views of river and cathedral and great police palace, extended. All rooms except five — which are soberly pretty and quieter but give onto a dull courtyard (they're the cheapest) — have at least two windows onto this picture. Rooms are very attractive, not big but uncluttered and full of light from the river. Double-glazing keeps the noise out, air conditioning keeps the air cool. Fine new fabrics are all from the house of Pierre Frey; a light cherry-wood laminate covers desktops, bedheads and modern panelling; there are hand-enamelled bedside lights from northern France and framed prints from England; dark green marble bathrooms with bright white fittings are smart behind their translucent doors and the top-floor duplex suites are fun and full of character.

Rooms: 26 including 3 suites for three.
Price: Singles/doubles 850-1100 Frs
(€ 129.58-167.69); suites 1500 Frs.
Breakfast: 40 Frs.
Meals: Available locally.
Closed: Never.

Metro: *St Michel*, **RER** *St Michel-Notre Dame*.

ASP Map No: 4

Le Sainte Beuve

9 rue Sainte Beuve
75006
Paris

Tel: (0)1 45 48 20 07
Fax: (0)1 45 48 67 52
E-mail: saintebeuve@wanadoo.fr
web: www.hotel-sainte-beuve.fr

Jean Pierre Egurreguy

Designer flair pervades this beautifully-refurbished hotel that was known and loved during the wilder days of Montparnasse — all's quiet in the street now. The atmosphere is of light, restful, unstuffy luxury — quiet good taste in gentle tones and thick furnishings. The gold and ivory silk curtains are superb. In winter a log fire burns in the old marble fireplace. The attentive efficient staff are a vital element in your sense of well-being. It is small and intimate, and so are the bedrooms. The general tone is Ancient & Modern. Decorated with soft colours and contemporary 'textured' fabrics, the pastel effect modulated by more colourful chintzes and paisleys. Every room has at least one old piece of furniture — a leather-topped desk, an antique dressing-table, a polished *armoire*, old brass lamps — and 18th-19th-century pictures in rich old frames. The bathrooms are superbly modern with bathrobes and fine toiletries. Lastly, breakfast is a feast of croissants and brioches, from the famous Mulot bakers, home-made jams and freshly-squeezed orange juice. *Book early.*

Rooms: 22 including 1 junior suite & 4 apartments.
Price: Doubles & suite 760-1700 Frs (€ 115.86-259.16); apartments 1800 Frs.
Breakfast: 80 Frs.
Meals: On request 40-200 Frs.
Closed: Never.

Metro: *Notre Dame des Champs, Vavin;*
RER *Port-Royal.*

Le Madison

143 boulevard Saint Germain
75006
Paris

Tel: (0)1 40 51 60 00
Fax: (0)1 40 51 60 01
E-mail: resa@hotel-madison.com
web: www.hotel-madison.com

Maryse Burkard

Opposite the vastly celebrated *Deux Magots* café, this is 1800's French elegance set off by lovely designer materials and staff with just the right mix of class and cheerfulness. Luxurious public rooms have antiques from the owner's collection: a portrait of his mother as a young girl dominates the breakfast area where a powerful porcelain cockerel crows and the grand buffet on its tiled 18th-century sideboard cannot fail to tempt. The solemn *salon*, all pillars and plush, awaits your company in its silent mirrors. Some bedrooms feel small after these great spaces but all have pleasing modern-smart décor in rich colours and textures with good, coordinated, tiled bathrooms. We loved the big double-windowed rooms over the boulevard. One has a fine dark green china lamp on an antique desk and a deep red marble bathroom. Next door is a smaller room that you love or loathe — deep raspberry walls, bright yellow fabrics, royal blue lamp... vital and provocative! The top-floor suite is a triumph of space, wraparound views of Paris, good paintings, shower room AND bathroom.

Rooms: 54: 53 doubles/twins & 1 suite.
Price: Singles 800-900 Frs
(€ 121.96-137.2); doubles 1050-1600 Frs;
suite 1600-2500 Frs.
Breakfast: Included.
Meals: In room on request 100-300 Frs.

Metro: *St Germain des Prés;* **RER** *Châtelet-Les Halles.*

Hôtel Louis II

2 rue Saint Sulpice
75006
Paris

Tel: (0)1 46 33 13 80
Fax: (0)1 46 33 17 29
E-mail: louis2@club-internet.fr

François Meynant

Imagination has triumphed in this charming hotel, often to dramatic effect (how about pink satin bamboo wallpaper in the loo?), so that even the smallest rooms (some are very snug with little storage) have huge personality. Two rooms have dazzling wraparound *trompe-l'oeil* pictures set into the timber frame by the artist who painted the lift doors. On the top floor, sleep under ancient roof timbers in a long flower-papered room where crochet bed and table coverings are so fitting and there's an old rustic *armoire* or a 1920's cheval glass. One bathroom has brass taps and a yellow cockleshell basin, another has an oval bath and burnished copper fittings. Every room is different, sheets are floral, bath/shower rooms are small but fully equipped. In the morning, admire the slightly worn elegance of the big sitting/breakfast room with fanned beams to carry the ceiling round the corner, gilt-framed mirrors, fine antiques and candelabras. You will be enthusiastically welcomed by manager and staff and properly cared for: they tend to treat guests like visiting friends.

Rooms: 22 doubles/twins.
Price: 600-900 Frs (€ 91.47-137.2).
Children under 5 free.
Breakfast: 59 Frs.
Meals: Available locally.
Closed: Never.

Metro: *Odéon;* **RER** *St Michel-Notre Dame.*

Grand Hôtel des Balcons

3 rue Casimir Delavigne
75006
Paris

Tel: (0)1 46 34 78 50
Fax: (0)1 46 34 06 27
E-mail: resa@balcons.com
web: www.balcons.com

Denise & Pierre Corroyer

Yes, it is balconied, and moulded, and corniced. But the delight is the Art Nouveau interior. Denise Corroyer, who teaches *ikebana* and flowers the hotel, copied the voluptuous curves of irises and bindweed from the 1890's staircase windows onto panels, screens and light fittings. There's a touch of humour in the lifesize 'negro boy' smiling on a shelf; a tinge of eroticism in the full-bodied Venus at breakfast; a sense of lightness and pleasure that owners and staff communicate. Service is the key here and Jean-François (Jeff to English-speakers), the owner's son, is enthusiastic about providing an ice machine, a superior selection of bathroom consumables, a clothes line over every bath and a practical meeting room where clients can work or children play. Rooms are not big but judiciously-designed units use the space cleverly and front rooms have, of course, balconies. At the back, you may be woken by the birds. It is all in prime condition with firm beds, good bathrooms, simple, pleasantly bright colours and fabrics. And breakfast is a feast which is FREE on your birthday!

Rooms: 50: 45 doubles/twins & 5 suites.
Price: Doubles 425-610 Frs
(€ 64.79-92.99); suites 950 Frs.
Child under 10 in parent's room free.
Breakfast: 55 Frs.
Meals: Afternoon tea available in winter from 4pm-8pm.
Closed: Never.

Metro: *Odéon;* **RER** *Luxembourg.*

ASP Map No: 4

Hôtel de l'Odéon
13 rue Saint Sulpice
75006
Paris

Tel: (0)1 43 25 70 11
Fax: (0)1 43 29 97 34
E-mail: hotelodeon@wanadoo.fr
web: www.hoteldelodeon.com

M & Mme Pilfert

The pretty Parisian façade deceives: behind is a feast of elegant panelling and attention to detail round a delicious green and flowery corner. The Pilferts' collection of antique beds would make any dealer envious — maybe a canopied four-poster (or two), or a pair of decorated cast-iron beds. You will have crochet bedcovers, a nice old mirror, probably a table and chairs, a window onto the narrow street or the patio. Beams abound, carefully-coordinated colour schemes convey quiet traditional comfort, bathrooms are marble. The owner has used his ingenuity and sense of architectural volumes to make even the small rooms feel special (e.g. two windows cantilevered out over the patio transform a narrow single room into a real space). Wherever feasible, the antique beds have been adapted to take extra-wide mattresses. The generous breakfast is in the 'garden room' that gives onto that little patio with its creepers, flowers and figurines, or in the soft sitting area beside the antique-fitted glass telephone box — quite a feature. It's quiet and friendly and there's room to move.

Rooms: 29 including 3 triples.
Price: 880-1350 Frs (€ 134.16-205.81).
Breakfast: 65 Frs.
Meals: Available locally.
Closed: Never.

Metro: *Odéon;* **RER** *St Michel-Notre Dame.*

Hôtel de la Tulipe
33 rue Malar
75007
Paris

Tel: (0)1 45 51 67 21
Fax: (0)1 47 53 96 37
web: www.hoteldelatulipe.com

M & Mme Fortuit

The utterly delightful Tulipe, once a convent, became an hotel for the 1890 *Exposition Universelle* and has rooms around the honeysuckled courtyard or over the quiet street. Most seem small but they all represent at least two cells. There are beams and stone, some yellow-sponged walls with deep red carpets, simple pine or cane furniture, patchwork bedcovers and white curtains, or bright Provençal prints and cream covers. Many bath/shower rooms have blue-pattern, country-style tiling; the renovated ones have bright sunflower-yellow paint. Two rooms, one for disabled guests, lead directly off the patio: it makes them feel specially connected. The new breakfast/tea room is utterly charming with its pale stone tiles, blond timbers, slim-legged conservatory furniture and interesting paintings... and croissants fresh from the local bakery. Above all, together with the unpretentiousness of the friendly, intelligent Fortuit family and their hotel, we remember their smiles and relaxed manner and so, most certainly, will you. *The one room without a loo has its own across the landing.*

Rooms: 22 doubles/twins.
Price: 600-800 Frs (€ 91.47-121.96).
Breakfast: 45 Frs.
Meals: Available locally.
Closed: Never.

Metro & RER: *Invalides, Pont de l'Alma, La Tour Maubourg.*

ASP Map No: 4

Hôtel Relais Bosquet-Tour Eiffel

19 rue du Champ de Mars   **Tel:** (0)1 47 05 25 45
75007   **Fax:** (0)1 45 55 08 24
Paris   **E-mail:** hotel@relaisbosquet.com
     web: www.relaisbosquet.com

Dora & Philippe Hervois

Surprise! Beyond the unprepossessing doorway is a colourful, cushioned *salon*, two attractive breakfast rooms (one for smokers), a long, Persian-rugged vista past twin patios with chairs and magnolia. 23 rooms give onto the courtyard, 17 onto the street. With space and peace comes remarkable service: owners and staff are quietly attentive; each room has a tea-maker, iron and ironing board, four pillows, modem socket, masses of hangers. The careful décor is either red, blue or green themed, with pretty prints for curtains and head cushions, white quilted bedcovers, big upholstered stools as suitcase racks and a fine modern white bathroom where the trim reflects the room's colour scheme. Bedrooms and bathrooms have space, the furniture is good new/trad, beds are zippable twin doubles (extra long in 'Superiors') and the lighting is just right. Every print has been chosen for its character and framed accordingly. The occasional antique adds a personal touch and staff will organise baby-sitters or secretarial workers for you. A most likeable hotel two minutes from the Eiffel Tower.

Rooms: 40 doubles/twins.
Price: 600-1000 Frs (€ 91.47-152.45).
Extra bed 100 Frs.
Breakfast: 60 Frs & à la carte.
Meals: Available locally.
Closed: Never.

Metro: *Ecole Militaire;* **RER** *Pont de l'Alma.*

Eiffel Park Hotel

17 bis rue Amélie
75007
Paris

Tel: (0)1 45 55 10 01
Fax: (0)1 47 05 28 68

Françoise Testard

The Eiffel Park was a cleancut, shiny business hotel — and had a change of heart, involving lots of Asian furniture and *objets*. The granite floor of the high yellow hall is warmed with a big oriental rug, colonial armchairs, a low table made from a pair of Indian shutters and a gigantic Provençal urn with sunflowers. Pass a carved Indian gate to the soft-smart bar and *salon* then to the breakfast room with its high-tech furniture and patio. All most comforting. Each bedroom has some rustic Far-Eastern furniture — little chests, bedside tables, highly polished or hand-painted to match the colour scheme, which may be blue and sunny gold or vibrant pink and red. Rooms are not big but there are quirky shapes and angles that give space and bathrooms have fine classic white tiles and fittings. The crowning glory is the roof terrace where grapes grow, lavender flowers and you can breakfast while gazing across the roofscape. A lively, friendly welcome completes the picture. *Four apartments can be arranged and ASP readers who stay three nights get their third breakfast free!*

Rooms: 36 doubles/twins.
Price: Singles/doubles/twins 550-770 Frs (€ 83.85-117.39); deluxe 940 Frs.
Breakfast: Buffet 55 Frs. Free your third morning.
Meals: Available locally.
Closed: Never.

Metro: *La Tour Maubourg;* **RER &** *Air France bus: Invalides.*

ASP Map No: 4

Hôtel Newton Opéra

11 bis rue de l'Arcade
75008
Paris

Tel: (0)1 42 65 32 13
Fax: (0)1 42 65 30 90
E-mail: newtonopera@integra.fr
web: www.integra.fr/newtonopera

M Simian

Little attentions that count: a pretty flask of mandarin liqueur and two tiny goblets in your room, a superb bathroom with grey pinstripe tiling, makeup remover pads, a gilded soap dish, a magnifying mirror. On a quiet street, not far from Paris's renowned department stores, the Newton Opéra will enfold you in soft, peaceful elegance. The big *salon* is peach plush with period pieces on oriental rugs: a good place to read the day's papers; the breakfast room is a stone vault with high-backed chairs, a generous buffet and prints to remind you of the artistic heyday of the 1900s. Bedrooms, not big but attractive in their yellow and green or pink and green or all blue garb, have 16th-century or polished rustic furniture, a delicate chair... and a modem socket. On the sixth floor, two rooms have private, shrubbed balconies with tables and loungers (book early, they are much coveted). Or try the bargain weekend offer with room, champagne and a night out included in the price. As one loyal client said: "The room is deliciously cosy, the bathroom has everything you need and they are so friendly here".

Rooms: 30 including 1 triple.
Price: Singles/doubles 760-850 Frs
(€ 115.86-129.58); triple 920 Frs.
Breakfast: Buffet 60 Frs.
Meals: On request from 160 Frs.
Closed: Never.

Metro: *Madeleine, Havre-Caumartin;*
RER *Auber.*

Hôtel de Banville

166 boulevard Berthier
75017
Paris

Tel: (0)1 42 67 70 16
Fax: (0)1 44 40 42 77
E-mail: hotelbanville@wanadoo.fr
web: www.hotelbanville.fr

Marianne Moreau-Lambert

A deliciously Parisian hotel, with the elegance of inherited style, soft and welcoming like a private home. The Lambert family love their *métier* and are proud of their excellent interior design. The gracious reception area has a bar, deep sofas and a piano beneath Old Masters, mirrors and clocks. Top-floor rooms are magnificent: 'Marie', subtle tones of stone and earth, from palest eggshell to rich red loam, with a gauzily canopied bed, a sitting room onto a delicious little terrace (with Eiffel Tower view) and a brilliant bathroom behind thick, soft curtains; 'Amélie', sunnily feminine in pale yellow and soft ginger, rejoicing in her own balcony and a fine, old-style, bathroom (separate wcs in both). The other rooms, full of light, pale colours and intimacy, have a gentle, airy, soft-quilt-on-firm-mattress touch, period and modern furniture and good bathrooms. Staff — many have been here for years — are as friendly as the owners: the motto of the house might be 'Know what they want before they say it'. *Good public transport to all parts of Paris.*

Rooms: 38 doubles including 1 suite.
Price: Singles/doubles 795-1100 Frs
(€ 121.2-167.69), suite 1525 Frs.
Breakfast: 65 Frs.
Meals: Light meals 50-150 Frs.
Closed: Never.

Metro: *Porte de Champerret, Pereire;*
RER *Pereire.*

ASP Map No: 4

Hôtel Cheverny

7 villa Berthier
75017
Paris

Tel: (0)1 43 80 46 42
Fax: (0)1 47 63 26 62

M Alaya

The Cheverny is made of unexpected vistas and twists, a series of tiny hanging gardens and patios overlooked by glazed landings and little sitting areas; there are plants everywhere, flowers of all colours in summer. The style is cleanly modern with 1930's touches. Colours are pale and restful, dove-grey with dark blue, deep biscuit with pale cream and 'ethnic' woven patchwork for a splash of brightness. The bedroom units are elegant and unobtrusive with suitcase spaces beneath (an intelligent detail) and firm beds. Bathrooms are just as coolly attractive with a neat clothes-line (another good mark). The junior suites are stunningly, warmly chic — e.g. deep grey and bright gold stripes on thick dark blue carpet with two smart red French armchairs. Other rooms are smaller (so are their prices), all have good storage and the latest telephone systems plus modem sockets. Just a stone's throw from the lively boulevard, 5 minutes' walk from the Porte Maillot conference centre, 15 from the Arc de Triomphe — here is a place to sleep peacefully in stylish surroundings.

Rooms: 48: 45 doubles & 3 suites.
Price: Singles & doubles 600-910 Frs (€ 91.47-138.73); suites 960 Frs.
Breakfast: Buffet 60 Frs.
Meals: On request 90-150 Frs.
Closed: Never.
Metro: *Porte Champerret;* **RER** *Pereire.*

Hôtel Pergolèse

3 rue Pergolèse
75116
Paris

Tel: (0)1 53 64 04 04
Fax: (0)1 53 64 04 40
E-mail: hotel@pergolese.com
web: www.hotelpergolese.com

Édith Vidalenc.

So near the Arc de Triomphe, old Paris gives way to a festival of contemporary design as you pass the intriguing doors: use of light and materials — wood, leather, polished metal — and custom-designed furniture all contribute. Édith Vidalenc works with designer Rena Dumas to keep a sleek but warm, colourful, curvaceously human hotel. Her own sense of hospitality governs staff attitudes: the team at reception are professional but don't take themselves too seriously — leagues away from the frostiness that often passes for 'deluxe' treatment. Hilton McConnico did the pictures and the brilliant carpet in the bar. An arch shape is the theme: in ash bedheads, lobby sofas before curved glass walls onto the patio, table legs, chrome washbasins. Tones are mutedly smart pastels so the dark-coloured breakfast room is a friendly morning nudge. The fairly small rooms are furnished in ash and leather with thick curtains and white bedcovers of soft skin-like material. The star *Pergolèse* room is a small masterpiece in palest apricot with a few spots of bright colour and a superb open bathroom.

Rooms: 40 doubles/twins.
Price: 1050-1900 Frs (€ 160.07-289.65).
Breakfast: 70 Frs (in room); buffet 95 Frs.
Meals: Very light meals from 150 Frs.
Closed: Never.

Metro: *Argentine;* **RER** *& Air France bus Porte Maillot.*

Les Jardins du Trocadéro

35 rue Benjamin Franklin
75116
Paris

Tel: (0)1 53 70 17 70
Fax: (0)1 53 70 17 80
E-mail: jardintroc@aol.com
web: www.jardintroc.com

Katia Chekroun

Intimate, relaxed, lavish and fun — a listed building with exuberantly Napoleon III décor, when the motto was "Too much is not enough". Behind the bronze-leafed door, two Egyptian torch-bearers salute; Muses beckon from landing walls; musical monkeys gambol across doors (all painted by Beaux Arts students). The atmosphere is young and casual — you are greeted by a sweet alabaster Beatrice — but efficiency and service are there, discreet and unobsequious. Lovers of the small and intimate will like it here; so will fans of French style. The gilt-mirrored, bronze-lamped *salon* has pure Second Empire furniture on a perfectly aged marble floor and drinks are served at a genuine custom-made bistro bar, *le zinc*. Don't expect big bedrooms (the 'executive' rooms are larger and very good suites can be organised) but enjoy their soft generous draperies and the genuine ormolu antiques that the owners took such trouble finding; surrounded by marble, luxuriate in your whirlpool bath and fluffy bathrobe, then descend for the 'worldwide tapas' served in the pretty basement dining room.

Rooms: 23: 18 doubles & 5 suites all with whirlpool bath.
Price: Doubles/twins 890-1800 Frs (€ 135.68-274.41); suites 1790-2600 Frs.
Breakfast: 'Unlimited' buffet 75 Frs.
Meals: Menus from 100 Frs at the 'La Petite Muse' restaurant.
Closed: Never.

Metro: *Trocadéro*; **RER** *Charles de Gaulle-Etoile*.

Hôtel Kléber

7 rue de Belloy
75116
Paris

Tel: (0)1 47 23 80 22
Fax: (0)1 49 52 07 20
E-mail: kleberhot@aol.com
web: www.kleberhotel.com

Samuel Abergel

The gilt-framed mirrors come from a derelict château — the owners love hunting for such delights. Behind the iron balconies, the atmosphere is determinedly French *romantique* — witness the gilt-bronze-encrusted curly chests, elaborate lamps (one astounding 'desk' light with hefty bronze stems and three big bunches of electrified (sic) grapes), period paintings and orientalisms (lifesize statues). The suite has a beautiful roll-top desk with Chinese inlay in its generous *salon* (which clients often use as a meeting room), a king-size bed and a kitchenette. All is rich in colour — reds, yellows, blues — and texture, in the smaller rooms too; bedding is new and twins can be zipped into king-size; tiled or mosaic bathrooms have all the necessary bits including power showers. The basket of fruit and chocolates in your room is part of Samy's warm welcome. In the refurbished ground-floor area, the breakfast buffet includes homemade jams and croissants as well as cereals, cheese and eggs for a fine start to the day. English, Spanish, Hebrew, Japanese and Arabic spoken!

Rooms: 22: 21 doubles/twins & 1 apartment.
Price: Singles & doubles 690-1390 Frs
(€ 105.19-211.9); apartment 990-1990 Frs.
Breakfast: Buffet 75 Frs.
Meals: On request 100-150 Frs.
Closed: Never.

Metro: *Kléber;* **RER** *Charles de Gaulle-Étoile.*

67

Hôtel Le Lavoisier

21 rue Lavoisier
75008
Paris

Tel: (0)1 53 30 06 06
Fax: (0)1 53 30 23 00
E-mail: info@hotellavoisier.com
web: www.hotellavoisier.com

Ludovic Peressini

In a small street close to bustling boulevards, this handsome hotel on the Right Bank has been transformed. Behind the stone façade, everything is clean and comfortable. Good, subdued lighting, soft colours, a mix of squidgy sofas, brass stair stays, modern furniture and antique pieces create a mood both relaxed and smart. Even the manager, Ludovic Peressini, is helpful and approachable. Traditional, with a designer touch, the bedrooms are immaculate, the bathrooms great; there's plenty of hanging space, good mirrors and simple, good quality covers and drapes; the odd clever flea-market find too. Traffic noise can't be kept out entirely, but it's not too bad considering where you are. There's no noise from bars or late-night pavement cafés, and the views across Paris roof-tops are an engaging sea of slate and slopes. Fresh flowers on the reception desk and plenty of towels in the bathroom are a welcome sight after a day out exploring the city. The peace of the cosy bar is good to absorb before heading out again for the evening.

Rooms: 30 including 1 junior suite & 1 suite.
Price: 1190-2500 Frs (€ 181.41-381.12); junior suite 1490-1890 Frs; suite 2500 Frs.
Breakfast: 70 Frs.
Meals: Available locally.
Closed: Never.
Metro: *St Augustin.*

Hotel Danemark

21 rue Vavin
75006
Paris

Tel: (0)1 43 26 93 78
Fax: (0)1 46 34 66 06

M Jean Nurit

Cleverly tucked away between the hustle and bustle of Montparnasse with its cafés, theatres, and cinemas and the elegant tranquility of Luxembourg Gardens, you might almost miss the Hotel Danemark if you didn't know it had sliding doors and a blue exterior. The red and blue scheme of the painting in the reception is echoed in the thick cubist-patterned rugs leading to another small sitting area; tobacco-coloured leather armchairs and sofa making a comfy place for planning your day. The rooms are not large but are well-equipped and the walls warmly clothed in delicate pastel stripes or tiny flower patterns. Ask for a room on the street (double-glazed windows) so that you can gaze out upon a forest of green foliage and flowered balconies. A surprising 'ecologicial' building (a first, they say) designed by architect Henri Sauvauge in the '30s; each apartment is equipped with a huge planted area set against a white tile exterior. The continental breakfast is a copious one including cheese, fruit *compôtes*, yoghurt and bread brought in from a bakery reknowned for its *baguettes*.

Rooms: 15: 11 doubles, 4 twins.
Price: 620-890 Frs (€ 94.52-135.68).
Breakfast: 55 Frs.
Meals: A varied choice of restaurants within 5 minutes walk.
Closed: Never.

Metro: *Vavin, Notre Dame des Champs;*
Car Park: *Montparnasse.*

ASP Map No: 4

Abbaye des Vaux de Cernay

Route d'Auffargis D24
78720 Cernay la Ville
Yvelines

Tel: (0)1 34 85 23 00
Fax: (0)1 34 85 20 95
E-mail: aby_vau@club-internet.fr
web: www.chateauxandcountry.com/chateaux/vauxdecernay

André Charpentier

It may seem rather large but the buildings are so atmospheric, the place waves such a magical wand of respectful sophistication that people stop, feel and lose their restlessness. From thriving Cistercian abbey, through Revolution and ruin to Rothschild ownership in the 1870s, Cernay bears the marks of European history. The owners have turned it into a luxurious hotel that preserves the spirit and forms of the old place — you can almost hear the monks scurrying along those underground passages while you listen to the Cernay Music Festival in the roofless abbey church or wine and dine in hedonistic splendour under the vaults of the brothers' refectory. There may be little trace of the 'Strict Observance' Trappist rule for daily life that once reigned here — bedrooms have every modern comfort, *salons* are of the highest elegance, there is a lake for meditation and a 'fitness garden' — but you cannot fail to be deeply influenced by the vibrations from those glowing stones and Gothic arches and glad that the hotel business keeps them alive today.

Rooms: 55 singles/double/twins + 3 suites.
Price: Singles 490-790 Frs
(€ 74.7-120.43); doubles 790-1590 Frs;
suites 1900-3880 Frs. Various weekend
packages available.
Breakfast: 80 Frs. Buffet brunch Sundays
& holidays.
Meals: Weekday lunch from 160 Frs.
Dinner & weekend lunch 265-405 Frs.
Closed: Never.

From Paris Pont de Sèvres dir.
Chartres/Orléans. Exit Saclay/Gif sur Yvette dir. Gif sur Yvette/Chevreuse on N306.
In Saint Rémy les Chevreuse D906 becomes D306 dir. Chevreuse/Rambouillet;
signposted in Cernay La Ville dir. Auffargis D24.

Cazaudehore — La Forestière

1 avenue Kennedy
78100 Saint Germain en Laye
Yvelines

Tel: (0)1 39 10 38 38
Fax: (0)1 39 73 73 88
E-mail: hotel@cazaudehore.fr
web: www.cazaudehore.fr

M Cazaudehore

The rose-strewn 'English' garden is like an island in the great forest of St Germain and it's hard to believe the buzzing metropolis is just a short train journey away. The first Cazaudehore built the restaurant in 1928, the second built the hotel in 1962, the third generation apply their imaginations to improving both and receiving their guests with elegant French charm. The buildings are almost camouflaged among the greenery, summer eating is deliciously shaded under rose-red parasols; or hotel guests have the elegant, beamed dining room with its verandah to themselves (there are several seminar and reception rooms). Food and wine are the main focus — the wine-tasting dinners are renowned and chef Jacques Pactol has developed a lighter, more refined version of the Périgord style, skilfully mixing tradition and invention: you will eat supremely well here. But bedrooms are much cared for too, renovated in refined but unostentatious style with good fabrics, original colour schemes (saffron, blue and lightning green, for example), period furniture and prints, and masses of character.

Rooms: 30: 25 doubles/twins & 5 suites.
Price: Doubles 1100 Frs (€ 167.69); suites 1500 Frs. Extra bed 150 Frs.
Breakfast: 85 Frs.
Meals: Lunch & dinner 200-370 Frs; children 130 Frs. À la carte also available.
Closed: Never. Restaurant closed Mondays, except for residents.

A13 dir. Rouen exit 6 dir. St. Germain en Laye on N186; N184 dir. Pontoise. Hotel is on left 2.5km after the château.

Normandy

The Casino, I hasten to add, has quite the air of an
establishment frequented by gentlemen who
look at ladies' windows with telescopes.
Henry James

Auberge du Val au Cesne

Le Val au Cesne
76190 Croix Mare
Seine-Maritime

Tel: (0)2 35 56 63 06
Fax: (0)2 35 56 92 78
web: www.pageszoom.com/
val-au-cesne

M Carel

Cupola-shaped cages of parrots, rare chickens, doves and parakeets hint at the exotic; the garden is hidden in an emerald, rolling-hilled Norman valley. Monsieur Carel, a self-made *patron*, will serve a leisurely meal outside on a sunny day or invite you into the half-timbered farmhouse and place you in one of the two dining rooms separated by the chimney (he makes a point of mixing the locals with the visitors, contrary to some owners who segregate the English language speakers). The low ceilings, raw timbers and sepia photographs of his ancestors are an appropriate Norman background for the regional dishes he creates. His customers come in droves now, so the cottage next door has been transformed into five little independent apartments, four of them on the ground floor. Each one has its own personality and the colours are as vibrant as his pet ducks: royal blues and reds, canary yellow and iris purple. Padded textiles on the walls make good soundproofing. The last one, lighter and bigger, is at the top of an outside stairway.

Rooms: 5 doubles/twins.
Price: 480 Frs (€ 73.18).
Extra bed 80 Frs.
Breakfast: 50 Frs.
Meals: Lunch & dinner from 150 Frs.
Closed: Never.

*From Rouen A15/N15 for approx. 20km. Left on D22 to Fréville then D5 dir. Yvetot for 3km. **Do not go into Croix Mare** (postal address).*

Hôtel de la Cathédrale

12 rue Saint Romain
76000 Rouen
Seine-Maritime

Tel: (0)2 35 71 57 95
Fax: (0)2 35 70 15 54
E-mail: arttra@club-internet.fr
web: www.hotel-de-la-cathedrale.com

Laurent Delaunay

In one of the cobbled streets of historic old Rouen, the Archbishopric looming over it, this is the only half-timbered hotel in a city of timber-frame houses. From some windows you see two Gothic marvels: the Cathedral towers and the magnificent tracery of St Maclou — your soul will be safe here. But a wind of material change is blowing over the hotel. The newly-arrived, dynamic Delaunays plan to renovate the rather old-fashioned décor and bathrooms with all due respect to the original features. The little half-timbered courtyard is a delight in summer with myriad flower pots and riotous creeper, a lovely spot for breakfast. The indoor breakfast room has cotton tablecloths and a great old fireplace: it's friendly and fresh and there are armchairs. Rooms are simple, some of them a decent size, some bathrooms have already been renovated and there are some interesting pieces in the motley mixture of furniture. Laurent Delaunay, attentive, eager to please and keen to put his plans into action, is running a remarkable-value hotel plumb in the middle of a city that cries out to be explored. *No-smoking in some rooms.*

Rooms: 25 doubles/twins.
Price: 280-370 Frs (€ 42.69-56.41).
Breakfast: 37 Frs.
Meals: Available locally.
Closed: Never.

In Rouen centre, park in Parking Hôtel de Ville, take 'Rue piétonnière' exit from car park, walk towards cathedral. Rue St Romain is first street along east side of cathedral.

Auberge de Vieux Carré

3 rue de la Ganterie
76000 Rouen
Seine-Maritime

Tel: (0)2 35 71 67 70
Fax: (0)2 35 71 76 96

Patrick Beaumont

If our description is a little thin it is because the hotel is slap in the middle of major changes as we write! So to put it in this book is an act of faith, made possible by the solid charms of the old establishment and the good taste of the young owner. He has already made a success of the unusual and delightful Hotel Carmes in Rouen. He is spending a small fortune on the make-over, planning Art Deco à la anglaise with a raised bookshelf and wood panelling behind the reception, open fire places, leather armchairs and sofas. In the bedrooms there will be wrought-iron bedside tables, heavy curtains — all very minimalistic, simple and refined. The building is gloriously Rouenais, with beams galore and a little courtyard in front with a cherry tree and lots of other things growing. Monsieur Beaumont will put old prints of Rouen on the walls and wash the wood-work with light pastel colours. To crown it all he will put a Japanese garden on the roof, with chairs for sun-soaking. Our inspector waxed lyrical about the place, utterly convinced that it will be a triumph. And Rouen is worth a long stay.

Rooms: 14: 13 doubles/twins & 1 triple.
Price: 350-400 Frs (€ 53.36-60.98).
Breakfast: 34 Frs.
Meals: Lunch & snacks from 60 Frs.
Closed: Never.

From autoroutes exit Rouen Rive Droite dir. Hotel de Ville. In centre of town on pedestrian street. Public parking 30m.

Château de la Rapée

27140 Bazincourt sur Epte
Eure

Tel: (0)2 32 55 11 61
Fax: (0)2 32 55 95 65

M Bergeron

A winding road through 80 hectares of forest in the Epte valley. With those 10km in mind, just keep going and going, a slight slant up and up; not a house, cabin, animal, or car in sight, wondering what on earth will greet you at the end of the road. A little plateau at the edge of the world, and an extraordinary vision of happy Hitchock film; a Norman baroque manor of angles, curlicues, overhanging roofed windows, turrets and towers, blue crenellated trim, from every angle a different vision. Shake your head in disbelief. The circular glassed-in dining room has pink table cloths and pink trim. Monsieur Bergeron, who bought the house (to the dismay of his wife who spent the next years with nowhere to go), is quite a gentleman rake; he never uses green anywhere in the hotel as it is "not flattering for the ladies". He's very proud of this almost-museum. One room, with romantic baldaquin, is scrupulously clean in soft satiny pastels, not a nick or a smudge in the paint. Good mattresses and linen, carpet on the walls, working chimneys in the *salon* in winter. Mad, wonderful, passionate — special.

Rooms: 13 doubles/ twins.
Price: 480-580 Frs (€ 73.18-88.42).
Extra bed 90 Frs.
Breakfast: 60 Frs.
Meals: Lunch & dinners 170-230 Frs.
Closed: August 16-30. Restaurant closed February.

From Gisors D915 north for approx. 10km. Signposted.

Le Moulin de Connelles

40 route d'Amfreville sur les Monts
27430 Connelles
Eure

Tel: (0)2 32 59 53 33
Fax: (0)2 32 59 21 83
E-mail: moulin.de.connelles@wanadoo.fr
web: www.cofrase.com/hotel/moulindeconnelles

M & Mme Petiteau

Bring your boater, hop in a green and red-trimmed flatboat right out of a Monet painting and slip along a quiet arm of the Seine after a morning at Monet's Giverny garden, twenty minutes away. Watery greens, pinks and that scintillating veil of haze that is so particular to this part of Normandy intensify the Impressionist mood. Then look up at the vision of an extraordinary half-timbered, checker-boarded, turreted manor house and you will have to pinch yourself, hard. What's more, you are a treasured guest here. The Petiteau's quiet attentions extend from the tinted glass on the restaurant veranda to the in-house baked croissants and pre-dinner, just warm *amuse-bouches*. Step around to the garden and gaze at the rows of copper pots through the kitchen windows. It's only after a moment that you realise that part of the house is on an island; hidden paths lead through flowering bushes to a private pool and the tennis courts. We loved room 9 with its yellow walls, blue trim and a balcony on the river. Our favourite was suite 7 in the tower, with double exposure. Bring your paintbrushes.

Rooms: 13: 7 doubles/twins &
6 suites for 4.
Price: Doubles 600-850 Frs.
(€ 91.47-129.58); suites 850-1250 Frs.
Breakfast: 70 Frs.
Meals: Lunch & dinner 140-315 Frs.
Children 70 Frs.
Closed: January-end March.

From A13 exit 18 on N15 dir. Pont de l'Arche for 4km; right to Andé and Connelles. Signposted.

Château de Brécourt

Douains
27120 Pacy sur Eure
Eure

Tel: (0)2 32 52 40 50
Fax: (0)2 32 52 41 39
E-mail: chateau-brecourt@wanadoo.fr
web: www.chateauxandcountry.com/chateaux/brecourt

Mme Langlais

It's worth a night here just to get the instant access to Monet's Gardens at Giverny that the miracle-working Madame Langlais will conjure up. On top of that it's quite a nice little place. It is moated, a national Historic Monument, with a low, raw-beamed dining room that catches the breath and a heart-melting feast of brick and stone. There are chimneys you can hide in, floor tiles polished by centuries of leather soles, a triple staircase with sculpted oak balustrade that would probably not fit into your house, a Louis XV wood-panelled dining room of rare elegance, mosaics on some bathtubs, tissue on the walls and, perhaps most importantly, well-worn leather sofas in front of the fireplace. The red of some of the walls is as bold as the blues of the nearby curtains. Needless to say, the bedrooms are gigantic and look over the great park of 20 hectares, enough to lose yourself in if the crowds at Giverny have got to you. On Fridays you can, if you have planned ahead, eat a 17th-century meal; on other days you eat just as well. There's even a faint smell of burning logs — perfect.

Rooms: 30: 25 doubles/twins & 5 apartments.
Price: 500-1085 Frs (€ 76.22-165.41); apartments 1225-1425 Frs.
Breakfast: 80 Frs.
Meals: Lunch & dinner from 240 Frs.
Closed: Never.

From A13 exit 16 onto D181 Pacy sur Eure then very soon left on D75 to Douains. Signposted.

Hôtel de France

29 rue Saint Thomas
27000 Evreux
Eure

Tel: (0)2 32 39 09 25
Fax: (0)2 32 38 38 56

M Meyruey & M Wantier

Without question the attraction is the food: Monsieur Wantier's cooking has won three forks from the inspectors of the exacting *Michelin Guide*. Behind the slightly worn but pretty exterior, the restaurant is elegant — deep pink tablecloths, delicate glassware, polished silver and (how French!) a posy of artificial flowers on each table. Sliding glass doors open on to a charming garden with a stream and flower-strewn bank. The service is discreet and professional. Breakfasts are excellent, and served in a recently renovated, rustic reception area at round tables. The courteous and capable Monsieur Meyruey fronts the house, which is co-owned with his partner, *le chef*. Corridors, white-walled and purple-carpeted, are spotless. Bedrooms are nothing special but perfectly adequate, with white walls, modern floral fabrics, spotlights by the beds. You can be sure of a good night's sleep — mattresses are exceptionally comfortable, pillows thick — but ask for one of the rooms over the garden; they're much quieter than those over the road.

Rooms: 16: 15 doubles/twins & 1 suite.
Price: Doubles 270-345 Frs
(€ 41.16-52.59); suite 450 Frs.
Breakfast: 40 Frs.
Meals: Lunch 150 Frs;
dinner 150-210 Frs.
Closed: Never. Restaurant closed Sunday
evenings & Mondays.

Look for signs for Centre Ville — hotel behind tourist office.

Hostellerie du Moulin Fouret

27300 Saint Aubin le Vertueux
Eure

Tel: (0)2 32 43 19 95
Fax: (0)2 32 45 55 50

M & Mme Déduit

Go fishing for a while before lunch under pink parasols on a rose-covered terrace overlooking a quiet garden and vine covered walls. The Déduits can get you a day-tripper permit. Or you may just want to be beside the bubbling Charantonne river and wonder what a miller's life was like in the 16th century when this mill was built between two arms of the river. The gear wheels now house a cleverly structured multi-tiered bar in the entrance where a cocktail can be had before dining. If the weather turns grim it doesn't really matter as the dining room, a cosy union of massive, dark beams, biscuit-clothed chairs with matching drapes and pink table linen, combined with Monsieur's cooking skills, will keep you happy. The rooms and bathrooms are smallish but adequate; ask for the one furnished with natural wood. All overlook the river. If you arrive late, Edwige will be delighted to prepare a meal for you in your room. On a weekend, do book ahead for your meals — this is a most popular place. *There is a delightful path of 12km along the old railroad tracks exploring the Charenton valley.*

Rooms: 8 doubles.
Price: 250 Frs (€ 38.11).
Breakfast: 45 Frs.
Meals: Lunch & dinner 100-330 Frs.
Closed: Never. Restaurant closed Sunday nights & Mondays from Sept. 1-April 30.

From A13 dir. Rouen exit Pont Audemer. D130 dir. Monfort/Le Bec Hellouin. Take N138 at Brionne dir. Bernay. 3km behind railway station dir. St Quentin des Isles on D33.

Hôtel de la Poste
27210 Beuzeville
Eure

Tel: (0)2 32 57 71 04
Fax: (0)2 32 42 11 01

M & Mme Bosquet

Generations ago this was an old coaching inn and now the Bosquet family have proudly created a small, town-centre hotel of traditional, solid, French quality. Entering through blue archways you are warmly met in a friendly reception area. From here you will be led up a dramatic stairway to carpeted, floral bedrooms with generously-sized double beds. Rooms on the garden side are quiet, but perhaps there could be disturbance at the front on Tuesday, the weekly market day. The restaurant is perfect for the place, in a slightly bistro-ish way — fresh flowers on the tables, views to the newly planted garden and a majestic bar which spans the room. The regional food is specially well cooked and served. The Bosquets welcome families and their *prix fixes* menus and modest room prices should leave change for future exploration of this rich area — Beuzeville is only ten minutes drive from Honfleur is only ten minutes drive from Honfleur and has some interesting antique shops of its own. Engagingly, unpretentiously 'correct'.

Rooms: 14: 11 doubles/twins, 2 triples & 1 quadruple.
Price: Doubles 250-350 Frs (€ 38.11-53.36); triples 360 Frs; quadruple 450 Frs.
Breakfast: 40 Frs.
Meals: Lunch & dinner 130-195 Frs. Weekday lunch from 100 Frs.
Closed: November 15-Easter. Restaurant closed Thursday mid-September-mid-June.

From Paris/Rouen A13 exit 28 Beuzeville, left N175. Between Pont Audemer, Rouen and Pont l'Evêque.

Auberge de la Source

La Peleras
61600 La Ferté Macé
Orne

Tel: (0)2 33 37 28 23
Fax: (0)2 33 37 28 23

Christine & Serge Volclair

Using reclaimed beams and stone, Christine and Serge built the Auberge de la Source — they did a lot of the work themselves — on the site of his parents' 18th-century apple press. Unfortunately that means no more cider, but they serve a superb one made just down the road. Both the restaurants — one smaller and cosier, the other with huge sliding windows — and the bedrooms were designed to make the most of the view down to the lake, which is the hub of a huge sports complex. Apart from windsurfing and a sailing school, this offers riding, a climbing wall, archery, fishing and something called 'swing-golf', easy to learn apparently. Children have a play area, pony rides, mini-golf and pedal boats. If you want "natural" nature the forest is nearby where you will see huge stags without too much searching. The auberge has big rooms catering for families, all cosy with huge beams and chunky antiques mixed in with more modern furniture. The food is simple, centering on steaks cooked over a wood fire, with fresh farm produce to go with it. A great choice for families with either small children or sporty teenagers.

Rooms: 5: 3 triples & 2 quadruples.
Price: 280-440 Frs (€ 42.69-67.08).
Breakfast: Included.
Meals: Lunch & dinner 75-120 Frs.
Picnic 50 Frs.
Closed: January-February.

From Ferté Macé, D908 dir. Domfront Mont St Michel. After 2km right to auberge. Well signposted.

Auberge Saint Christophe

Saint Christophe
14690 Pont d'Ouilly
Calvados

Tel: (0)2 31 69 81 23
Fax: (0)2 31 69 26 58

M & Mme Lecoeur

You can canoe on the river or rock climb if you are brave, while the beaches are a short drive away. This could be a useful stopover, or a base for a long weekend exploring Normandy. It is right on a road (you would have to watch small children), but in a quiet village so your nights should not be broken. Bedrooms are fresh and flowery — two pink and three dominated by green — and all but one look onto a pretty, though not huge, garden. Bathrooms are small but have all the essentials and everything is kept spotlessly clean. The Saint-Christophe started out as a tiny auberge selling *friture*, pan-fried tiny fish from the river that flows through the village. Monsieur and Madame Lecoeur have built up a reputation for their food; he is the chef. The dining room is light and airy and in summer meals are served on the pretty terrace behind the auberge. M. Lecoeur prides himself on the lightness and freshness of his menus and food comes on striking plates with abstract flowers around the rim.

Rooms: 7 doubles/twins.
Price: 280 Frs (€ 42.69).
Breakfast: 40 Frs.
Meals: Lunch & dinner 103-220 Frs.
Closed: Sunday nights & Mondays.

From Pont d'Ouilly centre right (before bridge over R. Orne) and follow river for approx. 2km. Left on D23 dir. St Christophe. Auberge on left 500m.

MMap 231-30   **ASP Map No: 2**

Aux Pommiers de Livaye

RN 13 Notre Dame de Livaye
14340 Crèvecœur en Auge
Calvados

Tel: (0)2 31 63 01 28
Fax: (0)2 31 63 73 63

Germain & Marie-Josette Lambert-Dutrait

Some have come for a day and stayed for a fortnight; all have been delighted with the warmth of the welcome and the quality of the food. A long drive bordered by chestnut and apple trees leads to the 300-year-old half-timbered Norman farm house smothered in climbing roses and wisteria. The entrance and glassed-in dining room are full of country-farm style tables and chairs and have a beautiful view of the Lambert's lush green fields where horses, cattle and the occasional deer graze. One wall is lined with homemade jams and dried flowers and antique plates vie for space above the timbers. The gound floor bedrooms are charming; water-green painted brass beds against pale yellow walls, and a joyful selection of pink and green eiderdown coverlets. Marie-Josette judiciously uses *pochoir* patterns to repeat the colours. The towels are prettily presented wrapped with a ribbon — a nice touch. No tourist office could give you such a personal introduction to the region as do Germain and Maire-Josette; an invaluable asset to guests. They have even mapped out a series of walking tours for you.

Rooms: 5: 1 double, 1 triple, 2 quadruple & 1 suite.
Price: 420-720 Frs (€ 64.03-109.76).
Breakfast: Included.
Meals: Dinner 100-150 Frs.
Closed: December 16-end February.

From Lisieux N13 W dir. Crèvecœur. Hotel 1km before Crèvecœur — signposted.

Hostellerie de Tourgéville

Chemin de l'Orgueuil
14800 Tourgéville-Deauville
Calvados

Tel: (0)2 31 14 48 68
Fax: (0)2 31 14 48 69
E-mail: hostellerie@hotel-de-tourgeville.com
web: www.123france.com/hostellerie-de-tourgevil

Wilhelm Stoppacher

There were real stars in the '70s, when film director Claude Lelouch built his glorified 'Norman quadrangle' as a club for friends; now there are just giant photographs. But his adorable private cinema is still here, as are pool, gym and sauna. Timbers and stones are genuinely old; the all-glass ground floor is thoroughly modern. Open-plan sitting and dining areas are in blond oak, soft cushions and warm colours. The chef has an excellent reputation, by the way. Most rooms are soberly decorated with high-quality fabrics, matt satin curtain stuff, beige carpet, the odd antique and those ubiquitous film stars. Ground-floor rooms have small private terraces and triplexes (effectively up-ended suites with the bathroom on a balcony between *salon* and bedroom), fine double-height fireplaces on their stone-flagged floors, plus two deep sofas. The friendly manager is gradually redecorating with a more lively, contemporary touch, interesting, amusing furniture and some superb, strong-colour co-ordinates. A very special place to stay; Lelouch calls it "an hotel for people who don't like hotels".

Rooms: 19: 6 doubles & 13 suites.
Price: Doubles 650-900 Frs
(€ 99.09-137.2); suites 850-1600 Frs.
Breakfast: 75 Frs.
Meals: Dinner 190-295 Frs.
Closed: 3 weeks in February or March.

From A13 exit Deauville dir. Deauville.
After Canapville left at roundabout on D27
dir. Caen; first left; first left again (D278);
first right (chemin de l'Orgueuil); entrance
600m up on left.

Manoir de la Rivière

14310 Saint Louet sur Seulles
Calvados

Tel: (0)2 31 77 96 30
Fax: (0)2 31 77 96 30
web: www.chateaux-france.com
E-mail: manoir-de-la-rivière@wanadoo.fr

Docteur Jean-Claude Houdret

A theatrical B&B tucked away in the hills of rural Normandy! The outbuildings of this traditional, mellow-stoned 16th-century farmhouse have been converted into guests' extravagantly themed rooms. The *Angel Room* is painted an iridescent white and blue; a fresco of the pyramids graces the *Explorer's Room* — painted by monsieur himself — and the *Colonel's Room* is eccentrically kitted out with guns, swords, military coins and a life-sized model of a 19th-century soldier. Lots of the artefacts, including the embroidered bathrobes, are for sale. Bathrooms are spotless and immaculate. The guests' sitting room is stone-walled and coir-carpeted, with a wonderful suite of pink, gold and white Louis XV armchairs upon which the Princess of Wales, we are told, once sat, and a big open fire. The *manoir's* warm welcome extends even to your dogs, whose kennels are centrally-heated. More plans are in the pipeline from the unstoppable Docteur Houdret: a concert room, a beauty treatment room, a reception room for grand occasions and yet more improvements to the formal gardens and grounds.

Rooms: 4: 3 doubles & 1 suite for four.
Price: Rooms 500-650 Frs
(€ 76.22-99.09); suites 800-1000 Frs.
Breakfast: Included.
Meals: Dinner 180 Frs.
Closed: Never.

From Caen N175 to Villers Bocage. There, right to St Louet sur Seulles; pass church — house is second on right up poplar-lined drive.

Ferme de la Rançonnière

Route d'Arromanches
14480 Creully
Calvados

Tel: (0)2 31 22 21 73
Fax: (0)2 31 22 98 39

Mme Vereecke & Mme Sileghem

A matronly farmer was unloading vast quantities of fresh eggs from a wrinkled grey *deux chevaux* as I drove through the crenellated carriage gate, past the 15th-century tower into the vast grassy courtyard around which are the reception, restaurant and bedrooms of the La Rançonnière. Some went into a tiny corner store set in the massive sandstone wall to sit with local cheeses, cream and potatoes. The others were whisked into the oak-beamed, vaulted restaurant laid for lunch; white linen, tiny pink bouquets and a cheerful wood fire at one end. (In summer you can dine in the courtyard.) Young, efficient Isabelle Sileghem and her husband, with help from a devoted staff, keep this place humming. There are exposed timbers everywhere, and the comfortable bedrooms have small windows and rustic, sometimes heavy furniture. An antique butter churn in the corridor and a well-worn kneading trough in a large family room remind you that this is a working farm. A new annexe in an old farmhouse down the road might be quieter on the weekends. Reserve ahead for the best rooms. A wonderful old place.

Rooms: 45: 35 doubles/twins, 10 junior suites in Manoir 600m away.
Price: Doubles 295-580 Frs (€ 38.11-88.42); suites 680 Frs. Extra bed 100 Frs.
Breakfast: 50 Frs.
Meals: Lunch & dinner 60-280 Frs.
Closed: Never.

From Caen by-pass exit 7 dir. Creully/Arromanches on D22 for 19km. In Creully right at church dir. Arromanches on D65. In Crépon, hotel is first on right.

Le Château de Sully

Route de Port en Bessin
14400 Sully
Calvados

Tel: (0)2 31 22 29 48
Fax: (0)2 31 22 64 77

M & Mme Brault

From the veranda, the view of giant crescent-shaped flower beds filled with flamboyant mixtures of tangled flowers is quite stunning. This elegant 18th-century building combines classical architecture with an exquisite setting, every detail inside and out carefully orchestrated. Yellow is the dominant colour for the formal dining room, whilst russet reds tone in with the bar and sober leather sofas in the main *salon*. In another lounge, table-games and a billiard board guarantee some fun too. The first-floor bedrooms looking out over neat lawns are beautifully decorated, and the attic rooms one floor up are cosy and inviting. There are more bedrooms, an indoor pool and fitness centre in the *petit manoir* annexe. There are traces of children's paintings still to be seen in the 16th-century chapel, and lots of outdoor space for today's children. Inside, however, the little darlings will have to resist the temptation to thunder past delicate objects, as well as promise to sit up straight in the dining room. Good value, remarkably, for this really is a most magnificent place.

Rooms: 22: 19 doubles, 2 triples & 1 suite.
Price: Doubles 520-950 Frs (€ 79.27-144.83); triples 740-790 Frs; suite 785-950 Frs.
Breakfast: 65-75 Frs.
Meals: Lunch & dinner 150-350 Frs.
Closed: December-end February.

From Bayeux D6 dir. Port en Bessin. Château is on right side of road approx. 4km after Bayeux.

La Chenevière

Escures Commes
14520 Port en Bessin
Calvados

Tel: (0)2 31 51 25 25
Fax: (0)2 31 51 25 20
E-mail: la.cheneviere@wanadoo.fr

M Esprabens

Pure tranquility — La Chenevière seems to have found the perfect formula. The owners have taken the green of Normandy using the hotel's magnificent park, the finely-proportioned rooms of a 19th-century manor house and added soft pastels, honey-coloured hardwood floors, and curtains that gently frame the light. A strong detail is added here and there: a framed collection of vermillion wax stamps or a series of architectural drawings decorating whole walls in the two bars (one for non-smokers). The rooms, all of which overlook the park, are so vast (and quiet) that brighter flower-patterned materials are used, the curtains are swagged and the bathrooms are truly royal. Add the 'nose and mouth' to this experience with freshly cut flowers and Claude Esprabens's expertise in the kitchen. He does both the local seafood and local farm produce. A most successful marriage of a country home and a first class hotel, done with restrained good taste and no surprises. If you turn up with this book you'll be offered afternoon tea! *There are paths galore for walking, biking or riding in the nearby forest of Cerisy.*

Rooms: 19 doubles/twins.
Price: Doubles 820-1220 Frs
(€ 125.01-185.99); junior suite
1020-1120 Frs; suite 1220-1420 Frs.
Breakfast: Included.
Meals: Lunch & dinner 175-380 Frs.
Closed: January 3-February 8.

From Bayeux D6 NW to Port en Bessin for 8km. Signposted.

Hôtel du Vieux Château

4 cours du Château
50260 Bricquebec
Manche

Tel: (0)2 33 52 24 49
Fax: (0)2 33 52 62 71
E-mail: Hubert.Hardy@ wanadoo.fr
web: www.hotelrestvieuxchateau.com

Hubert Hardy

It is the *château fort* of the old town's defences — extraordinary, with a fully documented history going back to 1066 and beyond. It was badly neglected and then rescued from ruin to become a *cabaret misérable* (seedy dive) in the 18th century. Another century rescued the remains and the town council did its best, and still does so — for it now owns the castle and hotel. This may explain the somewhat lacklustre management and the gap between expectation and reality, but you come here to wallow in this remarkable piece of history... and the beds and little bathrooms are fine. Actually much of it is fine, with ancient stone walls and plain carpets, beams and the odd bit of good, old furniture. If you know France you will know what I mean. The views onto the floodlit courtyard are to tell your grandchildren about, together with the imprisonment here by Joan of Arc of the Duke of Suffolk in 1429. There is a fine old dining room, rather incongruously equipped with stainless steel cutlery and bread baskets, inter alia. Be bold and stay here en route to and from the ferry. It is all very real, and rather endearing.

Rooms: 16: 13 doubles & 3 quadruples.
Price: Doubles 300-495 Frs
(€ 45.73-75.46); quadruples 615 Frs.
Breakfast: 45 Frs.
Meals: Lunch & dinner 65-170 Frs.
Closed: January.

From Cherbourg D900 dir. Bricquebec for approx. 26km. Hotel in centre of town, easily found by its high medieval tower dominating horizon.

Hôtel Restaurant Le Mesnilgrand

Négreville	**Tel:** (0)2 33 95 09 54
50260 Bricquebec	**Fax:** (0)2 33 95 20 04
Manche	**E-mail:** mesnilgrand@wanadoo.fr

James & Pascal Boekee

Deep in the countryside lies a converted 18th-century cider farm, now a restaurant, small hotel and creative activity centre in one. The owner and chef, both English, of this deeply rural centre provide rare opportunities. You could find yourself wild-mushrooming, nature trailing or seeking the finest fish, cheese or cider, with the chef, from the local market. The energy and creativity of your hosts know few bounds. Le Mesnilgrand has but five bedrooms and you will pay very little extra for children under three. The rooms are comfortable, silent and simply decorated with good bathrooms. You can play tennis, paint by the lake or just recline in the English-style long bar. The chef's reputation is big in the area and his organically chosen menu will vary from day to day (or even from person to person). You eat in a setting to match Michael's culinary skills (which he will share on pre-arranged short cookery courses). Or there are horse-riding opportunities with or without specialist instruction. Everything can be arranged.

Rooms: 5 doubles/twins.
Price: Double 520 Frs (€ 79.27); half-board 750 Frs (for two). Children under 3 free. Extra bed 100 Frs.
Breakfast: Included.
Meals: Dinner 135-200 Frs, organic whenever possible. Menu changes daily.
Closed: Restaurant closed Sunday evenings & Mondays to non-residents.

From Cherbourg (20 mins) RN13 exit St Joseph to D146 dir. Rocheville; 5km after dual carriageway hotel is signposted.

Château de la Roque

50180 Hébécrevon
Manche

Tel: (0)2 33 57 33 20
Fax: (0)2 33 57 51 20
E-mail: mireille.delisle@wanadoo.fr
web: www.chateau-de-la-roque.fr

M & Mme Delisle

As we came up the poplar-lined drive into the circular courtyard at the end of the day, the windows blinked like diamonds. The land falls away to a lake on the other side of this 16th- and 17th-century country house. Young daughter, Gladys, led me through the entrance passing collections of precious stones, pictures of ancestors on the farm, leather-covered bellows, a majestic grandfather clock framed by two long windows and Norman statues — all among potted plants. Continuing up a circular stone staircase, you reach the large, light bedroom furnished with the same care for detail, colour and comfort: oriental rugs, an antique writing desk, and good bed linen. The Delisles raise organic chickens, pigs, sheep, cows, turkeys and ducks and make their own bread in a wood-fired oven. Dinner comes after a refreshing glass of their *pommeau* (a Norman speciality of cognac and apple juice). You may ask for a picnic lunch and stroll around their lake or explore the nature reserve nearby. Raymond and his wife, Mireille, were off on a tandem bicycle trip through England visiting former guests, now friends.

Rooms: 15: 9 doubles, 3 twins,
3 suites for 3/4.
Price: Doubles 400-420 Frs (€ 60.98-
64.03); triples 480 Frs; suites 560 Frs.
Breakfast: Included.
Meals: Dinner, including wine, 100 Frs;
children 90 Frs.
Closed: Never.

*From St Lô D927 dir. Coutances to St Gilles.
In village, D77 dir. Pont Hébert for 3km;
signposted.*

Les Hauts

7 avenue de la Libération
50530 Saint Jean Le Thomas
Manche

Tel: (0)2 33 60 10 02
Fax: (0)2 33 60 5 40
E-mail: leshauts@club-internet.fr
web: www.chateau-les-hauts.com

André & Suzanne Leroy

You will either really love or hate the inside of this house, with its ornate reception rooms, very Art Deco, and unusual interior design. Everyone, however, will love the spot: perched in a beautiful garden above the sea, with views to Mont St.Michel. Madame Leroy is warm and bubbly, something of a chatterbox, and very proud of the house. The beach, 400 metres away, is pebbled but there are others just a short drive away. Breakfast might keep you going until supper; a buffet of proper French food, it includes charcuterie, cheese, five different breads, 12 different jams and home-made cake. The bedrooms range from a big room with a canopied four-poster and Art Deco frieze to a delicately pretty room in pale pink, with blue-green paintwork and chintz curtains and bed covers. One room is bold black with white and brown patterns. Our inspector loved it, but some might find it too much. The bathrooms have their original 19th-century porcelain fittings but the plumbing works effortlessly.

Rooms: 8: 7 doubles & 1 quadruple with 2 double beds.
Price: 370-650 Frs (€ 56.41-99.09).
Extra bed 150 Frs.
Breakfast: Buffet included.
Meals: Good restaurants nearby.
Closed: Never.

From Cherbourg, N13 to Valognes then D2 to Coutances then D971 to Granville then D911 (along coast) to Jullouville and on to Carolles and St Jean le Thomas (6.5km from Jullouville).

Le Gué du Holme

14 rue des Estuaires
Saint-Quentin-sur-le-Homme
50220 Ducey
Manche

Tel: (0)2 33 60 63 76
Fax: (0)2 33 60 067 7
E-mail: gue.holme@wanadoo.fr

M Leroux

A mouth-watering story can be told about the sea, the meadows, and the orchards of Normandy by dining here on the oysters, foie gras with apples and the renowned *pré salé*, lamb grazed on the sea-flooded grass. Michel, the hugely enthusiastic owner-chef, has a deeply rooted commitment to his Norman food — the more local the better. It is hard to spot the simple elegance of the Gué du Holme from the outside. It was all the more surprising to find the new rooms overlooking a small lavender-spiked rose-trellised garden. Breakfast is served outside on cheerful pink and white porcelain, sweet Normandy butter under silver cupolas, a delightful mix of breads — a special moment for planning the day or just a relaxing read. The Lerouxs are sensitive to detail and colour; the rooms feel crisp, an exquisite antique trunk lives in the corridor, the warmth and brightness of the welcome is reflected in the dining room with brass light fixtures, wood trim and ochre walls. Well away from the summer crowds, low-key, impeccable.

Rooms: 10: 9 doubles/twins & 1 suite for 3.
Price: 420-500 Frs (€ 64.03-76.22).
Breakfast: 55 Frs.
Meals: Menus 150-390 Frs. Half-board minimum 3 days 500-600 Frs.
Closed: January 2-4. Sunday evening from mid-September to Easter. Restaurant closed Fridays, & Saturday lunchtime.

From Caen N175 dir. Avranches. Exit Cromel at War Museum. Left on roundabout D103. Straight on second roundabout dir Saint Quentin sur le Homme. Hotel across from church. From Rennes N175 exit Cromel. Right on roundabout. 2km.

Brittany

Bless you, you do not, cannot know,
How far a little French will go;
For all one's stock, one need but draw
On some half dozen words like these
comme ça -par-là - la bas, ah ha!
They'll take you all through France with ease.
Thomas Moore

La Korrigane
39 rue le Pomellec
35400 Saint Malo
Ille-et-Vilaine

Tel: (0)2 99 81 65 85
Fax: (0)2 99 82 23 89

Mme Dolbeau

Small antique daybeds and vast gilt-framed mirrors, carved *armoires* and ancestral portraits — it's like stepping back into an elegant private mansion of the 1930s, with that deliciously old-fashioned refinement and sense of welcome. The 1990s have contributed all the requisite modern communication and bathroom bits. Madame Dolbeau, enchantingly 'just so', fits utterly into her surroundings and nothing is too much trouble for her. There is elegant stucco in front, solid Breton granite behind where the peaceful walled garden contains your reading corner or your breakfast table beneath the mature trees. In poor weather, the breakfast room is attractive, tall-windowed, chandeliered and the *salon* has comfortable armchairs, log fires and that ever-amazing trick of a window above the fireplace. Bedrooms are big and supremely comfortable, with thick matching covers and curtains, subtle lighting and pretty antiques. Light floods in, there is an irresistible softness, a sense of luxury and good manners — and all this within walking distance of the old walled town and the ferry port.

Rooms: 12: 11 doubles & 1 triple.
Price: Doubles 450-950 Frs
(€ 68.6-144.83).
Breakfast: 65 Frs.
Closed: Never.

From ferry port take Quai de Trichet, at roundabout take Rue le Pomellec.

Hôtel Elizabeth

2 rue des Cordiers
35400 Saint Malo
Ille-et-Vilaine

Tel: (0)2 99 56 24 98
Fax: (0)2 99 56 39 24

Joëlle Dolbeau

Built in 1558, the Hotel Elizabeth's stone walls look as comfortingly solid against the chilly winds as they were against the pirates who used to make this part of France less than welcoming to outsiders. Apparently the presence of privateers can still be felt in the breakfast room, which is a cave under the house reached by a stone spiral staircase (or a lift if you're feeling prosaic); presumably these are not the kind of privateers who steal your breakfast from under your nose before throwing you off the city walls. You can even call in for breakfast as a non-resident, before walking the plank onto the ferry. The bedrooms have internal wooden shutters and the other accoutrements of history such as 'period' furnishings but also their full complement of 21st-century comforts. Monsieur Dolbeau's welcome is particularly warm to foreigners and this makes an ideal place to treat yourself to a romantic week-end exploring the old stone streets of St Malo or to a night before or after the rigours of the ferry-crossing.

Rooms: 17: 4 doubles/twins & 13 small apartments.
Price: 400-690 Frs (€ 60.98-105.19).
Breakfast: 56 Frs.
Meals: Available locally.
Closed: Never.

Enter walled city via the Porte Saint Louis and take second right.

Hôtel Manoir de Rigourdaine

Route de Langrolay
22490 Plouër sur Rance
Côtes-d'Armor

Tel: (0)2 96 86 89 96
Fax: (0)2 96 86 92 46
E-mail: hotel.rigourdaine@wanadoo.fr
web: www.hotel-rigourdaine.fr

Patrick Van Valenberg

At the end of the lane, firm on its hillside, Rigourdaine breathes space, sky, permanence. The square-yarded manor farm, originally a stronghold with moat and all requisite towers, now looks serenely out over wide estuary and rolling pastures to the ramparts of St Malo and offers sheltering embrace. The reception/bar in the converted barn is a good place to meet the friendly, attentive master of the manor, properly pleased with his excellent conversion. A double-height open fireplace warms a sunken sitting well; the restfully simple breakfast room — black and white floor, solid old beams, plain wooden tables with pretty mats — looks onto courtyard and garden. Rooms are simple too, in unfrilly good taste and comfort: Iranian rugs on plain carpets, coordinated contemporary-chic fabrics in good colours, some nice old furniture, pale bathrooms with all essentials. Six ground-floor rooms have private terraces onto the kempt garden — ideal for intimate breakfasts or sundowners. Good cleancut rooms, atmosphere lent by old timbers and antiques, and always the long limpid view. We liked it a lot.

Rooms: 19 doubles/twins.
Price: 300-450 Frs (€ 45.73-68.6).
Breakfast: 40 Frs.
Meals: Restaurant very close in Plouër.
Closed: Mid-November-Easter.

From St Malo N137 dir. Rennes. After Châteauneuf right on N176 dir. Dinan/St Brieuc. Cross bridge over river Rance then exit dir. Plouër sur Rance; dir. Langrolay for 500m. Follow lane to Rigourdaine.

Manoir de La Hazaie
22400 Planguenoual
Côtes-d'Armor

Tel: (0)2 96 32 73 71
Fax: (0)2 96 32 79 72
web:

Jean-Yves & Christine Marivin

Chunks of Breton history — violence, greed and bigotry — happened here where country peace now reigns. The Marivins, she an artist/pharmacist, he a craftsman/ lawyer, love every minute of its past and have filled it with family treasures. The *salon* combines grandeur and warmth, ancient stones, antiques and a roaring fire. Ancestral portraits hang beside Madame's medieval paint and pottery scenes. *Tournemine's* blood-red ceiling inspired a powerfully simple colour scheme, plain furniture and a great canopied bed. Airily feminine *Tiffaine* has wildly gilded, curlicued Polish furniture and a neo-classical bathroom romp: statues, pilasters, a delicate mural of 'Girl in Hat'. Baths have sybaritic Jacuzzi jets. Rooms in the old mill-house, with fine old floor tiles and lovely rugs, open onto the garden — ideal for families. Row on the pond, glide from 'Hadrian's Villa' into the pool, sleep in luxury, enjoy your hosts' knowledgeable enthusiasm. Past owners have all left their mark (the admiral's anchors, the priest's colours).

Rooms: 6: 5 doubles/twins & 1 suite.
Price: Doubles 690-990 Frs
(€ 105.19-150.92); suite 1200 Frs.
Breakfast: 60 Frs.
Meals: Available locally.
Closed: Never.

From N12 Rennes-Brest road exit St René on D81 then D786 dir. Pléneuf Val André. Just before Planguenoual, right following signs to house (2.2km). Entrance opposite Ferme Musée.

97

MMap 230-9

ASP Map No: 2

Château Hôtel de Brélidy

Brélidy
22140 Bégard
Côtes-d'Armor

Tel: (0)2 96 95 69 38
Fax: (0)2 96 95 18 03

M & Mme Yoncourt-Pémezec

From upstairs you can see across bucolic fieldscapes to Menez-Bré, Armor's highest spot (302m). The old rooms here are cosy, quilty, family-antiqued. Below are the beamed *salon* and billiards room, their vast carved fireplaces built above the two great dining-room fireplaces — such strength. The owners have laboured 30 long years to restore 16th-century Brélidy, using authentic materials and preserving the sobriety. The worn stone staircase and the iron man fit well; so will you, enfolded in the personal attention that is Brélidy's keynote. In the West Wing, on the site of the original open gallery, guests in the suite can parade before waist-high windows like lords and ladies of yore. More modest rooms lie below, carefully decorated with soft colours, enriched with antiques; four have private entrances with little terraces and there's a huge terrace for all up above. In the gentle garden, the converted bakery is ideal for families and there's an indoor Jacuzzi. Beyond are two rivers, two ponds with private fishing, and everywhere is utter peace.

Rooms: 14: 12 doubles/twins & 2 suites.
Price: 450-830 Frs (€ 68.6-126.53).
Breakfast: Buffet 55 Frs.
Meals: Dinner 150-190 Frs.
Closed: November-Easter.

From N12 exit Lannion-Tréguier towards Tréguier. D712 then D8 then D15 to Brélidy. Hotel signposted.

Ti al Lannec

14 allée de Mézo-Guen
22560 Trébeurden
Côtes-d'Armor

Tel: (0)2 96 15 01 01
Fax: (0)2 96 23 62 14
E-mail: ti.al.lannec@wanadoo.fr
web: perso.wanadoo.fr/ti.al.lannec

Danielle & Gérard Jouanny

With dozens of English antiques, it is superbly French — soft and fulsome. An Edwardian seaside residence perched on the cliff, its gardens tumble down to rocky coves and sandy beaches; only pine needles and waves can be heard (the beach club closes at midnight). Inside, a mellow warmth envelopes you in armfuls of drapes, bunches, swags and sprigs. Each room is a different shape, individually decorated as if in a private mansion with a sitting space, a writing table, a good bathroom. Besides the florals, stripes and oriental rugs, the white bedcovers and views onto the sea or ancient cypresses give breathing space. Some bedrooms are big, with plastic-balconied loggias, some are ideal for families with convertible bunk-bed sofas (a brilliant discovery). *Salons* are cosily arranged with little lamps, mirrors, old prints; the sea-facing restaurant serves excellent food. The Jouanny family care immensely about guests' welfare and are deeply part of their community. They create a smart yet human atmosphere, publish a daily in-house gazette and provide balneotherapy in the basement.

Rooms: 24 doubles/twins including 5 family rooms for three.
Price: Doubles 680-1175 Frs (€ 103.67-179.13); triples 1100-1495 Frs. Extra bed 320 Frs.
Breakfast: 70 Frs, American 90 Frs.
Meals: Lunch & dinner 115-395 Frs; children 95 Frs.
Closed: Mid-November-mid-March.

From N12 Rennes-Brest road, exit 3km west of Guingamp dir. Lannion onto D767. In Lannion, follow signs to Trébeurden. Signposted in village.

Grand Hôtel des Bains

15 bis rue de l'Eglise
29241 Locquirec
Finistère

Tel: (0)2 98 67 41 02
Fax: (0)2 98 67 44 60
web: www.grand-hotel-des-bains.com

M Van Lier & M Dufau

Marine purity on the north Brittany coast: it's like a smart yacht club where you are an old member. The fearless design magician has waved a wand of natural spells — cotton, cane, wood, wool, sea-grass: nothing synthetic, nothing pompous. Sober lines and restful colours leave space for the scenery, the sky pours in through walls of glass, the peaceful garden flows into rocks, beach and sea. Moss-green panelling lines the deep-chaired bar where a fire leaps in winter. Pale-grey-panelled bedrooms have dark mushroom carpets and thick cottons in stripes and checks of soft red or green or beige or blue. Some have four-posters, some have balconies, others are smaller, nearly all have the ever-changing sea view. Bathrooms are lovely, with bathrobes to wear to the magnificent indoor sea-water pool and spa treatment centre. Staff are smiling and easy, the ivory-panelled dining room with its sand-coloured cloths is deeply tempting and children are served early so that adults can enjoy the superb menu. The luxury of space, pure elegant simplicity and personal attention are yours for the booking.

Rooms: 36 doubles/twins including 3 family apartments.
Price: Doubles 550-1000 Frs (€ 83.85-152.45). Extra bed 200 Frs.
Breakfast: Included.
Meals: Lunch & dinner 150-230 Frs. Excellent wine cellar.
Closed: Never. Restaurant closed January-February.

From Rennes-Brest N12 exit to Plestin les Grèves then continue to Locquirec. Hotel in town centre. Through gate to car park on right.

Manoir de Moëllien

29550 Plonévez-Porzay
Finistère

Tel: (0)2 98 92 50 40
Fax: (0)2 98 92 55 21
E-mail: manmoel@aol.com

M & Mme Garet

The sheer strength that pours from this stern stone manor was designed to withstand Atlantic storms, the decorative bits to demonstrate status. Now swishing pines protect the drive, hydrangeas bloom in October and the young garden of lawns and pond will flourish fast. Rooms are neatly arranged in converted outbuildings, each with its own entrance and little terrace. In the block of suites and duplexes, splendid luminous colour schemes are perfect foils for some delicious Breton antiques, fabrics are strong, bathrooms excellent, finishes unfussy. The 'older' rooms, although smaller and less contemporary, are perfectly comfortable, excellent value — and soon to be redecorated. The eating halls in the manor are superb in their deep-windowed, high-beamed authenticity and huge carved fireplaces. Your host, the chef, is as enthusiastic about his dinners as he is about his wife's décor and gardening plans. The 2-ton granite cider-press fountain is his own, most successful, design. Modern dynamics married to solid old stones in a place of peace.

Rooms: 18: 10 doubles/twins, 5 suites & 3 junior suites.
Price: Doubles 370-740 Frs (€ 56.41-112.81); suites 490-760 Frs; junior suites 650-740 Frs.
Breakfast: Buffet 50 Frs.
Meals: Lunch & dinner 126-250 Frs.
Closed: Mid-November-March. Restaurant closed Wednesday and Thursday lunchtimes.

From Quimper N dir. Locronan on D39 then D63 for 17km. Left on D7 dir. Douarnenez and Kerlaz for 3km; right on D107 dir. Plonévez. Manoir signed on right just before turn (20-25 mins).

Château de Guilguiffin

Le Guilguiffin
29710 Landudec
Finistère

Tel: (0)2 98 91 52 11
Fax: (0)2 98 91 52 52
E-mail: chateau@guilguiffin.com
web: www.guilguiffin.com

Philippe Davy

The bewitching name of the rough knight who became first Baron in 1010 (the King rewarding him royally for battle services with a title and a swathe of wild, remote Brittany), the splendidness of the place, its vast, opulent rooms and magnificent grounds, seduced us utterly: it is a powerful experience, grand rather than intimate, unforgettable. Built with stones from the ruined fortress that originally stood here, the present château is a jewel of 18th-century aristocratic architecture. Philippe Davy, the latest descendant, knows and loves old buildings, his ancient family seat in particular, and applies his energy and intelligence to restoring château and park. He repairs, decorates and furnishes in all authenticity; guestrooms are richly, thickly draped and carpeted; reception rooms glow with grandeur and panelling; superb antiques radiate elegance. In the park, he has planted thousands of bulbs and bushes and cleared 11km of walks. He likes to convert his visitors to his convictions and is a persuasive preacher. Guilguiffin is deeply, fascinatingly unusual.

Rooms: 6: 4 doubles & 2 suites.
Price: Doubles 650-800 Frs
(€ 99.09-121.96); suites 900-1300 Frs.
Breakfast: Included.
Meals: Choice nearby.
Closed: December-end February

From Quimper D785 dir. Pont l'Abbé until airport exit. Then D 56 for 5km to D784 dir. Audierne. 3km before Landudec look for signs to Guilguiffin.

Manoir de Kerhuel

Route de Quimper
29720 Plonéour-Lanvern
Finistère

Tel: (0)2 98 82 60 57
Fax: (0)2 98 82 61 79
E-mail: manoir-kerhuel@wanadoo.fr
web: perso.wanadoo.fr/manoir-kerhuel

M & Mme Lanvoc

The new managers are keen to make Kerhuel thoroughly welcoming. Breakfast is copious, in the intimate breakfast room for the few or, for the many, through some lovely carved panelling in the splendid banqueting room (once the stables), scanned by windows and tapestries. Your smilingly busy host/chef serves other meals in the pleasing modern restaurant that joins the old house to the old stables. This Kerhuel is just 100 years old, whence its rather stolid form in a flourishing green mantle of great trees and rhododendrons. The round, stone-walled, yellow-tented Bridal Chamber in the old dovecote is a tiny hideaway — go easy on the champers, though, the bathroom stairs are steep. Families are brilliantly catered for: bunk beds behind curtains, swings in the garden, a shallow children's pool beside the big one. Some rooms are pretty big, some have small high windows, beds may be canopied and quilted, there's always plenty of storage space behind modern sliding doors. You will find gentle colours, good repro furniture, the odd antique, space and a very easy atmosphere.

Rooms: 26: 21 doubles/twins & 5 suites for 2/4.
Price: Doubles 380-575 Frs (€ 57.93-87.66); suites 510-920 Frs.
Breakfast: Buffet 60 Frs.
Meals: Lunch & dinner 110-270 Frs.
Closed: Mid-Nov-mid-Dec, Jan-Mar & Weds during low season. Restaurant closed Weds from Oct-April. Mon & Tues lunchtimes except during school holidays.

From Quimper D785 dir. Pont l'Abbé for 10km; exit Plonéour-Lanvern on D156 for 4km. Hotel entrance on left.

Hôtel Restaurant Sainte Marine

19 rue du Bac
Sainte Marine
29120 Combrit
Finistère

Tel: (0)2 98 56 34 79
Fax: (0)2 98 51 94 09
web: www.guydiquelou.fr

Guy Diquelou

The friendliest little hotel imaginable, down by the pretty boating harbour, where you are grateful that the ugly great cruiser boats stay across the water in Bénodet (there's a ferryman if you really want to go there). Inside, variations on the marine theme are played with a sure, light touch and brilliant *trompe-l'œil* murals. Here, you sleep with your head on the deck and your dreams out to sea; there, gulls perch as you slip under your sailcloth bedcover and there's a second bed up the gangway under the 'fo'c'sle peak'. Other rooms are attractive but less unusual: yellow, blue and tan are favourite colours, walls are sponged, coordinated cottons clothe beds, cushions and windows. Bathrooms are small too, but simplicity, minimal furniture and no clutter leave room to breathe. Like everyone else in the village, you will soon become friends with your humorous host, so fiercely loyal to the wet days, grey skies and watery world of his beloved Brittany (though he admits to lots of sunshine too), and with his delightful, wild-alive Irish assistant. And the food is very good indeed.

Rooms: 11: 7 doubles/twins,
1 triple & 3 suites for 4.
Price: Doubles 310-450 Frs
(€ 47.26-68.6); suites 350 Frs.
Breakfast: 35 Frs.
Meals: Lunch & dinner 99-250 Frs. Not always open in evenings.
Closed: Mid-November-mid-December. Restaurant some evenings.

From Quimper dir. Bénodet. At entrance to Bénodet take bridge dir. Sainte Marine, first left dir. Le Port.

Manoir du Stang

29940 La Fôret Fouesnant
Finistère

Tel: (0)2 98 56 97 37
Fax: (0)2 98 56 97 37

Famille Hubert

There is ancient grandeur in this 'hollow place' (*stang*) between the remarkable dovecote arch and the wild ponds. On the tamed side: a formal French courtyard, a blooming rose garden, lines of trees, some masterly old stonework. But the welcome is utterly natural, the rooms not at all intimidating. The Huberts like guests to feel at home in their family mansion with a choice antique here, an original curtain fabric there, an invigoratingly pink bathroom to contrast with a gentle Louis Philippe chest — always solid, reliable comfort and enough space. Views are heart-warming, over courtyard, water and woods, the peace is total (bar the odd quack). Communal rooms are of stupendous proportions, as befits the receptions held here. The dining room can seat 60 in grey-panelled, pink-curtained splendour, its glass bays looking across to the gleaming ponds. Masses of things sit on the black and white *salon* floor — a raft of tables, fleets of high-backed chairs, a couple of sofas, glowing antique cupboards — and you still have space and monumental fireplaces. A magnificent place.

Rooms: 24 doubles/twins.
Price: 500-920 Frs (€ 76.22-140.25).
Breakfast: 50 Frs.
Meals: Dinner 190 Frs.
Closed: Occasionally & October-April
Restaurant closed September-June.

From Quimper N165 exit Concarneau/Fouesnant on D44 then D783 dir. Quimper. Enter property by private road on left.

Château-Hôtel Manoir de Kertalg

Route de Riec sur Belon
29350 Moëlan sur Mer
Finistère

Tel: (0)2 98 39 77 77
Fax: (0)2 98 39 72 07
web: www.manoirdekertalg.com

M Le Goamic

So many contrasts. Driving through thick woods, you expect the old château in its vast estate, but the hotel is actually in the big, blocky stables, built in 1890 for racehorses (who even had running water): it became an hotel in 1990 when the tower was added. The *salon* is formal and glitzy with its marbled floor, modern coffered ceiling, red plush chairs — and intriguing dreamscapes by Brann. You will be welcomed with polished affability by the charming young owner, and possibly by visitors who come for tea and ice-cream. Even the 'small' bedrooms are big; château décor is the rule — brocading, plush lace, satin and gilt-framed mirrors. The 'big' rooms are exuberant: one has full Pompadour treatment in gold, pink and white, another is richly Directoire in curved cane and coffee-coloured velvet. The tower rooms are cosier, old-fashioned posh, but have space for a couple of armchairs. Some bathrooms are to be modernised, yet all are solid quality and the value is remarkable. Wild woodland walks beckon and there's a helipad — two worlds meet and embrace.

Rooms: 9 doubles/triples including a suite.
Price: 490-1200 Frs (€ 74.7-182.94).
Breakfast: 65 Frs.
Meals: Five restaurants within 2-8km.
Closed: November-March (Easter).

From N165 westwards exit Quimperlé Centre to Moëlan sur Mer; there, right at traffic light dir. Riec and follow signs (12km from N165). Helicopter pad.

Château de Kerlarec

29300 Arzano
Finistère

Tel: (0)2 98 71 75 06
Fax: (0)2 98 71 74 55

Monique & Michel Bellin

The plain exterior belies the 19th-century festival inside — it's astonishing. Murals of mountain valleys and Joan of Arc in stained glass announce the original Lorraine-born baron ('descended from Joan's brother') and the wallpaper looks great, considering it too was done in 1830. In the gold-brocade-papered *salon*, Madame Bellin lavishes infinite care on every Chinese vase, gilt statuette and porcelain flower: sit in an ornate black and green chair by the red marble fireplace and soak up the atmosphere. Staircase and bedrooms have more overflowing personality, mixing fantasy with comfort, some fascinating furniture, lovely old embroidered linen on new mattresses and bathrooms of huge character. On the top floor, slip through a 'slot' in the rafters from sitting to sleeping space and discover a gold and white nest. Expect porcelain and silver at breakfast and reserve your *crêpes* or seafood platter for a candlelit dinner one night. Your enthusiastic hostess lavishes the same attention on her guests as on her house — and the bassets will walk with you in the park.

Rooms: 6: 1 double & 5 suites.
Price: 380-500 Frs (€ 57.93-76.22).
Breakfast: Included.
Meals: Lunch & dinner 150 Frs crêpes,
225 Frs shellfish platter, by arrangement.
Closed: Never.

From Quimperlé D22 E dir. Pontivy for 6km; château on left — narrow gate.

Château du Launay

Launay
56160 Ploërdut
Morbihan

Tel: (0)2 97 39 46 32
Fax: (0)2 97 39 46 31
E-mail: info@chateaudulaunay.com
web: www.chateaudulaunay.com

Famille Redolfi-Strizzot

A dream of a place, another world, another time, beside bird-swept pond and quiet woods. Launay marries austere grandeur with simple luxury, fine old stones with contemporary art, rich minimalism with exotica. In the great white hall, an Indian monk shares the Persian rug with a bronze stag. The staircase sweeps up, past fascinating art on the huge landing, to big light-filled rooms where beds are white, bathrooms are plainly, beautifully modern, light and colour are handled with consummate skill. The second floor is more exotic, the corridor punctuated with an Indian gate, the rooms slightly smaller but rich in carved colonial bed, polo-player armchairs, Moghul prints. For relaxation, choose the gilt-edged billiards room, the soberly leather-chaired, book-filled library or the stupendous drawing room, stuffed with pieces including a piano (concerts are given), a giant parasol and many sitting corners. A house of a million marvels where you take unexpected journeys and fabulous parties are thrown. Your charming young hosts know how to receive — and food is deliciously varied.

Rooms: 10 doubles/twins.
Price: 600-750 Frs (€ 91.47-114.34).
Breakfast: 40 Frs.
Meals: Dinner 135 Frs, by reservation only.
Closed: January-end February.

From Pontivy D782 (21km) to Guémené; continue on D1 dir. Gourin to Toubahado (9km). Don't go to Ploërdut. In Toubahado right on C3 dir. Locuon for 3km. Entrance immediately after 'Launay' sign.

Le Logis de Parc Er Gréo

9 rue Mané Guen Le Gréo
56610 Arradon
Morbihan

Tel: (0)2 97 44 73 03
Fax: (0)2 97 44 80 48
E-mail: logisparc.er.greo@wanadoo.fr
web: members.aol.com/morbihan1/hotels.html

Eric & Sophie Bermond

The neat new building is a metaphor for Breton hospitality. The front is a high north wall — it may seem forbidding but once inside you know that it shelters house and garden from the wild elements, that fields, woods, sea and the coastal path are just yards away. Eric prepares itineraries for guests, boating is on the spot, swimming a little further away. Warm colours, oriental rugs and fine family pieces sit easily on the tiled floors of the many-windowed ground floor, Eric's father's watercolours lend personality to all the rooms, the unusual candlesticks in the hall and ancestral portraits, including a large Velazquez-style child in a great gilt frame, are most appealing. *Salon* and dining room open widely onto terrace and garden — wonderful places to relax or play with the children on the big lawn. Rooms, attractive in shades of red, green and salmon, are functionally furnished. Your hosts, their charming young family and their enthusiasm for their project — to stop being clients in boring hotels and do things properly themselves — make this an easy, friendly place to stay.

Rooms: 12 doubles/twins.
Price: 320-560 Frs (€ 48.78-85.37).
Breakfast: 55 Frs.
Meals: Available locally.
Closed: Occasionally in winter.

From Vannes D101 dir. Ile aux Moines.
Ignore left turns to Arradon, turn left to Le
Moustoir then on to Le Gréo and follow signs
(10km in total).

Domaine de Rochevilaine

Pointe de Pen Lan
56190 Billiers
Morbihan

Tel: (0)2 97 41 61 61
Fax: (0)2 97 41 44 85
E-mail: domaine@domainerochevilaine.com
web: www.domainerochevilaine.com

Bertrand Jaquet

Once just a smugglers' path and a customs house out on a rocky spur, now a hamlet of 16th-century Breton manors brought, astoundingly, stone by stone from their original sites and rebuilt here as a splendiferous hotel. It has endless sea space — all rooms have sea views — a sheltered garden, superb service that is never obsequious and a thoroughly relaxed, welcoming atmosphere: people wander in bathrobes from the great indoor pool to the spa treatment rooms (exclusive ancient Phoenician methods are used). *Suites* are private manor-houses under the cliff's edge; *Prestige* rooms are huge, some with four-posters; all rooms have excellent bathrooms and stylish contemporary comfort with the occasional antique wardrobe or carved fireplace. The great white breakfast room looks both out to sea and to the pool; the dining room is tapestried, beamed and luxurious (food's good too). Add an outdoor pool, an art gallery and lots more ancient Breton stone-works. While you indulge in top-quality comforts, the ocean beats everlastingly at the foot of the cliff and the gulls mew overhead.

Rooms: 38: 34 doubles/twins & 4 suites.
Price: Doubles 590-1545 Frs
(€ 89.94-235.53); suites 990-2500 Frs.
Breakfast: Buffet 85 Frs.
Meals: Lunch & dinner 270-470 Frs.
Closed: Never.

*From Vannes N165 E dir. Nantes 24km;
right on D5 through Billiers to Pointe de Pen
Lan. Domaine at end of road.*

Auberge du Parc
La Mare aux Oiseaux
162 Ile de Fédrun
44720 Saint Joachim
Loire-Atlantique

Tel: (0)2 40 88 53 01
Fax: (0)2 40 91 67 44

Eric Guérin

A perfect little inn in a low-lying village deep in the watery wilderness of the Brière Regional Park — people even come for lunch by boat — it has the charm and simplicity of a remote staging post and the exquisite sophistication of an increasingly reputed table. Eric Guérin, an adventurous and attractive young chef, trained with the best in Paris and now applies his lively culinary creativity on his own account. Appropriately in this amphibious land, he delights in mixing earth fruits and water creatures — he calls it "good French traditional with a zest of young Parisian". His pretty, low-ceilinged dining room, with rough rustic walls and smartly-dressed chairs, is the ideal setting for this experience; bedrooms under the thatch are for quiet nights after days of marshy discoveries and evenings of gourmet pleasure. Eric's art-world background is evident in his choice of gently contemporary, uncluttered décor and country antiques. He has some modern but approachable art, too. The garden is green, the canal watery, the welcome genuine and the food... out of this world.

Rooms: 5 doubles/twins.
Price: 380 Frs (€ 57.93).
Breakfast: 40 Frs.
Meals: Lunch & dinner 150-200 Frs.
Half-board 850 Frs.
Closed: March. Restaurant closed Sunday evenings & Mondays, except July & August.

Nantes dir. La Baule, exit Montoir de Bretagne, dir. Parc Naturel Brière, dir. St Joachim. In St Joachim, left at lights to Fédrun (2km). Auberge opposite La Maison du Parc.

111   MMap 232-26   **ASP Map No: 2**

Hôtel Villa Flornoy

7 avenue Flornoy
44380 Pornichet
Loire-Atlantique

Tel: (0)2 40 11 60 00
Fax: (0)2 40 61 86 47
E-mail: hotflornoy@aol.com
web: www.villa-flornoy.com

Luc Rouault

Villa it is, a large one, in a quiet road just back from the vast sandy beach and protected from the sea-front bustle. Built as a family boarding house in the 1920s, Flornoy still stands in the shade of a quieter age: high old trees, nooked and crannied seaside villas in stone, brick and wood. Inside it is just as peaceful. After being greeted by the delightful young owner and admiring the clock over the desk — his family have made clocks for generations — enjoy sitting in the *salon*: garden view, four tempting 'corners', well-chosen marine prints and the occasional interesting *objet*. Rooms — mostly a good size, a few with balconies — have a pretty, fresh, padded feel, nothing frilly, just plain or Jouy-style wall fabrics, coordinated colours and patterns, good mod/trad furniture, excellent beds and white bathrooms with fine new fittings. It is simple, solid, attractive and extremely comfortable and in the morning you will be glad to breakfast, generously, in the light dining room or under the trees in the green and blooming garden. Really good value and relaxedly welcoming.

Rooms: 20: 13 doubles/twins & 7 triples.
Price: 325-540 Frs (€ 49.55-82.32)
(an extra 50 Frs for triples).
Breakfast: 42 Frs.
Meals: Dinner 120 Frs (residents) or 145 Frs (non-residents).
Closed: November-mid-February.

Pornichet dir. town centre. At big market place, right onto av Général de Gaulle for 300m; ave Flornoy is on right just after Hôtel de Ville on left.

L'Abbaye de Villeneuve

Route de la Roche sur Yon
44840 Les Sorinières
Loire-Atlantique

Tel: (0)2 40 04 40 25
Fax: (0)2 40 31 28 45
E-mail: abbayevilleneuve@aol.com
web: www.chateauxand country.com/chateaux/villeneuve

Frédéric Brevet

This ancient foundation has waxed and waned for 800 years. Today's hotel is the abbey's 18th-century hostelry. One corridor is atmospherically frugal in its coconut matting and deep brown curtains held by heavy unbleached ropes — a cypher for a monk's sandals, robe and belt. The rich-coloured, thick-curtained rooms are less austere. Even the sober-*saloned* suite with ancient chest and grey plush chairs, has a bedroom warmly clothed in old rose and a capacious bathroom. Warm fabrics, *armoires*, marble-topped tables and French armchairs abound, with not a single furbelow. 'Standard' rooms are small, well decorated, warmly beamed. Down the superb barrel-vaulted staircase you come to the authentic touch of the public rooms: hung with blue or red cloth, flaunting carved fireplaces and beamed ceilings, they hum with history — and the scent of good food. The quiet 'cloister' garden with its round swimming pool balances the duck pond by the fairly busy road (we gather it's less so at night) at the bottom of the drive and banishes all memory of the plastic lettuce tunnels opposite!

Rooms: 20: 17 twins/doubles & 3 apartments for 2.
Price: 450-1245 Frs (€ 68.6-189.8).
Breakfast: 75 Frs.
Meals: Lunch & dinner 140-380 Frs.
Closed: Never.

Nantes A83 S, exit 1 dir. La Roche sur Yon; right on D178 dir. Viais.

The Loire Valley

Conseil Général du Loiret, D. Chauveau

One of the most wonderful rivers in the world,
mirroring from sea to source a hundred
cities and five hundred towers.
Oscar Wilde

Le Domaine de Mestré

49590 Fontevraud l'Abbaye
Maine-et-Loire

Tel: (0)2 41 51 75 87
Fax: (0)2 41 51 71 90
E-mail: domaine-de-mestre@wanadoo.fr
web: www.dauge-fontevraud.com

Dominique & Rosine Dauge

History oozes from every corner of Mestré. A Roman road, a cockleshell for the pilgrims who stayed en route to Compostela, part of a 13th-century chapel, the mill and tithe barn remind us that monks farmed here when Mestré was part of the vast Abbey. Most of the present building is 18th century: the family have farmed here for 200 years and keep the traditions of French country hospitality. Monsieur runs the eco-conscious farm, milking by hand. Madame makes fine natural soaps, and cooks; two daughters help out. All take pride in providing wholesome, home-grown food and elegant service. Big, rustic-style rooms are furnished with old family furniture, some of it well lived in — huge *lits bateaux* or brass beds with wool-stuffed mattresses and fluffy eiderdowns; armchairs, including a pair of fine old American rocking chairs — and some have great views over to the wooded valley. The sitting room is pure 'Victorian parlour' with its dark panelling, red wallpaper, card table and leather-bound books; the dining room is simply delightful. A sense of timeless welcome and class enfolds the privileged guest.

Rooms: 12: 9 doubles/twins, 2 singles & 1 suite.
Price: Doubles 325-395 Frs (€ 49.55-60.22); suite 590 Frs.
Breakfast: 40 Frs.
Meals: Dinner 145 Frs, by reservation.
Closed: November 20-February (March weekends only).

From Saumur D947 dir. Chinon. Right in Montsoreau dir. Fontevraud l'Abbaye. First right 1.5km after Montsoreau — signposted.

Château de Beaulieu
Route de Montsoreau
49400 Saumur
Maine-et-Loire

Tel: (0)2 41 67 69 51
Fax: (0)2 41 50 42 68
E-mail: chbeaulieu@club-internet.fr

Andréa Michaut

French to the core, the *petit château* exudes a natural, quiet charm, thanks to the delightful young family who run it. The classic, austere building with its wedding-cake frontage is set in lovely sloping gardens, screened from the main road by ancient cedar trees, with guest bedrooms at the back. These spacious rooms are the height of understated elegance, most of them furnished with beautifully draped four-posters, classic wallpapers and fine antiques. Stylish, yet irresistible. Bathrooms are commodious, with baths to wallow in. Their most recent project is a new suite in the attic. Your hosts are warm, friendly but unintrusive, and include children, dogs and a pretty Burmese cat. In spite of its polish and grace, this is at heart a family home. Choose a book from the billiard-room/library and sink into a squishy leather sofa in the guests' sitting room (it's beamed, with an open fire, and cosy). An idyllic place to unwind after a tiring day's touring château and wine country: it is so quiet that it's hard to believe you are only a mile from the centre of Saumur.

Rooms: 7: 5 doubles & 2 apartments.
Price: 290-420 Frs (€ 44.21-64.03).
Breakfast: 40 Frs.
Closed: December-January.

From Saumur D947 dir. Chinon. Château on right, 2km from Saumur centre, just after Gratien & Meyers wine cellars.

Hôtel Anne d'Anjou

32 quai Mayaud
49400 Saumur
Maine-et-Loire

Tel: (0)2 41 67 30 30
Fax: (0)2 41 67 51 00
E-mail: hotel-anneanjou@wanadoo.fr
web: www.hotel-anneanjou.com

Jean-René Camus

Any malign inhabitants of the château could have tossed rocks onto the roof of this elegant townhouse. It is just below, on the banks of the Loire in a picture-book position. The main staircase is listed and has a fine wrought-iron balustrade and *trompe l'oeil* that gives the impression of a dome. The main reception area, big and filled with light, has just a discreet desk to welcome you. The bedrooms on the first and second floors look either onto the river and the road, or onto the courtyard and château. Two of the rooms are especially fine: the *Salle Empire* (listed) has terracotta panelling and moulded friezes, and the *Salle Epoque* has a splendid old chequered tiled floor and grey panelling. Another room has a fine parquet floor and a balcony overlooking the river. Top floor rooms have solid old ceiling beams and views of the château through dormer windows. Some front rooms are plainer and look over the road, but the traffic is light, especially at night. The new owners are breathing fresh life into this lovely old building, and doing so with a mixture of dynamic (ex-naval) efficiency and Seychellois flair.

Rooms: 45: 41 doubles/twins, 2 quadruples & 2 apartments.
Price: 440-790 Frs (€ 67.08-120.43).
Breakfast: Buffet 52 Frs.
Meals: Lunch & dinner 100-350 Frs.
Closed: Never. Restaurant closed Sundays from October-Easter.

Arriving at Saumur follow signs to Saumur Centre. Continue along south bank of Loire on Chinon-Fontevraud road. Hotel is below castle 500m after theatre.

Château de la Beuvrière

49220 Grez Neuville
Maine-et-Loire

Tel: (0)2 41 37 67 67
Fax: (0)2 41 95 24 16

Mme Vandenberghe

The gargoyle-strewn façade of this Gothic fantasy (rebuilt 1830) is like something out of the pages of Mervyn Peake. Hidden away in the heart of rolling, wooded countryside it is one of the most striking château-guesthouses we have seen. Encircled by a dry moat, reached by a flight of stone balustraded steps, its twirled chimneys and turrets are circled by rooks; in the grounds stands a Gothic chapel with splendid stained-glass windows. Rooks aside, peace and tranquility reign. Magnificent lawns at the back sweep down to a huge lake. Guests find staying here inspirational and the visitors' book is filled with eulogies. Your courteous Belgian hosts have furnished the place with suitably heavy antiques — they were once in the antiques trade — and have done up each bedroom in an idiosyncratic style. There's an eclectic twist to the furnishings, furry bedspreads and 1970's wallpaper in one room, an amazing carved Gothic bedhead in another, a Spanish look in a third. Come if you're looking for somewhere different. Families will love it: the guestrooms are big and the park is a joy to explore.

Rooms: 10: 7 doubles, 2 triples &
1 apartment for 2/3.
Price: Rooms 395-780 Frs
(€ 60.22-118.91); triples 720 Frs;
apartment 3500 Frs.
Breakfast: 45 Frs.
Meals: Dinner 195 Frs.
Closed: November-Easter.

*From Laval N162 dir. Angers. 4km after Le
Lion d'Angers, at Grieul, right on D291 dir.
St Clémént de la Place. Château 3km from N162. Do **not** go to Grez Neuville.*

Château des Briottières

49330 Champigné
Maine-et-Loire

Tel: (0)2 41 42 00 02
Fax: (0)2 41 42 01 55
E-mail: briottieres@wanadoo.fr
web: www.briottieres.com

François de Valbray

The heavenly *petit château* has been in the same family for 200 years and is now occupied by the relaxed and endearing Monsieur de Valbray, his wife and six children. *La vieille France* is alive and well here and your hosts are more than happy to share it with guests. A magnificent library/billiard room leads into a small sitting room, but if it's grandness you're after, share your pre-dinner aperitif with Monsieur in the huge, and hugely aristocratic *salon*, furnished with family portraits, tapestries and fine antiques. Go up the marble staircase and along the corridors lined with *toile de jouy* to the bedrooms on the first floor, feel the comfort of the beds (the newest are king-sized), relish the park views. Several bedrooms have been recently redecorated but traditional furniture and fabrics prevail. Some beds are charmingly canopied, while the sumptuous family suite includes a small governess' room. Some bathrooms are marbled; the more expensive include towelling robes. In the grounds is a delightful country-style *orangerie*, let out as a gîte, and a large swimming pool in the walled garden beckons. It is the perfect aristocratic retreat.

Rooms: 10: 8 doubles/twins, 1 suite & 1 cottage.
Price: Doubles 750-1200 Frs (€ 114.34-182.94); suite & cottage 1500-1800 Frs.
Breakfast: 60 Frs.
Meals: Dinners, including wine & aperitif, 300 Frs.
Closed: December-February 15.

From A11 exit 11 at Durtal onto D859 to Châteauneuf sur Sarthe, then D770 to Champigné, D768 towards Sablé and left after about 4km to Les Briottières. Signposted.

Château du Plessis Anjou

49220 La Jaille Yvon
Maine-et-Loire

Tel: (0)2 41 95 12 75
Fax: (0)2 41 95 14 41
E-mail: plessis.anjou@wanadoo.fr
web: perso.wanadoo.fr/plessis

Paul & Simone Benoist

Built in the 16th century, Le Plessis has always belonged to the Benoist family and has been taking guests for 14 years. Soon, Paul and Simone Benoist plan to hand over to their charming, friendly daughter Valérie and her husband. Though large and very elegant, the château, set in 14 hectares of wooded park is inviting rather than imposing, with curving tiled roofs, white walls and creeper-covered shutters. You can play tennis or fish or sail off from the grounds in a balloon; two of the best *Sons et Lumières* are within easy reach; so are the châteaux and wineries of the Loire. Dinner, at a long table in a rather ornate dining room with Roman friezes, could include salmon, pork fillet with apricots, cheese and a crisp fruit tart. Although a grown-up sort of place, children would be made welcome; the owners are particularly friendly and Valérie has a young child herself. While one bedroom is very striking, with a lofty beamed ceiling and beds set in a deep turquoise alcove, some of the others are less so.

Rooms: 8 doubles/twins.
Price: 600-820 Frs (€ 91.47-125.01).
Breakfast: Included.
Meals: Dinner, including aperitif, 270 Frs .
Closed: November-February

From A11 exit Durtal on D859 to Châteauneuf sur Sarthe; D770 dir. Le Lion d'Angers for 18km. Right on N162 dir. Château Gontier. After 11km right on D189 dir. La Jaille Yvon.

Auberge du Roi René

53290 Saint Denis d'Anjou
Mayenne

Tel: (0)2 43 70 52 30
Fax: (0)2 43 70 58 75
E-mail: roi.rene@wanadoo.fr

Marie-Christine & Pierre de Vaubernier

Monsieur is the original *bon viveur*, and looks the part — a fund of culture and wit, a passionate believer in the art of good living. There are no airs and graces to Madame either: she is friendly, straightforward and chief gastronome. Food is a way of life here: Marie-Christine has passed muster with several top chefs, the *Trois Gros* brothers included, and cooks a *cuisine d'amour*. The stately Auberge, which dates from the 15th century, lies in the centre of St Denis, a delightful village (let Monsieur be your guide). An attractive grassy courtyard fronts the restaurant and with full disabled facilities, leads directly off here. The bedrooms on the first floor are reached via ancient stone stairs in the tower and have magnificent old oak doors and terracotta floors; they are narrow, cosy, charming, well lit. There are two dining rooms to choose from: one in the medieval part, warm-carpeted with a huge and handsome stone fireplace; the other, pure 18th century, elegant gracious and light. It is everything, and more, that an auberge should be.

Rooms: 4: 3 doubles & 1 suite.
Price: 350-550 Frs (€ 53.36-83.85).
Breakfast: 50 Frs.
Meals: Dinner 80-250 Frs.
Closed: Never.

From Sablé sur Sarthe D309 to St. Denis d'Anjou. Auberge in centre of village.

Château de Saint Paterne

72610 Saint Paterne
Sarthe

Tel: (0)2 33 27 54 71
Fax: (0)2 33 29 16 71
E-mail: paterne@club-internet.fr
web: www.chateau-saintpaterne.com

Charles-Henry & Segolène de Valbray

A 20th-century fairytale: a 15th-century château and a great park abandoned by The Family for 30 years, rediscovered by the heir who left sunny yellow Provence for cool green Normandy to resurrect the old carcass. He and his wife, a charming young couple, have redecorated with refreshing taste, respecting the style and history of the building, adding a zest of southern colour to panelled, antique-filled rooms, pretty country furniture before ancient fireplaces and hand-rendered, rough and 'imperfect' finishes — nothing stiff or fixed. Sitting, dining and first-floor bedrooms are in château style (plus a South-American rug on a parquet floor); the *Henri IV* room (he had a mistress here, of course) has thrillingly painted beams; ancestors and *objets* adorn but don't clutter. The attic floor is fantasy among the rafters: nooks, corners and split levels, a striking green and red bathroom, another bath sunk below the floor. Your host, an excellent, unfrilly cook, uses exotic vegetables from his Laotian-tended kitchen garden. A brilliant, attractive mixture of past and present values and superb hosts.

Rooms: 10: 7 doubles/twins, 2 triples & a cottage for 2/3.
Price: 450-900 Frs (€ 68.6-137.2).
Breakfast: 50 Frs.
Meals: Dinner, including aperitif & coffee, 230 Frs.
Closed: Mid-January-mid-March.

From Alençon D311 dir. Chartres/Mamers. St Paterne is on outskirts of Alençon. Drive through village; entrance to château is on right opposite garage (Elf).

Château d'Esclimont

28700 Saint Symphorien le Château
Eure-et-Loire

Tel: (0)2 37 31 15 15
Fax: (0)2 37 31 57 91
E-mail: esclimont@wanadoo.fr

Stéphane Jitiaux

The château that has everything, including an illustrious past. Built in 1543 by the Archbishop of Tours, owned by the Rochefoucauld family until 1968, it was then transformed into an impressive hotel. Superb architectural features, swish decor and a great setting — not only the immediate moat, gardens and mature parkland but Paris only an hour away. The La Rochefoucauld motto *c'est mon plaisir* could have been devised for the present staff; they are immensely courteous and genuinely seem to have the guests' best interest at heart, whether they arrive by helicopter for a business meeting or come for a romantic week-end. Bedrooms and bathrooms, especially those in the château itself, are pretty splendidly comfortable, as you would expect; there is always renovation work in progress, Forth Bridge-style. Dining rooms are plushly traditional (and have menus to match) with chandeliers, padded chairs and carefully restored *cuir de Cordue*. You can eat on the terrace or by the pool, if you prefer. There are musical evenings and cookery courses, tennis courts, bicycles and boating on the lake — you'll need the exercise.

Rooms: 53: 47 doubles/twins &
6 apartments.
Price: 1000-3300 Frs (€ 152.45-503.08).
Breakfast: 110 Frs; buffet 150 Frs.
Meals: Lunch 290 Frs; dinner 360-495
Frs. Children's menu 150 Frs.
Closed: Never.

*A10/A11, exit 1 Ablis. N10 dir. Chartres.
After 6km right on D168.*

Château de Beaujeu

18300 Sens Beaujeu
Cher

Tel: (0)2 48 79 07 95
Fax: (0)2 48 79 05 07
E-mail: info@chateau-de-beaujeu.com
web: www.chateau-de-beaujeu.com

M & Mme Wilfrid de Pommereau

Sweep up the tree-lined avenue, pass the stables and the dovecotes in the yard, step back in time: your turretted 16th-century château has been in the family since the French Revolution. Mme Pommereau is elderly and hard of hearing and stays in the background, but will recount reams of family history when asked. And every item tells a story: the stags' heads on the wall were shot by his grandmother a century ago! It is a rare pleasure to spend a night under the roof of a château so untouched by modernity. No carefully renovated 'features' here — everything is as it was. The paintwork may be peeling, the wallpapers faded, but the colours are original and refreshingly unsynthetic. The *trompe l'oeil* on the walls is all of a piece, in spite of the cracks. Downstairs rooms are filled with generations of possessions, including magnificent Aubusson tapestries on the walls. Bedrooms are comfortable, with gracious windows overlooking the park; bathrooms, with '60s fittings, slightly eccentric. The suites in the tower are lovely, with splendid mouldings, windows and doorways in curved glass.

Rooms: 4: 2 doubles & 2 suites.
Price: Doubles 700 Frs (€ 106.71);
suites 750-950 Frs.
Breakfast: Included.
Meals: Dinner 200 Frs, by reservation.
Closed: November-Easter.

From Sancerre D955 dir. Bourges. Right on D923 dir. Aubigny sur Nère. Left on D7 to Sens Beaujeu. In village left at fountain, D74 dir. Neuilly en Sancerre. Down hill, château at end of tree-lined drive.

Château d'Ivoy

18380 Ivoy le Pré
Cher

Tel: (0)2 48 58 85 01
Fax: (0)2 48 58 85 02
E-mail: chateau.divoy@wanadoo.fr
web: perso.wanadoo.fr/chateau.divoy/

Marie France Gouëffon-de Vaivre

Every antique bed is appropriately canopied (*Kipling*: frothy mosquito net on a carved Anglo-Indian bed, *Lord Drummond*: an Olde-English feel), every superb bathroom a study in modern fittings on period washstands. Ivoy is home to an interior designer who has achieved miracles since buying it from a famous entomologist who had planted a tropical rainforest in one stateroom, now the fine-furnished, "Spode" dining room. It was built for Mary Stuart's Purser, Drummond: the Stuarts were allowed to create a Scottish duchy here that lasted 200 years and it became the Drummond family seat after the battle of Culloden. The front is stern, the back opens wide onto sweeping lawns, park and hills — all guest rooms face this way. The house radiates rich refinement and your hostess's infectious delight. She will welcome you in her grey-green hall with its lovely sandstone floor and ceramic stove, invite you to use the library (home to a huge hairy spider... emprisoned in a glass paperweight) or the *salon*, and will then retire discreetly. A very special place to stay. *Children over 12 welcome. No smoking in some rooms.*

Rooms: 6/7: 5 doubles, 1 twin, all with four-poster beds (can combine rooms to make suite for 3).
Price: 820-1120 Frs (€ 125.01-170.74). Extra small bedroom 400 Frs.
Breakfast: Included.
Meals: Available locally.
Closed: Never.

From A10 exit Salbris on D944 dir. Bourges to Neuvy sur Barangeon; left on D926 to La Chapelle d'Angillon; there D12 to Ivoy le Pré. Château entrance on right after church.

Le Manoir des Remparts

14 rue des Remparts   **Tel:** (0)2 54 47 94 87
36800 Saint Gaultier   **Fax:** (0)2 54 47 94 87
Indre   **E-mail:** WILLEM.PRINSLOO@wanadoo.fr

Ren Rijpstra

Behind the imposing gates and the high walls — the house is built on the outside of the old city ramparts — lies this charming 18th-century manor. The place is a gem: a gravelled courtyard and wisteria-clad barn at the front, a large, tree-filled walled garden with summer house at the back. Your hospitable and punctilious Dutch hosts have renovated the house with sympathy and style, preserving the beautiful fireplaces, the parquet floors and the marvellous oak staircase. Bedrooms are really comfortable. The style is essentially Provençal — Ren is an interior designer — with *Soléidado* and *toile de Jouy* wallpapers, country antiques, old paintings and pillows decked in fine antique linen. One room has a metal-framed four-poster with red check curtains: very fresh and modern. Bathrooms are sumptuous, the traditional fittings offset by sea-grass flooring and elegant drapes. Dine on *mille-feuille* of salmon in the dining room in the adjoining barn; retire with a book to the guests' sitting room which is warm and inviting with its book-lined walls, soft lighting and ancient beams.

Rooms: 4: 3 doubles & 1 suite.
Price: 550 Frs (€ 83.85).
Breakfast: Included.
Meals: Dinner 160 Frs: 5-courses, three times a week.
Closed: December 15-January 2.

From Châteauroux A20 dir. Limoges, then N151 Le Blanc/Poitiers road. Entering St Gaultier stay on Le Blanc road; cross 2 sets of lights; right, then imm'ly left across Le Blanc road. Pass supermarket dir. Thenay, continue about 500m. Manoir is on right.

ASP Map No: 7   MMap 238-39   **125**

Château de Boisrenault

36500 Buzançais
Indre

Tel: (0)2 54 84 03 01
Fax: (0)2 54 84 10 57
E-mail: yves.dumanoir@wanadoo.fr
web: www.chateau-du-boisrenault.com

Yves & Sylvie du Manoir

Built by a 19th-century aristocrat as a wedding present for his daughter — well overdue, she'd had two sons by the time it was finished — this is a turretted, customised, Renaissance château. Noble and imposing on the outside, it's very much a family home within. Furniture, *objects*, pictures, all have a tale to tell and there are plenty of hunting trophies and stags' heads on the walls. Reception rooms are lofty, with huge fireplaces. One sitting room has a baby grand; another, smaller and cosier, is lined with books. Each bedroom is an adventure in itself. Named after the family's children and grandchildren, the rooms feature a hotch-potch of pieces from different periods, including some excellent antiques. A couple of stuffed pheasants make unusual lampshades in Hadrien's room and offset the yellow walls beautifully! Breakfast and dinner are shared with other guests at a vast table in the dining room. A delicious pool lies discreetly tucked away behind trees in the grounds; table-tennis and table-football are a godsend on rainy days. A super place for a family stay.

Rooms: 6 doubles.
Price: 395-560 Frs (€ 60.22-85.37).
Breakfast: Included.
Meals: Available locally.
Closed: January.

From A20 exit 11 and D8 to Levroux. There D926 dir. Buzançais. Château on left, 3km before town.

La Rabouillère

Chemin de Marçon
41700 Contres
Loir-et-Cher

Tel: (0)2 54 79 05 14
Fax: (0)2 54 79 59 39

Martine & Jean-Marie Thimonnier

Monsieur — a construction engineer by profession — built the traditional Solonge farmhouse himself. This building, with its timber frame and herringbone brickwork, and his first project, the delicious little house next door, bring together old and new: traditional materials, modern comforts. Not only is Monsieur full of plans — a barn to house garden equipment is next on his list — he is a civilized and articulate host. Madame is charming too, and has furnished the interiors with great skill. The first-floor suite of the main house is spacious and splendid, decorated in pretty Laura Ashley fabrics and with fine views over woodland and park. Other rooms are quite a bit smaller, but sympathetically decorated too, with good sized bathrooms (towels are changed every day, bed linen every other), communicating doors between two sets of rooms should you need them, and shared kitchenette. Some lovely old family pieces decorate the smaller house next door, which has a more rustic feel. Breakfasts are served in the spacious guests' dining/sitting room at tables beautifully laid with English china, and include eggs from the farm and homemade jam.

Rooms: 6: 4 doubles, 1 suite & 1 apartment.
Price: Doubles 360 Frs (€ 54.88), suite 550 Frs, apt 700-900 Frs.
Breakfast: Included.
Meals: Available locally. Can picnic in garden.
Closed: Never.

Leave A10 at Blois dir. Vierzon onto D765 to Cheverny; D102 dir. Contres. Chemin de Marçon is 6km beyond Cheverny on left.

Château de Chissay

Chissay en Touraine
41400 Montrichard
Loir-et-Cher

Tel: (0)2 54 32 32 01
Fax: (0)2 54 32 43 80
E-mail: chateau-chissay@wanadoo.fr
web: www.chateauxandcountry.com/chateaux/chissay

M Patrice Longet

One minute you can be discovering the delights of the famous châteaux of the Loire, the next, indulging in the delights of your own private one. The Château de Chissay is a Renaissance jewel and, though the last word in luxury, it's not in the least overwhelming. Built for the Chancellor of France during Charles VII's reign, the château was used as a royal residence for hundreds of years and became the meeting place of military bigwigs in World War II. Yet its public rooms feel surprisingly intimate. Light pours into the vast bedrooms, each different and special; imagine yourself the Sleeping Beauty as you climb to your room via a turretted stone stair. (Though you may take the lift!). The 'troglodyte' room in the rock face behind the château is some peoples' favourite. Suites have immaculate sitting rooms in more corner towers; a wooden-beamed room shaped like a boat under the eaves has a mosaic Jacuzzi in its 'prow'. Simpler rooms in the annexe near the outdoor pool are perfect for families. And there's an inner courtyard with splashing fountain from which you reach an Italian style portico with valley views. Glorious.

Rooms: 43: 32 doubles/twins, 2 triples
& 9 suites for 3/5.
Price: 450-1025 Frs (€ 68.6-156.26).
Breakfast: 65 Frs.
Meals: Lunch & dinner 185-295 Frs
(reserve dinner before 6 p.m.).
Closed: Mid-November-mid-March.

A10 from Paris exit Blois. Cross the Loire dir.
Montrichard then D176 to Chenonceaux.
The château is 4km after Montrichard on
right; signposted.

Hôtel Château des Tertres

Route de Monteaux
41150 Onzain
Loir-et-Cher

Tel: (0)2 54 20 83 88
Fax: (0)2 54 20 89 21
E-mail: chateau.des.tertres@wanadoo.fr
web: www.chateau-tertres.com

Bernard Valois

A classic mid 19th-century nobleman's house surrounded by mature wooded parkland in the Loire valley — but all is not traditional inside. The young and energetic Monsieur Valois is an artist, and his sense of fun pervades this lovely place. Many of the rooms *are* period pieces, including the sitting rooms and the largest of the bedrooms, some of which are remarkably ornate. The smallest rooms, though, are minimalist — symphonies of creamy yellow and white. That a creative spirit is at work is evident, too, in the gardener's lodge. Its four guest rooms have been furnished with real panache: one with a massive Italian four-poster, another with a perspex bedhead and a row of medieval steel helmets lined up on the wall! Older children will love staying here. Your arty host is extremely hospitable and will let you in on the secrets of the château if you ask: before it was restored to its original elegance it had an amazingly chequered career, having been a German military headquarters, a school for metal workers and a chicken farm, in three of its former lives.

Rooms: 22: 18 doubles & 4 in gardener's lodge in grounds.
Price: 400-600 Frs (€ 60.98-91.47).
Breakfast: Buffet 45 Frs.
Meals: Available locally.
Closed: Mid-November to week before Easter.

From A10 exit Blois. N152 dir. Amboise/Tours. Right to Onzain opposite bridge to Chaumont. Left in village dir. Monteaux. Château about 1.5 km on right.

Le Moulin de Saint Jean

Saint Jean-Saint Germain
37600 Loches
Indre-et-Loire

Tel: (0)2 47 94 70 12
Fax: (0)2 47 94 77 98

Andrew Page & Sue Hutton

A deliciously watery home. We love this place — a restored mill on an island. Having breakfast on the verandah over the mill stream is not the only reason guests return. Sue radiates generosity and charm; Andrew, equally relaxed and friendly, is an excellent cook. Dinners are extremely convivial affairs, shared with your hosts. All is ups and downs, nooks and crannies, big rooms and small ones, character and variety. Andrew and Sue plan to convert their garage into accommodation for themselves, so the guests' sitting room will move to the first floor. Comfy chairs and colourful cushions set the scene; bedrooms, too, are full of personality, and all different. Attractive, high-quality fabrics, interesting pictures and much evidence of Sue's spongeing and stencilling skills. Add a shady garden, the temptation of about 1,000 paperbacks and the colourful presence of a blue and yellow macaw. Everywhere there is the gentle murmur of running water — which is why this site, however idyllic, is not the most relaxing place for parents of very young children.

Rooms: 6: 4 doubles, 1 twin & 1 triple.
Price: 300-350 Frs (€ 45.73-53.36).
Extra bed 100 Frs.
Breakfast: Included.
Meals: Dinner, including aperitif, wine & coffee, 150 Frs.
Closed: December-January.

From Loches, N 143 dir. Châteauroux; pass Perusson then left at sign to St. Jean-St Germain; house is last over bridge on left.

Hôtel du Bon Laboureur et du Château

6 rue du Docteur Bretonneau   **Tel:** (0)2 47 23 90 02
37150 Chenonceaux   **Fax:** (0)2 47 23 82 01
Indre-et-Loire

Isabelle & Antoine Jeudi

This little hotel, in the middle of the village of Chenonceaux, a short stroll from the château, started life as a coaching inn in the 18th century. Now it has expanded into an adjoining building, the old village school and into a somewhat grander building with a rather pretentious tower known tongue-in cheek as 'the Manor'. The bedrooms are all light and airy with plenty of space and are kept in tip-top condition. One is in psychedelic green and yellow, another is more traditional in pink and another, smaller, in fresh blue and white. A good spot for seeing the châteaux with children as there are good family rooms and the pretty garden has a pool. The heart of the hotel is in the original building, with an elegant 18th-century style dining room and a simpler, more relaxed one adjoining it. In summer, proper tables with starched white cloths, candles and flowers are set on the terrace under the trees. Amboise, Chaumont, Chambord and the other châteaux are within easy reach so you can make time for a swim and a cocktail before dinner. A large potager behind the hotel supplies vegetables.

Rooms: 26: 22 doubles/twins & 4 apartments.
Price: Doubles 400-600 Frs (€ 60.98-91.47); apartments 700-1000 Frs.
Breakfast: 45 Frs.
Meals: Dinner 155-315 Frs. Picnic lunch 50 Frs.
Closed: Mid-November-mid-December & January. Restaurant closed Wednesday lunchtimes & Thursdays during low season.

From Blois, cross R. Loire onto D751 then D764 to Montrichard. Follow signs to Chenonceaux. Hotel on right in village centre.

ASP Map No: 7   MMap 238-14   **131**

Château des Ormeaux

Nazelles
37530 Amboise
Indre-et-Loire

Tel: (0)2 47 23 26 51
Fax: (0)2 47 23 19 31
E-mail: chateaudesormeaux@wanadoo.fr
web: perso.wanadoo.fr/chateaudesormeaux/

Xavier Merle

The charming owners of Des Ormeaux were happy to swap the small-town mentality of Savonnières for the grandeur of their turreted 19th-century château in its 67 acres. They live in 'cave' rooms built into the rock face behind the hill-top château. Corner guestrooms on two floors — original panelling on the first floor, sloping ceilings on the second — have tiny little *boudoirs* off the main room in the turret; all are named after classical composers. A decent size, with elaborate bedcovers and drapes and massive bathrooms attached, they are very grand in a turn-of-the-century way. One room, blue and gold, has a marble fireplace and an *armoire à glace*, a wall of mirrors hidden behind an apparently ordinary cupboard; another, decorated in ochre and maroon, a crystal chandelier and plushly canopied bed. Yet more crystal chandeliers in the dining room, where evening meals, shared with one or more of your several hosts — there are six in total — are enhanced by background Bach and candlelight. Best of all, from wherever you stand (or swim) the valley views are superb.

Rooms: 6 doubles/twins.
Price: 550-650 Frs (€ 83.85-99.09).
Breakfast: Included.
Meals: Dinner 250 Frs, by reservation.
Closed: Never.

From Tours N152 dir. Blois. After Vouvray, left to Noizay and from there D1 dir. Nazelles. Château on left about 2km after Noizay.

Le Manoir Les Minimes

34 quai Charles Guinot
37400 Amboise
Indre-et-Loire

Tel: (0)2 47 30 40 40
Fax: (0)2 47 30 40 77
E-mail: manoir-les-minimes@wanadoo.fr
web: www.amboise.com/les-minimes

Eric Deforges & Patrice Longet

Every detail has been thought out with tender care, lovingly chosen antiques and *objets* placed to create a light sophistication. A far cry from the *Minimes* monastic order who had a convent here until it was destroyed in the French Revolution — then this noble townhouse took the site. Between majestic Loire and historic castle, the manor has 18th-century grace and generous windows onto its big courtyard, the castle and the lustrous river. Before opening Les Minimes in 1998, the charmingly young and enthusiastic Eric Deforges was in fashion design, hence his faultless eye for fabric, colour and detail. Exquisitely-decorated rooms are big — slightly smaller on the top floor with beams and river views from their dormers — with luxurious bathrooms. The masterpiece is the suite where the *toile de Jouy* wall fabric seems to be one single piece. The elegant chequered hall leads to a series of interconnecting *salons*. There's a smaller, more intimate television room and a breakfast room in soft yellow and grey. With fresh flowers everywhere, it feels like a classy home, not a formal hotel.

Rooms: 13: 11 rooms & 2 suites.
Price: Doubles 590-820 Frs
(€ 89.94-125.01); suites 1200-1400 Frs.
Breakfast: 58 Frs.
Meals: Prepared dinners on request & arrangement with 4-star restaurant nearby (incl. taxi service).
Closed: Never.

From A10 exit Amboise. D31 dir. Amboise. Cross R. Loire, D31 dir. town centre. Hotel on left approaching town centre.

Le Fleuray Hôtel

37530 Cangey
Indre-et-Loire

Tel: (0)2 47 56 09 25
Fax: (0)2 47 56 93 97
E-mail: lefleurayhotel@wanadoo.fr

Peter & Hazel Newington

Perfect if, like most of our readers, you have a helicopter — or a hot-air balloon. Pretty perfect, too, for ordinary mortals, for Peter and Hazel have created a haven of pure peace. The raw material was ideal: a solid, handsome old manor-house with duck-pond and barns, mature trees and bushes, all that was needed to persuade them to settle. The rooms in the barn are just right for families; slightly cut off from the rest, their French windows open onto the garden, so children may roam unfettered. The Newingtons are unstuffy and easy-going, genuinely enjoying the company of visitors. They have created a slightly English mood, with lightly floral sofas into which you can sink, book-cases, flowers (always fresh) and prints — and a plain carpet in the sitting room. The bedrooms are big and fresh; one, for example, has white cane furniture and floral covers on the huge bed. It must be fun to dine outside, under the old roof and its arched entrance; or under huge parasols, on pink table cloths and green chairs. It is fun in the winter, too, with an open fire and Hazel's superb cooking.

Rooms: 14 doubles/twins.
Price: Doubles 375-550 Frs
(€ 57.17-83.85). Extra bed 95-115 Frs.
Breakfast: 68 Frs; children's 55 Frs.
Meals: Lunch & dinner 155-265 Frs.
Children 80 Frs.
Closed: French school holidays in
February/March.

*From A10 exit 18 Amboise/Château
Renault. D31 to Autrêche. Left on D55 to
Dame Marie Les Bois. Right on D74 dir. Cangey.*

Domaine des Bidaudières

Rue du Peu Morier
37210 Vouvray
Indre-et-Loire

Tel: (0)2 47 52 66 85
Fax: (0)2 47 52 62 17
E-mail: info@bandb-loire-valley.com
web: www.bandb-loire-valley.com

M & Mme Pascal Suzanne

In the three years they've been here, Sylvie and Pascal Suzanne have made their mark on this classic, creamy-stoned ex-wine-grower's property. Unstuffy and outgoing, this young couple lend a stylish sophistication to the place — and plan to produce a small quantity of their own wine, having planted new vineyards to the terraced rear. Bedrooms are fresh and contemporary, each wallpapered and carpeted differently, each immaculate. All are light, south-facing and have valley views. The dining room, where the kitchen used to be, was actually built into the rock — a hugely attractive, stone-floored room with a low rocky ceiling, a sitting area and an open fire at one end. Guests can idle away the afternoon in the elegant swimming-pool on the lower terrace which lies alongside the carefully restored *orangerie*. Families are welcome to stay in the more rustic 'troglodyte' apartment nearby.

Rooms: 5: 3 doubles, 1 suite for three, 1 (troglodyte) apartment for four.
Price: Doubles 650 Frs (€ 99.09); suite 750 Frs; apartment 700 Frs.
Breakfast: Included.
Meals: Available locally.
Closed: Never.

From Paris, A10 exit 20 Vouvray onto N152 dir. Amboise. In Vouvray D46 dir. Vernou sur Brenne. House is second on left after railway bridge.

Château de Jallanges

Vernou sur Brenne
37210 Vouvray
Indre-et-Loire

Tel: (0)2 47 52 06 66
Fax: (0)2 47 52 11 18
E-mail: chateaudejallanges@wanadoo.fr
web: www.chateaux-france.com/-jallanges

Stephane Ferry-Balin

The château is four centuries old, built in the time of Louis XI, and Monsieur is immensely proud òf this heritage. It's listed of course — and so are the castle's lovely Renaissance gardens. Bounding with energy, Monsieur Balin, who loves a chat, tells us he has been receiving guests for 15 years; an accountant by day, a hotelier by night, he is also the energetic organiser of concerts, conferences and wedding receptions. The château opens its doors to the public most of the year — which is why bells ring when you enter the *cour d'honneur*, the magnificent courtyard round which the castle is built. The dining room, dotted with antique pieces and precious porcelain, provides a fitting backcloth to the sumptuous breakfasts guests are treated to each morning. Bedrooms are splendidly old-fashioned; the *Henri XIV* sports a magnificently sculpted fireplace, the *Suite Romantique* is made up of two cosy bedrooms and a small salon. Bathrooms are big and comfortable and the rooms on the upper floor have fine views of the park or the lovely formal gardens. A truly stately place.

Rooms: 7: 5 rooms & 2 suites.
Price: Doubles 750-800 Frs (€ 114.34-121.96); suites 900-1500 Frs.
Breakfast: Included.
Meals: Dinner, including wine, 260 Frs.
Closed: Never.

From Tours N152 dir. Blois. Left in Vouvray on D46 to Vernon sur Brenne, then D76. Château signposted.

Prieuré des Granges

37510 Savonnières
Indre-et-Loire

Tel: (0)2 47 50 09 67
Fax: (0)2 47 50 06 43
E-mail: salmon.eric@wanadoo.fr

Eric & Christine Salmon

An oasis in an encroaching sea of suburbia, Le Prieuré is a dream. Hidden away in three acres of landscaped gardens and mature trees, the main building, long, low, ornate, is 400 years old, but behind its magnificent stone walls there's a refreshing lightness of touch and lack of pretension. The dining room, sitting room and breakfast room — long, light, painted white and blue — are discreet, comfortable and very charming. The generous bedrooms are equally elegant affairs, each one with a character of its own, and the occasional rustic touch. (One has its own bread oven.) Stone floors are softened with Persian rugs; ceilings are beamy; bathrooms are large, white (mostly) and luxurious. Downstairs rooms open onto their own little courtyards. At the back is a large grassy garden with a pool. Your host, a relaxed Anglophile with a taste for fine beer, takes huge pleasure in making sure his guests have everything they need. Eric and Christine have achieved the near impossible: that elusive mix of the sophisticated and the down-to-earth.

Rooms: 6: 5 doubles & 1 suite for 4.
Price: Doubles 580 Frs (€ 88.42);
suite 750 Frs.
Breakfast: Included.
Meals: Available locally.
Closed: December-February.

*Leave A10 at exit 24 Joué lès Tours dir.
Villandry. In Savonnières, left at Hôtel
Faisan dir. Ballan Miré. House on left after
approx. 1km. Signposted.*

Le Vieux Château d'Hommes

37340 Hommes
Indre-et-Loire

Tel: (0)2 47 24 95 13
Fax: (0)2 47 24 68 67
E-mail: hubert.hardy@wanadoo.fr
web: www.hotelrestvieuxchateau.com

Famille Hardy

The moat and the ruins of the old castle, with one little tower still standing, make a thoroughly romantic setting for this great house, originally the tithe barn built just outside the castle wall. Inside, a vast baronial hall and fireplace welcome you and the atmosphere becomes more formal. In the big, luxurious bedrooms, antique furniture (beautifully Italian in one case) goes hand-in-hand with the lavish bathrooms. Two rooms give onto the fine courtyard bounded by outbuildings containing a couple of gîtes; two look out to open fields and woods. In contrast, the stone walls and terracotta tiles of the Tower Room, which overlooks the moat, give it a more rustic feel — its bathroom is down a narrow spiral staircase. In an area not particularly renowned for stunning countryside, the courtyard setting is certainly splendid, and the Hardy couple are interesting though they are often away, leaving daily management to permanent staff.

Rooms: 6 doubles/twins.
Price: 420-650 Frs (€ 64.03-99.09).
Extra bed 135 Frs.
Breakfast: Included.
Meals: Dinner, including aperitif, wine & coffee, 165 Frs.
Closed: Never.

From Tours N152 dir. Saumur. In Langeais D57 to Hommes. There, D64 dir. Giseux. Château on right as you leave village

Château de Montgoger

37800 Saint Epain
Indre-et-Loire

Tel: (0)2 47 65 54 22
Fax: (0)2 47 65 85 43
E-mail: contact@chateau-mongoger.com
web: www.chateau-montgoger.com

M & Mme Paul O.Thilgès-Porté

The setting of what Monsieur calls his "little piece of paradise" is, indeed, heavenly. For guests the magic starts the moment the gates swing open and you ride up the long sweeping drive through wooded slopes — carpeted with white cyclamen in autumn — and pass ancient ruins. The original castle was gutted by fire; the present building has a 19th-century *orangerie* with an elegant parquet-floored, crystal-chandeliered dining room and a lovely sitting room for guests. The elaborately furnished bedrooms are spacious, have fabulous views of parkland and the Vienne Valley, and are lavishly draped and decorated in deep reds and greens. Madame is a talented artist and her paintings are throughout the house, with other treasures. Beyond the house lies a swathe of lawn with an ancient oak under which Joan of Arc is supposed to have slept. Guests may rest in the greater comfort of a rough-hewn shelter — or seek out the old stone lily pond and waterfall grotto. Monsieur is utterly charming and a generous host. His spaniel and even his peacocks come running when he calls!

Rooms: 5: 2 doubles, 2 twins & 1 suite.
Price: Single 400 Frs (€ 60.98); doubles 500 Frs; twins 550 Frs; twin suite 650 Frs.
Breakfast: Included.
Meals: Available locally.
Closed: October 20-March 31.

27km S of Tours. A10 exit 25 Ste Maure de Touraine; D760 dir. Ile Bouchard for about 3km; right at roundabout on D57 dir. St Epain. Château signposted on main square of St Epain opposite town hall.

La Commanderie

16 rue de la Commanderie
37220 Brizay
Indre-et-Loire

Tel: (0)2 47 58 63 13
Fax: (0)2 47 58 55 81
E-mail: info@lacommanderie.com
web: www.lacommanderie.com

Christian Vaurie

Some of the makers of this stupendous grandeur — Knights Templar, Princes and Prime Ministers, Presidents and Financiers — look down as you eat in the magnificent dining room, a favourite restaurant for discerning Grenoblese. But the owners' passion for their superbly-restored château-hotel and the enthusiastic welcome they give their guests give it the feel of an intimate family-run hotel. The place is awash with family antiques and heirlooms, unquestionable good taste prevails and fresh flowers add that touch of life and genuine attention. Bedrooms are in four separate buildings, each quite small so adding to the sense of intimacy. Rooms in *château* and *chalet* are more traditional with carved wooden beds and gilt-framed mirrors, though some of them give onto a small road. The *orangerie* has rooms that, once you have negotiated the plainish corridors, look out over fine parkland and are deliciously peaceful. The *petit pavillon* houses the cheapest rooms, also onto the road. But whichever you choose you will feel thoroughly welcome and pampered, and it's excellent value for families.

Rooms: 11: 4 doubles & 7 others sharing showers and wcs.
Price: 250-330 Frs (€ 38.11-50.31).
Breakfast: Included.
Meals: Dinner, including wine & coffee, 130 Frs by reservation.
Closed: Never.

From Chinon cross R. Vienne & take D749 then D760 to Ile Bouchard. After entering town, 2nd right and follow signs.

Domaine de la Tortinière

Les Gués de Veigné
37250 Montbazon
Indre-et-Loire

Tel: (0)2 47 34 35 00
Fax: (0)2 47 65 95 70
E-mail: domaine.tortiniere@wanadoo.fr
web: www.silencehotel.com/domainedelatortiniere

Xavier Olivereau

It seems unreal, this pepperpot-towered château on a hill above the River Indre, the bird-filled woods where wild cyclamen lay a carpet in autumn and daffodils radiate their light in spring, the view across to the stony keep of Montbazon — an exceptional spot with tennis, a heated pool, fishing or rowing on the river. Bedrooms are perfect, decorated with flair and imagination, be they in the château or in a converted outbuilding. One of these, an adorable Renaissance dolls' house, has two smaller rooms and a split-level apartment; the orchard cottage, for playing shepherdesses *à la Petit Trianon*, is big and beautifully furnished — the desk invites great writings. Bathrooms are luxurious, some smaller than others. Guests enjoy taking the underground passage to the orangery to dine in simple elegance, inside or on the terrace. Soft lighting, panelled reception rooms, deep comfort, discreet friendliness are the marks of this real family-run hotel: the warm, humorous owners are genuinely attentive, their sole aim is to make your stay peaceful and harmonious.

Rooms: 21: 15 doubles/twins & 6 suites.
Price: Doubles 530-950 Frs
(€ 80.8-144.83); suites 1150-1450 Frs.
Breakfast: 85 Frs.
Meals: Dinner 295 Frs;
picnic lunch 100 Frs.
Closed: December 21-end February.
Restaurant closed Sunday evenings from
November-March.

2km north of Montbazon. From Tours N10 S
dir. Poitiers for 10km. In Les Gués, right at second set of traffic lights. Signposted.

Poitou
The Atlantic Coast

La Rochelle… I perceived to be a fascinating little town,
a most original mixture of brightness and dullness.
Henry James

Le Palais Briau

Rue de la Madeleine
44370 Varades
Loire-Atlantique

Tel: (0)2 40 83 45 00
Fax: (0)2 40 83 49 30
E-mail: palaisbrio@aol.com
web: welcome.to/palais_briau

Thérèse & François Devouge

A glorious Palladian residence perched high on the hillside overlooking the Loire valley. Built in the 1850s by François Briau, an early industrialist who made his fortune constructing railways, the house is palatial, lovingly restored and saved from commercial modernisation by the present owners. Faithful to the era in which the house was built, they have even held on to Briau's original furniture and fittings (of which he was immensely proud). Madame radiates exuberance and charm; Monsieur is an artist and designer whose impeccable taste has been stamped on every interior. A remarkable colonnaded stair sweeps up to the guests' sitting and dining rooms — pure Napoleon III. Bedrooms are light and large; three are blessed with magnificent views. Exquisite wallpapers, brocade canopies above polished mahogany beds, fine linen, fresh flowers — all elegant and glamorous. Bathrooms are sumptuous and orientally-tiled. The grounds too are fabulous; large areas are completely wild and overgrown and contain the remains of a vast *orangerie*. A breathtaking place.

Rooms: 4: 3 doubles & 1 suite with children's bed.
Price: 550-850 Frs (€ 83.85-129.58).
Breakfast: Included.
Meals: Three very good restaurants nearby.
Closed: Never.

From Angers N23 dir. Nantes. Château is signposted left at roundabout as you enter Varades.

Saint Christophe

Place Notre Dame
44502 La Baule
Loire-Atlantique

Tel: (0)2 40 60 35 35
Fax: (0)2 40 60 11 74

Calixte Jouon

An easy walk from the "finest beach in Europe", the exceptionally attractive Saint Christophe is a trio of 1920's seaside villas with a family-house atmosphere where you never feel the weight of 30 rooms. There are no corridors, just hallways and landings, each one an opportunity for a fine old table, a glass-fronted cabinet with family treasures or a deep sofa with a good reading light: books are an essential part of this exceptionally civilised hotel. Your host, a charming, urbane and humorous man of great height and much heart, and his artist wife, whose works enliven many walls, genuinely enjoy people. They "cultivate the informal", provide excellent food in the invigoratingly red and electric-blue dining room, fresh flowers and space for families (five rooms have bunk beds). Rooms vary greatly in size but each has at least one old piece of furniture, one object or picture to arouse your curiosity. Décor varies too — there are stripes and florals, pastels and powerfuls, patchwork and *piqué*, all gently put together in a personal, relaxing style. One does indeed feel at home here.

Rooms: 33: 28 doubles/twins & 5 family rooms.
Price: 280-430 Frs (€ 42.69-65.55) (except July & August: half-board only).
Breakfast: 50 Frs.
Meals: July & August half-board only: 445-545 Frs p.p.
Closed: Never.

La Baule dir. La Baule Centre. Place des Victoires, right on Avenue de Gaulle to sea front. Right along beach; second right (Avenue des Impairs); hotel 100m facing you.

Hôtel du Martinet

Place de la Croix Blanche
85230 Bouin
Vendée

Tel: (0)2 51 49 08 94
Fax: (0)2 51 49 83 08

Françoise Huchet

Madame Huchet describes the Martinet as a country hotel that is by the sea. This is a fair description: sitting by the pool in the garden you feel very much in the country, but the sea is just down the road. Halfway down the Vendée coast, Bouin is a working seaside village — the pretty church was built in the 14th and 15th centuries — not somewhere that has sprung up for the tourists. Madame Huchet's son Emmanuel runs oyster beds off the village and busy little fishing ports are clustered along the coast. This is a real family hotel and Emmanuel is also the chef, specializing, not surprisingly, in fresh fish and seafood. Meals are either in a cosy blue-panelled dining room or in a more summery one in a veranda looking onto the garden. The rooms are simply but attractively decorated, some in the main house, which has only been a hotel for 14 years, and some like little cottages alongside the swimming pool. A great place to bring children for a holiday: the hotel is relaxed and informal, there are country walks as well as beaches and Emmanuel will be happy to take you to see his oysters.

Rooms: 22: 21 doubles & 1 studio for 4.
Price: Doubles 240-370 Frs
(€ 36.59-56.41); studio 400-420 Frs.
Breakfast: 50 Frs.
Meals: Lunch & dinner 100-120 Frs.
Closed: Never.

51km SW of Nantes on D751 past Bouaye then D758 through Bourgneuf en Retz dir. Noirmoutier for 9km.

Hôtel du Général d'Elbée

Place du Château
85330 Noirmoutier en l'Ile
Vendée

Tel: (0)2 51 39 10 29
Fax: (0)2 51 39 08 23
E-mail: general-delbee@wanadoo.fr
web: www.chateauxandcountry.com/chateaux/delbee

Céline Renaud

The General in question came to a sorry end, shot on the square for raising an army of Vendéen royalists against the Revolution, but was allowed, as an officer, to face the firing squad in his armchair. This house is where the rebellion was planned, a solid, powerful residence down by the bridge, just below the castle, at the heart of life on Noirmoutier. The sea air makes the colours soft and limpid, the land and seascapes are flat and bewitching (Renoir was very taken with this spot), the inner garden and swimming pool are a haven for the general's privileged guests. Inside, the atmospheric old building is fittingly furnished with excellent country antiques, 18th-century fireplaces and fresh flowers. Bedrooms in the wing over the garden have been recently redecorated and are very pleasant indeed. Those in the 18th-century part, which also has a big terrace over the canal, may be in need of a little face-lift. But all bathrooms are excellent, the suites under the rafters on the second floor are ideal for families and a quiet, careful welcome is waiting for all.

Rooms: 28: 24 doubles/twins & 4 suites for 3/4.
Price: 595-950 Frs (€ 90.71-144.83); suites 725-1450 Frs.
Breakfast: 65 Frs.
Meals: Available locally.
Closed: Mid-October-end April.

Fom A11 exit Nantes from ring road, D751 and D758 through Bourgneuf en Retz dir. Beauvoir sur Mer. Crossing to Noirmoutier via Le Gois only possible at low tide. Otherwise take bridge.

Hôtel Fleur de Sel

Rue des Saulniers
85330 Noirmoutier en l'Ile
Vendée

Tel: (0)2 51 39 21 59
Fax: (0)2 51 39 75 66
E-mail: info@fleurdesel.fr
web: www.fleurdesel.fr

Pierre Wattecamps

Noirmoutier has a personality all its own: this group of simple white buildings in its Mediterranean garden is typical. Built in the 1980s, it sits peacefully between sea and salt marsh, long sandy beach and little yachting harbour. It is perfect for family holidays, with tennis court, golf driving range, big pool and superb outdoor Jacuzzi. Bedrooms are good too, some in classic cosy style with country pine furniture and fabrics, others more bracing with ship-shape yew furniture and yachting motifs; several have little ground-floor terraces. The delightful, caring owners have humour and intelligence; their daughter's paintings are sometimes shown here. The chef has worked with the very best in Paris and meals are served by courteous waiters in the airy, raftered dining room or on the oleander-lined terrace. It is all cleancut, sun-warmed, impeccable and welcoming. There is a bridge, but try and come by the Passage du Gois causeway, open 3 hours twice a day round low tide: an unforgettable 4km drive 'through the sea' where shellfish-diggers cluster. (The island is very popular in summer).

Rooms: 35: 30 doubles, 3 triples & 2 quadruples.
Price: 400-720 Frs (€ 60.98-109.76).
Breakfast: 55 Frs.
Meals: Lunch 138 Frs; dinner 185-285 Frs.
Closed: November 2-February 12.

From Paris A11 dir. Nantes. 82km SW of Nantes D751 Bouaye then D758 Bourgneuf en Retz, Beauvoir sur Mer to cross Passage du Gois at low tide or Pont de Fromentine. Hotel 500m behind church.

Le Château du Boisniard

Le Boisniard
85500 Chambretaud
Vendée

Tel: (0)2 51 67 50 01
Fax: (0)2 51 67 53 81

Joël Coutolleau

There's a grand piano in the entrance, a fire-place and a sofa — what more could you want even if you can't play? The restoration of this handsome 15th-century Breton château, destroyed in the Revolution when the Vendée fought back to restore the crown during some vicious wars, has been mammoth, a labour of passion rather than love. The Coutolleaus are devoted to the place, with good reason. It is a château on a human scale, in 30 acres of woodland. There are 2.5 miles of footpaths snaking their way through the park, two lakes, terraces and a tennis court. Swans are attracted here and grace the lake most delicately. Inside, there is a feeling of great space and solid good taste. The bedrooms all gaze over the park and one of them was once a little chapel; the quietness is within as well as without. The bedsteads are designer-sculpted and the colours are bright and fresh. English guests will feel particularly at home here in the library. Altogether lovely, charmingly formal yet utterly unpretentious, and peaceful.

Rooms: 10: 8 doubles/twins & 2 suites.
Price: 450-850 Frs (€ 68.6-129.58).
Breakfast: 45 Frs.
Meals: Lunch & dinner 90-295 Frs.
Closed: Never.

From Cholet N160 dir. Les Herbiers then left dir. Le Puy du Fou for 5km. (15km from Cholet).

147   MMap 232-42   **ASP Map No: 11**

Chalet de Venise

6 rue Square
86280 Saint Benoît Bourg
Vienne

Tel: (0)5 49 88 45 07
Fax: (0)5 49 52 95 44

M & Mme Mautret

St Benoît is a pretty little village with a fine Romanesque church and, despite being just outside the suburbs of Poitiers, has managed to keep its village atmosphere. Set in the wooded valley, on the edge of a rippling stream, the Venise was completely rebuilt in 1994. It is a low, rendered building with stone balconies curving round following the stream, a wide terrace spread out below its balustrades. The smallish bedrooms have French windows onto the balcony and are decorated with apricot sponged walls, floral fabrics in contrasting dark colours and stained wood beds and dressing tables, all in neat, new contemporary style. But most people come here for the food, which is superb. Monsieur Mautret is the chef, Madame manages the restaurant — they are a delightful and excellent team. Service is elegant, almost reverential (silver cloches) but quick. Madame welcomes children and says they enjoy eating in the lovely big, light dining room or out on the terrace. The breakfast room is attractive too in soft blue and peach colours with Turkish rugs, good prints and plenty of real plants.

Rooms: 12 doubles.
Price: 350-380 Frs (€ 53.36-57.93).
Breakfast: 45 Frs.
Meals: Dinner 150-295 Frs.
Closed: Two weeks in February & one weekend in August.

From A10 exit Poitiers Sud dir. Poitiers. At traffic lights dir. Limoges/Châteauroux. Right after 1km. Right at lights to St Benoît Bourg (careful: there are 4 St Benoits in the area!). Hotel in village centre.

Le Relais du Lyon d'Or
4 rue d'Enfer
86260 Angles sur l'Anglin
Vienne

Tel: (0)5 49 48 32 53
Fax: (0)5 49 84 02 28
E-mail: thoreau@lyondor.com
web: www.lyondor.com

Heather & Guillaume Thoreau

In one of France's most beautiful villages, this old hotel owes its revival to Heather and Guillaume's herculean efforts: they bought it half-ruined in 1994 as a place for their wedding, new home and business, then left their high-flying London careers to do it up. They now run renovation courses, with practical advice from their epic experience of problems with red tape, labour, time and money. Each room was rebuilt round its old flagstones, doors and beams, then decorated in warm natural colours with Heather's beautiful paint effects (ragged, distressed, veiled), patinas and stencils — she now gives courses in paint finishes, using her rooms as living examples. Marvellous they are too, in their rich fabrics, intriguing details and individuality, small, not overdone, with delicious bathrooms. It's like staying in a country house with delightfully relaxed and friendly hosts. The menu is varied and refined — they have an excellent chef; generous breakfasts are served in the pretty yard in summer. And there's also *La Source* for steam baths, massages, face and body care.

Rooms: 10: 9 doubles & 1 suite for 4.
Price: Doubles 370-450 Frs (€ 56.41-68.6); suite 600 Frs.
Breakfast: 40 Frs.
Meals: Lunch & dinner 110-190 Frs.
Closed: January & February. Restaurant closed Monday & Tuesday lunchtimes.

A10 exit Châtellerault Nord on D9/D725 E to La Roche Posay. Through La Roche Posay onto D5 to Angles sur l'Anglin. Hotel in village centre.

Château de Saint Loup sur Thouet

79600 Saint Loup Lamairé
Deux-Sèvres

Tel: (0)5 49 64 81 73
Fax: (0)5 49 64 82 06
E-mail: chdb@compuserve.com
web: www.chateaudesaint-loup.com

Comte Charles-Henri de Bartillat

This château inspired Perrault to write Puss in Boots! It has an ancient and fascinating history. The Black Prince incarcerated John the Good here after the Battle of Poitiers in 1356. It was rebuilt in the 17th century by the 'Marquis of Carabas', whose magnificence so impressed the fairytale writer. Count Charles-Henri de Bartillat visited the château on Christmas Eve 1990, fell in love with the place and 10 days later had bought it. Saint Loup is an Historic Monument and both the château and the gardens are open to the public. The count, charming and passionate about his home, is painstakingly restoring the house and the grounds (using the plans drawn up by Jacques Boyer de la Boissière in the early 18th century, when the gardens were at their best). If you are a gardener, you won't know where to turn: to the flower gardens, the orchard with 75 ancient varieties or to the enormous potager, recreated in 1998. Staying here will impress the grown ups as well: the guestrooms are full of atmosphere, with beautiful old beds.

Rooms: 15: 13 doubles & 2 suites.
Price: Doubles 550-1200 Frs
(€ 83.85-182.94); suites 950-1150 Frs.
Breakfast: 60 Frs.
Meals: Dinner 250 Frs in main dining room of dungeon tower (on request).
Closed: Never.

A10 exit 26 onto D725 E to Airvault (55km), there D46 to St Loup Lamaire. Château visible as you enter village.

Hôtel Le Chat Botté

2 place de l'Egliselle de Ré
17590 Saint Clément des
Baleines
Charente-Maritime

Tel: (0)5 46 29 21 93
Fax: (0)5 46 29 29 97

Mmes Massé-Chantreau

A perfect seaside house, pine-panelled, pale-chaired, decorated with pastels and peace, this is part of a family network: one sister is your hotel hostess, another has her beauty salon right here where you can be wrapped in seaweed and reflexologised, a third has a B&B nearby and two brothers have a restaurant each, one of them next door. So things are well organised, all is spotless and you can choose to have your *énergétique* breakfast in the sweet little patio, the flowery garden or the grey-blue dining room before shiatsu and a bicycle tour of the island. The garden provides fresh flowers for the house, the sea and sky provide that limpid light that filters into the simple country-furnished, quilted bedrooms which give onto the church square or the garden or the patio — we preferred the patio aspect but all are havens from the heat of the summer beaches. Bathrooms and linen are of excellent quality; the island has lots to offer — working salt marshes, one of Europe's biggest bird sanctuaries, the Baleines lighthouse for a stupendous view (257 steps up) — and peace at your hotel.

Rooms: 19 doubles/twins.
Price: 340-630 Frs (€ 51.83-96.04).
Breakfast: 46-65 Frs.
Meals: Menus from 135 Frs at family-owned restaurant next door.
Closed: December 1-15 & January 3-February 5.

From A10 exit 33 onto N248 then N11 dir. La Rochelle. Cross bridge to Ile de Ré and take northern itinerary dir. Le Phare des Baleines. Hotel opposite church.

Hôtel de l'Océan

172 rue Saint Martin
17580 Le Bois Plage en Ré
Charente-Maritime

Tel: (0)5 46 09 23 07
Fax: (0)5 46 09 05 40
web: www.iledere.com

Martine & Noël Bourdet

Seasoned travellers, Martine and Noël tried to find a hotel that felt like a home. Although they had worked in antiques and interior design, after a spell running a restaurant they realised this was what they should be doing — but where? They knew it had to be on an island and after toying with Corsica and the Ile de Ré, they stumbled upon a rather sad old hotel, the Océan, and knew they had found 'their' hotel. Set back from the dunes in a garden pungent with rosemary and lavender, the hotel has 24 bedrooms: some around an inner courtyard, others like tiny cottages among the hollyhocks. They are all different. Children will love the curtained cabin bed set in a buttercup yellow alcove. Floors are covered in sisal matting and Martine and Noël's ships, lighthouses and shells are dotted around against cool, soothing colours. After your pastis on the decked terrace, your supper will involve a lot of fresh fish and herbs. The dining room is another success, with cream boards on walls and ceiling and palest greeny-grey carved chairs. It's fresh without being cold and clean without being clinical.

Rooms: 24 doubles.
Price: 350-550 Frs (€ 53.36-83.85).
Breakfast: 50 Frs.
Meals: Lunch & dinner 140-180 Frs.
Closed: January 5-February 5.

A10 exit 33 dir. La Rochelle. N248 then N11 Rocade round La Rochelle dir. Pont de l'Ile de Ré. At Bois Plage hotel is in town centre.

Domaine de Rennebourg

17400 Saint Denis du Pin
Charente-Maritime

Tel: (0)5 46 32 16 07
Fax: (0)5 46 59 77 38

Michèle & Florence Frappier

A house that is truly loved, it has been in her family for many years and Michèle and her daughter Florence began taking guests in order to keep it. Standing under huge old trees in its own parkland, the long, low building with mellow tiles and white shutters really is deeply peaceful. Florence, who lives in a 'dependency' with her husband, is something of an artist — she was making a mosaic in the kitchen when we visited — and has set up a little museum of dresses, hats and toys. Each fascinating room is full of atmosphere: one has a tiled floor, antique sleigh beds and a desk with a candle where you feel you ought to be sitting and writing. Another is panelled in cloudy blue with wispy blue curtains at the windows. If you like good linen you will appreciate the lacy pillowcases, all ironed by hand. Michèle pampers her guests: when one group stayed 21 nights she "just managed to work out a different menu each night". Many stay in touch and write to her. Before cooking supper, she will be in the garden — milking her flock of 120 goats.

Rooms: 7 doubles/twins.
Price: 300-350 Frs (€ 45.73-53.36).
Breakfast: 35 Frs.
Meals: Dinner, including aperitif & wine, 110 Frs.
Closed: Never.

From A10, exit 34 for St Jean d'Angély. Left on N150 dir. Niort. Domaine signposted just after St Denis du Pin.

Résidence de Rohan

Parc des Fées
Route de Saint Palais
17640 Royan (Vaux sur Mer)
Charente-Maritime

Tel: (0)5 46 39 00 75
Fax: (0)5 46 38 29 99

M & Mme Seguin

A gloriously peaceful place: the pool sits lazily on the low cliff, the gardens drop down to the sea, you can lie secluded under the umbrella pines with the sea lapping below or enjoy the fashionable beach. The hotel, built in typical *Belle Époque* style by the Rohans as a seaside cottage, has many of its original features — floors and fireplaces, cornices and carvings, a seductive staircase twisting up to the top floor — and smells deliciously of floor polish. The owners, as affable, warm and open as their house, welcome families and pets into their lovely interior. There are polished *armoires* and upholstered chairs in the big recently-decorated rooms, skilfully-matched fabrics and wallpapers and excellent bathrooms with big old-style basins. Breakfast at low tables indoors or outside; dine in small, exclusive Vaux or big, bustling Royan, much favoured by Parisian families. There's masses to do: take bike and ferry across to the Médoc vineyards, visit 'the best zoo in Europe' at La Palmyre or historic La Rochelle. There's even a surfable Atlantic wave on the *Côte Sauvage*.

Rooms: 41: 35 doubles/twins & 6 triples.
Price: Doubles 450-750 Frs
(€ 68.6-114.34); triples 830 Frs.
Breakfast: 57 Frs.
Meals: Many restaurants within walking distance or 5-20 minutes drive.
Closed: November 18-end March.

A10 exit 35 Saintes dir. Royan. Dir. Pontaillac Plage. Continue to Vaux sur Mer and St Palais. Résidence de Rohan on sea side of D25 in private estate called Parc des Fées.

Château de la Tillade

Gemozac
17260 Saint Simon de Pellouaille
Charente-Maritime

Tel: (0)5 46 90 00 20
Fax: (0)5 46 90 02 23
E-mail: la.tillade@t3a.com

Vicomte & Vicomtesse Michel de Salvert

You can tell that Michel and Solange, the present Viscount and Viscountess, like people and love entertaining. Their impressive château sits at the end of an avenue of lime trees alongside the family vineyards that have produced grapes for Cognac and Pineau des Charentes (a local aperitif) for over two centuries. Much of the original distillery equipment is on display and well worth a visit. Your hosts make you feel instantly at ease in their comfortable, friendly home, even if you're secretly terrified of dropping the fine bone china. Solange's talents as an artist (she also holds painting courses in her art studio) are reflected in her choice of curtains and fabrics while traditional French beds with rolled headboards capture the elegance of your surroundings. Meals are a delight, with good conversation (in English or French) round the family table while you are waited on lavishly but without stuffiness. The de Salverts provide colourful descriptions of local sites or restaurants to visit, and golfers, too, will be spoilt for choice.

Rooms: 5: 4 doubles & 1 triple.
Price: Doubles 420-500 Frs
(€ 64.03-76.22); triple 650 Frs.
Breakfast: Included.
Meals: Dinner, including aperitif, wine, liqueur & coffee, 180 Frs.
Closed: Never.

From A10 exit 336 right dir. Gémozac. At r'about: Gémozac bypass dir. Royan, right on D6 dir. Tesson. Entrance about 3km on left, well signposted (château not in village of St Simon de Pellouaille but on D6).

Château des Salles

17240 Saint Fort sur Gironde
Charente-Maritime

Tel: (0)5 46 49 95 10
Fax: (0)5 46 49 02 81

Sylvie Couillaud

A pretty little château with great personality, Salles was built in 1454 (exactly) and scarcely touched again until 1860, when it was 'adapted to the fashion' (profoundly). 100 years later, the enterprising Couillaud family brought the estate (guest house, vineyard, stud farm) into the 20th century. Behind its fine old exterior, it exudes light, harmony, colour and elegant informality with spiral stone stairs, boldly-painted beams and warm, well-furnished bedrooms bathed in soft colours and gentle wallpapers. Salles is a friendly family affair: sister at guest house reception, brother at vines and horses, mother at her easel — her watercolours hang in the public rooms, her flowers decorate bedroom doors — and in the kitchen. At dinner, refined food made with local and home-grown produce is served with estate wines. Sylvie Couillaud will help you plan your stay — she knows it all and is almost a mini tourist office. It's a congenial, welcoming house: people come back again and again and one guest said: "She welcomed us like family and sent us home with goodies from her vineyard."

Rooms: 5: 4 doubles/twins & 1 triple.
Price: Doubles 430-550 Frs
(€ 65.55-83.85); triple 600 Frs.
Breakfast: 50 Frs.
Meals: Dinner 170 Frs.
Closed: October 15-end March.

A10 exit 37 Mirambeau. Château is between Lorignac and Brie sous Mortagne at junction of D730 and D125.

Maison Karina

Les Métairies
16200 Jarnac
Charente

Tel: (0)5 45 36 26 26
Fax: (0)5 45 81 10 93
E-mail: hotelkarina@easynet.fr
web: www.hotelkarina.fsnet.co.uk

Austin & Nikki Legon

This old house was built as a cognac distillery and the bar is arranged around the copper stills. The Legons have done an excellent conversion, the garden is most successful and they are still planning to extend the pool, build a stone barbecue, plant more trees and create better seminar facilities. The dining room has many-shaped tables clothed in many-coloured cloth and plate-laden dressers in a lovely converted barn with a huge open fireplace giving off the aroma of wood fires. In summer, they do barbecues where they join their guests and they're eager for people to have a good time. Some come back year after year, the village council meets here and many locals come for the restaurant. Inside, family photographs, knick-knacks and pictures have a welcoming, homely air. The bedrooms are a good size and very pretty, some chintzy, some flowery, some plainer, with lacey white bedcovers, oriental rugs on wooden floors, moulded ceilings or rafters, exposed stone walls or sober wallpaper and plenty of space in chests and *armoires*. And there's lots to see in the area.

Rooms: 10: 6 doubles, 2 suites for 3 & 2 suites for 4.
Price: 300-500 Frs (€ 45.73-76.22).
Breakfast: 30-65 Frs.
Meals: Lunch & dinner 95-150 Frs. Picnic lunch 45-85 Frs.
Closed: December 10-January 20.

From Cognac N141 to Jarnac. Over bridge to traffic lights, left D736 dir. Sigogne. Bear right. Les Métairies signposted in village: right, first left, first right — Maison Karina on left.

Hostellerie du Maine Brun

Asnieres sur Nouère
16290 Hiersac
Charente

Tel: (0)5 45 90 83 00
Fax: (0)5 45 96 91 14
web: www.hotel-mainebrun.com

Sophie & Raymond Menager

The only sounds to wake you in your luxurious bedroom come from the birds and the water gushing beneath the hotel — a 16th-century mill, sympathetically remoulded in the 1930s. You may even forget you are in an hotel at all. The rooms have a mix of French 18th- and 19th-century furniture, expensive wallpaper and heavily draped curtains loaded with gold and cream. The flowers look as if they have been freshly picked in the garden. Raymond and Sophie have managed the trick of making the Moulin sumptuous without being stuffy. The only modern touches are in the bathrooms, designed for wallowing rather than a mere splash. Children are welcome, but unless yours are period items — better seen than heard — they may not blend in. There is a big pool, however, with plenty of sunshades and chairs. You can breakfast in the sunny dining room or on the terrace, and if you are planning to explore — Cognac is nearby or Oradour-sur-Glan, preserved as the site of a horrific civilian massacre in the Second World War — the friendly, if formal, staff will prepare a picnic feast.

Rooms: 20: 18 doubles & 2 suites.
Price: Doubles/twins 590-750 Frs
(€ 89.94-114.34); suites 950 Frs.
Breakfast: 65 Frs.
Meals: Lunch & dinner 102-200 Frs.
Closed: October 15-end April. Restaurant closed Mondays.

From Angoulême N141 dir. Cognac for approx. 8km. D120 right dir. Asnières sur Nouère — Hostellerie just along on left.

Relais de Buissonnet

Safari Parc de Haute Saintonge
16480 Guizengeard
Charente

Tel: (0)5 45 98 99 31
Fax: (0)5 45 98 49 95

Xavier Benoît du Rey

If you have always wanted to shoot a stag or a wild boar, then come. It is certainly not where you bring the children to look at the 'bambis'. It is a shoot; the trophies all round the dining room wall confirm this. Several kinds of deer, wild boar and wild mountain sheep roam over 800 hectares, foraging for food and not at all 'farmed'. The large lakes, 25 hectares in all, are full of pike, carp, tench and eels, while ducks and pheasants nest in the reeds and bushes round their banks. The farmhouse, on the highest ground in the area, was renovated recently. Somewhat bleak outside, it is less so inside, with terracotta floors, wood beams and enormous fireplaces. The eight bedrooms all have pastel walls, country cotton bedcovers and curtains and superb views. Breakfast is typically French. Groups of ten or more can order dinner which — surprise, surprise — might be game. Xavier runs the estate to the highest standards and demands 'impeccable' attitudes, rather than triumphalist butchery, from his hunters. The aim here is primarily to enjoy an ancient pastime, and the countryside.

Rooms: 8 doubles/ twins.
Price: Doubles 280 Frs (€ 42.69).
Breakfast: Included.
Meals: On special request, for groups of 10 or more.
Closed: Never.

60km south of Angoulême, on N10 via Barbezieux for approx. 15km. Left for Brossac, first right for Boisbreteau. Look for Safari Parc sign.

Limousin Dordogne

D. Narbeburu

To change from England to France is almost the
transition from one planet to another.

John W Forney

La Borderie

Saint Pierre Bellevue
23460 Royère de Vassivière
Creuse

Tel: (0)5 55 64 96 51
Fax: (0)5 55 64 96 51

Marc & Maryse Deschamps

You are almost exactly in the middle of France — in a ruggedly beautiful area — and the choice of walking trails is endless. The enormous Lac de Vassivière is only 3km away with its clean, sandy beaches. You can ride, take a boat and send the children off on the little train for a ride. La Borderie is a stone farmhouse down a quiet lane through the pine forests. Marc and Maryse moved here 18 years ago from Paris to "get away from it all". Their children range from 15-year-old twins to a four year old and your offspring will be made very welcome (and may get a donkey ride). Marc runs the 'gîte' with Maryse and did most of the conversion work himself. Meals are eaten at a long table in front of a huge fireplace. A typical supper might be freshly-picked mushrooms, duck in honey and blackberry tart. Bedrooms have stone walls but look warm and cosy with big old wooden beds and crisp linen. Several have working fireplaces. A pretty little cottage under a massive tree is known as the "dolls' house" and is very popular. Very French and very friendly.

Rooms: 7 doubles.
Price: Doubles 190-250 Frs
(€ 28.97-38.11). Extra bed 60 Frs.
Breakfast: Included.
Meals: Dinner 90 Frs.
Closed: Never.

From Royère de Vassivière, D8 dir.
Bourganeuf. Just before Le Compeix, right to
La Borderie; signposted.

Au Pont de l'Hospital

B. P. 38 L'Hospital
19400 Argentat sur Dordogne
Corrèze

Tel: (0)5 55 28 90 35
Fax: (0)5 55 28 20 70

Jim & Fiona Mallows

Beside the little, trout-rich Maronne that rushes over rapids towards its destiny in the great Dordogne stands a house run with a minimum of rules and constraints by people who trust that guests will understand it is a family home. With a relaxed and helpful atmosphere and space for all to spread, it is ideal for fishing buffs and families (young children need supervision by that untamed water). Jovial Jim Mallows advertises snacks for passers-by, runs a real-estate business, knows the area backwards and will tell you exactly where to eat great meals of remarkable value — he and Fiona are the most delightful hosts. Bedrooms are small but adequate, some with bathroom, some without. Fiona's 'anatomical portraits' of fish and Jim's watercolours hang in the attractive breakfast room with its wooden tables and wood-burning stove. With warning, they will do a barbecue and salad meal on the wooden pontoon projecting over the river. Come for the fantastic position in great walking country with five fishing rivers within 20 minutes, lots of places to visit and such unspoilt simplicity.

Rooms: 11: 8 doubles/twins, 2 triples, 1 quadruple, some sharing bathrooms.
Price: 160-240 Frs (€ 24.39-36.59).
Extra bed 50 Frs.
Breakfast: 30 Frs, English 55 Frs.
Meals: Good restaurants in town. Picnic lunch 45 Frs; barbecue 80 Frs (June to Sept).
Closed: Mid-November-end February.

From Tulle N120 to Argentat; through town, 2nd right after bridge (opposite garage) onto D116 dir. l'Hospital for 2km. Hotel on right imm'ly after bridge over R. Maronne. (L'Hospital sometimes marked without 's'.)

ASP Map No: 13   MMap 239-27   **161**

La Maison des Chanoines
Route de l'Eglise
19500 Turenne
Corrèze

Tel: (0)5 55 85 93 43

Chantal & Claude Cheyroux

Originally built to house the canons (*les chanoines*) of Turenne, this ancient restaurant-hotel has been in Monsieur Cheyroux' family for 300 years! No wonder the family held on to it — this 16th-century, honey-stoned house is one of the loveliest we have seen and the village is beautiful. Madame, young, charming, *très soignée*, is a fan of fine English fabrics and has used them lavishly for curtains and cushions. Bedrooms are divided between this house and another (equally ancient) opposite, approached via a little bridge from the garden. These well-lit rooms have plain carpets and white walls; bathrooms are luxurious with fluffy towels. The breakfast room is stone-flagged with wickerwork chairs padded in duck-egg blue. The dining room is in the old canon cellar: small and cosy, with white-clothed tables and vaulted ceiling. You can dine under a fairy-light-strewn pergola in the garden covered with honeysuckle and roses. And the food is a delight; Monsieur is chef and will use only the freshest, most local ingredients, including vegetables and herbs from the garden. An enchanting place.

Rooms: 6: 4 doubles, 1 triple & 1 apartment for 2+.
Price: Doubles 370 Frs (€ 56.41); triple 400-470 Frs; apartment 500 Frs. Extra bed 70 Frs.
Breakfast: 40 Frs.
Meals: Lunch & dinner 160-200 Frs.
Closed: November 5-end March. Restaurant closed Tuesdays, Wednesdays & Thursdays except July & August.

From Brive D38 S for 8km to Monplaisir; continue D8 to Turenne/Vayrac for 8km. In village left uphill following sign for château — hotel on left before church.

Château de la Côte

Biras Bourdeilles
24310 Brantôme
Dordogne

Tel: (0)5 53 03 70 11
Fax: (0)5 53 03 42 84

Michel & Olivier Guillaume

For four centuries the du Lau family owned the château and the young new owners are passionate about the place; they are modern in outlook yet deeply aware of the privilege of history. Not only that, but they have created some of the grandest bathrooms; in the top-floor suite you can, as you soak, star-gaze through the glass ceiling. The panache can be seen everywhere, without the place looking as if an international designer has got at it. It is thoroughly French, with a huge range of styles and sizes in the bedrooms. Some walls are papered, some show the old stone, some show their age, some are worthy of several stars. The panache carries over to the food — try *magret de canard en croute de fruits secs* — served in a lovely, formal, half-panelled dining room with an open fire. You can play snooker in a panelled sitting room, formal again and very French; none of those sagging English sofas. It is all utterly quiet, thanks to the six hectares of parkland. There are some very beautiful places to visit nearby so you have a clutch of good reasons for staying here.

Rooms: 14: 7 doubles/triples & 7 suites.
Price: 460-520 Frs
(€ 70.13-79.27); suites 600-750 Frs.
Extra bed 120 Frs.
Breakfast: 57 Frs.
Meals: Lunch & dinner 170-300 Frs;
children 80 Frs.
Closed: November 15-March 15, except
for 15 days over Christmas.

From Périgueux D939 dir. Brantôme. Left
before Brantôme onto D106e. Château 3.5km on right.

L'Enclos

Pragelier
24390 Tourtoirac
Dordogne

Tel: (0)5 53 51 11 40
Fax: (0)5 53 50 37 21
E-mail: rornsteen@yahoo.com
web: lenclos.hypermart.net

Robert & Dana Ornsteen

Robert will tell the intriguing history of house and village. He and Dana, who live half the year in Mexico, will welcome you enthusiastically. L'Enclos is The Manor (two guestrooms here), a series of converted stone cottages, the former bakery (two bread ovens remain) and chapel in a skirt-roofed, blond-stone huddle round the courtyard — enormous personality! The sensational cobbled floor in the hall just begs for admiration; the dining room, marble floored and rustic walled, dark beamed and Turkish rugged, is the image of the Ornsteens' natural/sophisticated style. Light bathes the American potted plants in the *salon*. Each room/cottage has its own character, all use bright fabrics that lift and give vibrancy to the bare stone or off-white walls; most have sisal or sea-grass matting in simple unspartan good taste. And those menus? The smaller is served, candlelit, by the pool: possibly *foie gras*, salads and cheese; the other is several courses, candlelit, in the dining room. A lush, quiet place for Dordogne explorers, with space for all in its gorgeous garden.

Rooms: 7 cottages: 6 for 2; 1 for 3
(some self-catering).
Price: 400-850 Frs (€ 60.98-129.58).
Breakfast: 45 Frs.
Meals: Dinner 125-175 Frs.
Closed: October-April.

From Limoges N20 dir. Uzerche then right on D704 dir. St. Yrieix la Perche. Before Hautefort right on D62 for Tourtoirac then right on D67 — Pragelier signed approx. 1 km on left.

Manoir d'Hautegente
24120 Coly
Dordogne

Tel: (0)5 53 51 68 03
Fax: (0)5 53 50 38 52

Edith & Patrick Hamelin

The ancient manor, first a smithy, later a mill, has been in the family for 300 years but is paradoxically just 50 years old: burned down in the Second World War, it had to be rebuilt. The millstream has become a fabulous waterfall feeding a pond that shimmers beneath the bedroom windows and riot of colour in the thoroughly kempt garden. Hautegente is rich inside too, like a private house, with two sumptuous dining rooms clothed in silk and hung with well-chosen paintings and prints. There's a cosy drawing room where a large fireplace and a vast array of cognacs summon the sybarite. Lavishly-decorated bedrooms have fine thick curtains, antiques and pretty lamps; some are small, some enormous and the soft, expensive feel of padded wall fabrics contrasts with the lovely old staircase leading up from the hall. The rooms in the converted miller's house are more modern; four have mezzanines and the ground-floor room is truly vast. Bathrooms are all beautifully tiled and properly equipped. Madame rules this empire with regal authority and her more relaxed son. A splendid and peaceful place.

Rooms: 15: 11 doubles & 4 triples.
Price: Doubles 530-1010 Frs
(€ 80.8-153.97). Extra bed 140 Frs.
Breakfast: 70 Frs.
Meals: Dinner 150-380 Frs. Half-board only in high season. Picnic hampers.
Closed: November-end March.

From Brive N89 dir. Périgueux through Terrasson. Left at Le Lardin on D704 dir. Sarlat then left at Condat on D62 dir. Coly. Manoir signed on left just before village.

Auberge de Castel Merle

24290 Sergeac
Dordogne

Tel: (0)5 53 50 70 08
Fax: (0)5 53 50 76 25

Anita Castanet &
Christopher Millinship

The Auberge has been in Anita's family for five generations. Husband Christopher is English, and also devoted to this atmospheric place. They have renovated the old buildings with consummate care, keeping the traditional look (no short cuts), using wood from their own land to restore walnut bedheads and oak doors. Christopher is an enthusiastic hunter of truffles and head chef, serving up to 100 meals a day in the summer. (Note the vast cast-iron cauldron in the banquet room in which he once conjured up a cassoulet for the entire village!) This is *sanglier* (wild boar) country and cooking the beast is one of his specialities. Flowery curtains, pelmets and hand-painted flowers on the walls prettify the dining room. Bedrooms have a straightforward country look, with Provençal prints, beamed ceilings and exposed stone walls. Some rooms overlook the courtyard, others the woods. And the views! The glory of the place is its position, high above the valley of the Vézère, with river, forests and castles beyond — best admired from one of the check-clothed tables on the large, leafy terrace.

Rooms: 5 doubles/twins.
Price: 220-260 Frs (€ 33.54-39.64).
Half-board 480-520 Frs for two (mid-July to August).
Breakfast: 30 Frs.
Meals: Lunch & dinner 70-190 Frs.
Closed: December-February & last week of September.
Restaurant closed Mondays.

From Brive to Montignac, then D706 dir. Les Eyzies. At Thonac left over bridge then right to Sergeac. Signposted.

Le Cygne

2 rue du Cingle
24260 Le Bugue
Dordogne

Tel: (0)5 53 07 17 77
Fax: (0)5 53 07 17 06

Ann & Marc Denis

Yes, there is a swan (*cygne*) — on the pond over there, across the square — just out of sight. The River Vézère is just out of sight too, but the Cygne is virtually at the centre of all that makes this Dordogne-Périgord area so famous. The eleven good-sized rooms are spotlessly clean and unfussily decorated; efficient double-glazing protects those facing the busy high street and you can easily drop down to a café or to market (Tuesdays and Saturdays). The pleasant breakfast room has wooden tables and white cloths; the indoor dining room has deep red walls, white cloths, high-backed brocade chairs and white china with matching red rims: it's far more lush than many a similar country-town hotel. Outside, a light and leafy dining area, with sliding glass doors, stretches into the garden in summer. The food has an excellent reputation and is often appreciated by well-to-do clients of other hotels. The attractive, enthusiastic and welcoming young Denis couple who run the Cygne are determined to make it a success. Its position, value and good honest fare should make it so.

Rooms: 11: 7 doubles/twins, 2 triples & 2 quadruples.
Price: 260-280 Frs (€ 39.64-42.69). Extra bed 80 Frs.
Breakfast: 35 Frs.
Meals: Lunch & dinner 88-155 Frs.
Closed: October 1-15, December 20-January 20. Restaurant closed Sunday evenings & Mondays.

From Périgueux D710 to Le Bugue. On entering town hotel on right immediately after fire station and opposite tourist office.

Le Domaine de la Barde

Route de Périgueux
24260 Le Bugue
Dordogne

Tel: (0)5 53 07 16 54
Fax: (0)5 53 54 76 19

André Darnaud

A sensational place. Once a week-end cottage for the 14th-century nobility who owned it, the Domaine has now become a luxurious but immensely friendly and easy-going hotel. The owners, unlike most restorers of ancient buildings, began with the grounds which they arranged as a perfect *jardin à la française* saving several centuries-old trees in the process, before they tackled the mill, the forge and the manor house. There is an informal 'family' feel about the place which in no way detracts from the professionalism of the management: the Darnauds' priority is your comfort, and it shows in their staff and in the immaculate, lavish but personal decoration and furnishing of the bedrooms. They also have a flair for the dramatic visual touch — witness the glass floor under which flows the mill-stream in the old mill, the *oeil de boeuf* window in the forge and the 'menacing Eros' who surveys you as you stroll through the gardens. There's plenty to do; the swimming pool has a jet-stream massage, there's table tennis and, in the *orangerie*, a sauna.

Rooms: 18 doubles/twins.
Price: Doubles 440-1090 Frs
(€ 67.08-166.17). Extra bed 125-160 Frs.
Breakfast: 68 Frs.
Meals: Lunch & dinnner 140-220 Frs.
À la carte also available.
Closed: Mid-October-mid-April.
Restaurant closed Wednesdays.

From Périgueux N89 then D710 to Le Bugue. 1km before Le Bugue, Domaine signposted on right.

Hôtel Restaurant Le Château

1 rue de la Tour
24150 Lalinde
Dordogne

Tel: (0)5 53 61 01 82
Fax: (0)5 53 24 74 60

Guy Gensou

Overhanging the river Dordogne — a lovely hotel in a spectacular position — the narrow terrace and swimming pool built into the rocks above the river have views of both the rising and setting sun across the water. The entrance is up a one-way street then through an old arched doorway. You are in the town here but insulated from it. The reception area is small and unpretentious; what is sensational is the stone staircase that winds up from the foyer to an understatedly elegant sitting area. Then come the bedrooms: from the smallest attic room to the biggest suite with balcony, they have pastel painted walls and simple furnishings and are very refined, very calming. Most overlook the river, others have windows on two sides and overlook the pool and entrance cul-de-sac. Bathrooms are impeccable, with either white or champagne tiles or terrazzo marbled walls. The dining room couldn't be more inviting; it's light and airy with stone and soft apricot-coloured walls, beautiful china, linen napkins, fresh flowers and a spectacular river view through the French windows. M Gensou cooks, very well. A great place.

Rooms: 7: 6 doubles & 1 suite.
Price: 300-900 Frs (€ 45.73-137.2).
Breakfast: 68 Frs.
Meals: Lunch & dinner 125-300 Frs.
Closed: 3rd week in Sept & Dec 15-Feb 15. Restaurant closed Mondays all year & Sundays from Nov-Mar.

From Bergerac D660 to Lalinde; right at post office — hotel faces you at end of street.

Domaine du Pinquet

Cussac
24480 Le Buisson
Dordogne

Tel: (0)5 53 22 97 07
Fax: (0)5 53 22 97 07

Nicole & Yves Bouant

A perfect little cluster of old stone farm buildings round a courtyard, a squat, square-hatted tower in the corner, thick woods on three sides with long views over the valley on the fourth (*pinquet* means little hill in patois) — quintessentially Dordogne. One wing is entirely for guests, another for the owners with a covered terrace in between for summer suppers and an expanse of grass beyond for picnics under the trees (the swimming pool is at a distance so does not intrude). The expected dining room — beams, stone walls, old tiles, big fireplace — is unexpectedly enlivened with good abstract oil paintings. A real plus is use of the excellent kitchen next to this room, ideal for families. Bedrooms are pale, some with quiet wallpaper, some with fabric but always clean, modern lines and no fussy bric-à-brac. Now that they no longer do meals (there are first-class restaurants nearby), the owners have time to help guests organise their visit and are planning to map out woodland walks. And, a short walk from the house, Cussac has a gem of a tiny Romanesque church.

Rooms: 6: 3 doubles, 1 triple, 1 suite & 1 quadruple.
Price: Doubles 350 Frs (€ 53.36); suite 470 Frs; triple 450 Frs; quadruple 550 Frs.
Breakfast: Included.
Meals: Available locally.
Closed: October-end March.

From Bergerac D660 dir. Sarlat for 19km. Cross R. Dordogne at Lalinde, left on D8 then D29 dir. Le Buisson for 12km. Right for Cussac: Domaine is approx. 500m on left.

La Couleuvrine

1 place de la Bouquerie
24200 Sarlat
Dordogne

Tel: (0)5 53 59 27 80
Fax: (0)5 53 31 26 83

Annick & Isabelle Lebon

This is either a haven for grass-snakes or guns, depending on how you translate the name. It is more likely the latter, for the hotel, built right into the city walls of the medieval town of Sarlat, once shook under the recoil of the canon on the ramparts above as they defended the town against the perfidious English! If feeling vulnerable, you may sleep at the top of one of the city towers and take your shower in the thickness of the wall itself, or you may have a private balcony overlooking the pedestrianised centre of Sarlat. Each room has its individual character, with few reminders of the 21st century. Mesdames Lebon (mother and daughter) run the place with an enthusiasm and concern for the comfort of their guests which is rare in this much-visited part of France. Their attention to detail extends — of course — to the cuisine, *'du terroir'* but 'judiciously re-imagined' for modern tastes, and the choice of lovely old prints and drawings on the walls. Better avoided in high summer, this is a good place to be at those moments when you want to escape into history.

Rooms: 23: 20 doubles, 1 triple &
2 quadruples.
Price: Doubles 265-340 Frs
(€ 40.4-51.83); triple 380 Frs;
quadruples 460 Frs.
Breakfast: 40 Frs.
Meals: Lunch & dinner 98-210 Frs.
Closed: Never. Restaurant closed
January 11-31 & mid-end November.

*From A20/N20 exit Souillac to Sarlat. Hotel
signposted in town centre.*

Le Relais du Touron

Le Touron
24200 Carsac Aillac
Dordogne

Tel: (0)5 53 28 16 70
Fax: (0)5 53 28 52 51

Claudine Carlier

Such an attractive approach up the drive lined with neatly-clipped box hedges and spiræa — it is all very elegant-looking, surrounded by broad lawns and handsome, mature trees. Reception is in the main entrance hall, by the high open fireplace, but only the big triple bedroom is actually in the main house: all the other rooms and the dining room are in the converted barn and stable block with the pool just below. The new dining room has one all-glass wall overlooking the pool and the garden beyond and is flooded with light; it is most inviting with its pale pink tablecloths. Bedrooms give onto a narrow terrace above the dining area and have the same decoration in straightforward, unfrightening style: plain carpets and walls, bright bedcovers and curtains and adequate lighting. The nearby road is well screened by thick trees and shrubs. Indeed, the two-hectare garden, which also contains a small pond and a large goose, is a great asset with lots of private corners to be explored and exploited. A good base, not far from bustling Sarlat, from which to visit this richly cultural area.

Rooms: 12: 11 doubles & 1 triple.
Price: Doubles 300-375 Frs
(€ 45.73-57.17); triple 440-485 Frs.
Breakfast: 38 Frs.
Meals: Lunch & dinner 100-120 Frs.
Closed: Mid-November-end March.
Restaurant closed Tuesdays.

From Brive N20 S to Souillac then D703 dir. Sarlat for 21km. Hotel sign on right just before village of Carsac.

La Terrasse
46200 Meyronne
Lot

Tel: (0)5 65 32 21 60
Fax: (0)5 65 32 26 93
E-mail: terrasse.liebus@wanadoo.fr
web: www.hotel-la-terrasse.com

Gilles & Françoise Liébus

This is a fortress rather than a château and has stood guard over the Dordogne since the 11th century, though with the scars of much violence. A child might build a castle like this: tall and straight, with a mix of round towers, square towers, fat towers and thin towers. Gilles and Françoise have made it an inviting country retreat once again. Entered from the back through magnificent doors off a pretty courtyard, the entrance lobby has an amazing polished flagstone floor. The bedrooms are all different, with the more interesting ones in the oldest part of the building. Most overlook either the river or the pool — set high into the walls with a fantastic view, this is a rare swimming pool with atmosphere. The main dining room is a touch 'interior designed' but you will love the vaulted 'winter' dining room, or eating on the terrace under the vines. Food is real southwest: wonderful concoctions with *foie gras,* truffles and top quality ingredients. Save it for dinner or you'll miss seeing Rocamadour, the Lascaux caves or canoeing on the river.

Rooms: 19: 15 doubles, 3 triple, & 1 suite.
Price: Doubles & triples 300-500 Frs (€ 45.73-76.22); suite 800-1200 Frs.
Breakfast: Buffet 50 Frs.
Meals: Lunch & dinner 100-300 Frs.
Closed: Mid-November-end April.

From Limoges leave A20 at Souillac. Take D703 dir. Martel for 6km, right at Le Pigeon onto D15 dir. Figeac for 4km. Turn for Hotel (signed) on left immediately after crossing bridge at St Sozy.

Domaine de La Rhue

RN 140
La Rhue
46500 Rocamadour
Lot

Tel: (0)5 65 33 71 50
Fax: (0)5 65 33 72 48
E-mail: domainedelarhue@rocamadour.com
web: www.rocamadour.com/us/hotels/LaRhue/index.htr

Eric & Christine Jooris

In spectacular rolling countryside, in the grounds of the family château, this 19th-century converted stable-block has a warm embracing atmosphere. Lots of exposed beams and original stone-floored halls leading to bright airy rooms (each named after different colours of horses' coats) where modern comforts and eastern rugs blend perfectly with the overall rustic feel. A delightful young couple, Christine and Eric Jooris want you to feel at home and are as happy to leave you to laze by the swimming pool or read in front of the fire as they are to advise on visits, book restaurants or even come and pick you up if you've taken an evening stroll down to Rocamadour (45 minutes). Breakfast is served in the cosy main hall; there are also some garden-level studio apartments, with kitchenette and terrace, for those planning a longer stay. And for the more adventurous, a trip in the air with Eric (a licensed balloonist) could be the high point — as it were — of your stay, a fabulous way of discovering Rocamadour, one of the most visited places in France. *No smoking in some rooms.*

Rooms: 14 doubles, including 1 quadruple & 1 studio with kitchenette.
Price: Doubles 380-580 Frs (€ 57.93-88.42); quadruples 680-790 Frs. Extra bed 110 Frs.
Breakfast: 44 Frs; regional 65 Frs; children's 25 Frs.
Meals: Available locally.
Closed: November-Easter.

South on N140 from Brive la Gaillarde. 7km north of Rocamadour, right down signposted lane to La Rhue. Hotel behind château.

Hôtel Beau Site

46500 Rocamadour
Lot

Tel: (0)5 65 33 63 08
Fax: (0)5 65 33 65 30
E-mail: hotel@hw-beausite.com
web: www.bw.beausite.com

Martial Menot

The perfect way to see Rocamadour: stay in this old hostelry, enjoy the stupendous cliff-hanging view from the restaurant and terrace, visit the historic village in the early morning, leave for the day when it fills with trippers (Rocamadour cracks at the seams between 11am and 7pm) and return for dinner and a peaceful evening's stroll along by-then walkable streets. The Beau Site is seriously old with a fairly wild history — stones and timbers could tell many a tale. It has belonged to charming Monsieur Menot's family for five generations and the reception area dazzles with medieval antiquities and shiny brasses on old flagstones worn by endless pilgrims' feet. The *salon* and games room are in the old vaulted kitchens and pantries, but we found fake leather and spindly legs disappointing. Bedrooms vary in size; recently-renovated rooms have pleasant wooden furniture, rich fabrics, good bathrooms; the rest are being updated for 2000. A friendly, welcoming place in an exceptional site. *Hotel guests may drive right to the hotel and park in its private car park.*

Rooms: 42: 40 doubles/twins, 1 triple & 1 apartment for 4.
Price: Doubles 385-495 Frs (€ 58.69-75.46); triple 595 Frs; apartment 695 Frs.
Breakfast: Buffet 55 Frs.
Meals: Lunch from 110 Frs; dinner à la carte. Picnic lunch 45 Frs.
Closed: February 2-November 12.

In Rocamadour take road to Cité. Go through medieval gates into village and park in front of hotel. Only hotel guests may use this lane.

Château La Gineste

46700 Duravel
Lot

Tel: (0)5 65 30 37 00
Fax: (0)5 65 30 37 01

M & Mme André Lamothe

This wine-growing château, brilliantly restored by André Lamothe, breathes restraint without austerity, luxury without ostentation and spans some five or six centuries (Richard the Lionheart hunted here): a courtyard with a line of elegant classical columns, carved stone lintels, a fluted, fan-vaulted ceiling over a spiral staircase — photographs cannot do it justice. With vines as far as the eye can see, the château wines are M Lamothe's delight — he's happy to show you his restored old-style winery. Dinner is in the old stone-vaulted cellar or the smaller breakfast *salon*: both have fireplaces and an elegantly relaxed feel. Bedrooms are big, the yellow suite is very big, and done in faultless taste using generous quantities of rich materials that lend lushness to soft white walls, polished wooden floors and genuine antique furniture and doors. Bathrooms are just as luxurious with double basins, big mirrors, good lighting. Three rooms give onto a covered colonnaded terrace looking across well-kept lawns, ancient plane and chestnut trees and the sea of vines to the hills beyond. Superb.

Rooms: 4: 3 doubles & 1 suite.
Price: 572-946 Frs (€ 87.2-144.22).
Breakfast: Included.
Meals: Dinner 165 Frs
Closed: December-January. Restaurant closed October-end May.

From Fumel D911 dir. Cahors. Château just before Duravel.

Manoir de Roquegautier

Beaugas
47290 Cancon
Lot-et-Garonne

Tel: (0)5 53 01 60 75
Fax: (0)5 53 40 27 75

Christian & Brigitte Vrech

In its beautiful park with long views across the rolling hills of the Lot valley, the old house is wondrously French with masses of drapes, swags and interlinings — all done, but never overdone, by Madame. The rooms in the old tower of the main château are truly memorable with their own entrance and spiral stone staircase. Some are carpeted, some have polished wooden floors with good solid furniture that's not too ornate, there are claw-footed baths and huge old basins and taps, and each top-floor suite has one round tower room. Rooms in the converted outbuildings have character too, and are eminently comfortable. There are fine mature trees to shade your picnic lunches and superb local dinners (homegrown vegetables and lamb from the Vrechs' farm 2km away) are served outside at a convivial trestle table; children can sup early, giving adults the chance to eat and talk in peace. There are swings, a games and telly room, a pool that is hidden from view, gazebos and pergolas around the garden — and such a gentle, friendly welcome from the owners that you will want to relax and stay for ever.

Rooms: 6: 3 doubles/twins, 2 suites for 3/4, 1 apartment for 6/7.
Price: Doubles/twins 320-410 Frs (€ 48.78-62.5); suites 605-645 Frs; apartment 820 Frs.
Breakfast: Included.
Meals: Dinner, including wine, 105 Frs; children's menu 70 Frs.
Closed: October-end March.

From Villeneuve sur Lot N on N21 dir. Cancon for 15.5km. Manoir signed on left 3.5km before Cancon.

Aquitaine

Bordeaux is… dedicated to the worship of
Bacchus in the most discreet form.
Henry James

Manoir du Soubeyrac

Le Laussou
47150 Monflanquin
Lot-et-Garonne

Tel: (0)5 53 36 51 34
Fax: (0)5 53 36 35 20

Claude Rocca

Those high, wrought-iron courtyard gates dignify you as you pass through them and you never know quite what to expect. Here there's white paving, a central statue, climbing and potted plants. Walk into the well-planted garden and there's one of those amazing swimming pools, *une piscine à débordement,* that looks as if it spills over the edge of the hill. Most bedrooms have that same beautiful hillside view; their décor is opulently traditional with themed colours, chintzy touches, lots of paintings and prints, some genuine old furniture, and rugs on wooden or tiled floors. Bathrooms have all the cossetting extras; Jacuzzi-type massage sprays, hairdryers, colour co-ordinated dressing gowns and essential oils. The courteous M Rocca has thought it all through with great care and enthusiasm and cooks gastronomic dinners too. Exposed beams, stone and brickwork and an open fireplace in the dining room set the scene for those candlelit meals and there is plenty of space to relax (with books, games and music) in the huge living room above it. Just the place for an up-market country holiday.

Rooms: 4: 3 doubles & 1 suite.
Price: Rooms 580-680 Frs
(€ 88.42-103.67), suite 850 Frs.
Breakfast: 50 Frs.
Meals: Dinner 145 Frs.
Closed: November.

*From Villeneuve sur Lot D676 to
Monflanquin, then D272 dir. Laussou. After
bridge, left to Envals for 3km; left for
Soubeyrac.*

Château Camiac

Route de Branne
33670 Créon
Gironde

Tel: (0)5 56 23 20 85
Fax: (0)5 56 23 38 84
E-mail: chateau.camiac@camiac.archimedia.fr
web: www.archimedia.fr/camiac

Jean-Marc Perrin

Twenty minutes from Bordeaux you find yourself surrounded by wonderful trees and total peace and quiet as you make your way up the immaculate drive to the imposing façade of this 19th-century château. Recently restored and decorated in rather unexpected, but extremely luxurious, Scandinavian style by the previous owners (M Perrin is gradually replacing the more inappropriate furnishings with Louis XV — equally anachronistic but rather more in keeping with the building), the château offers warm hospitality and a positively sybaritic level of comfort, especially in the suites, whose sitting areas are in the towers at each corner of the house. The bedrooms in the converted outbuildings are a step or two down the social scale, though still comfortable and attractive. Here, of course, you don't need to be secretive about opting for the local wine. It is as noble as the food, which is so exquisitely presented on lovely Villeroy and Bosch porcelain. This is a perfect base for the wine buff, 15 minutes from St Emilion and 45 from Bergerac. The very names are enough to set your palate singing.

Rooms: 22: 16 doubles, 2 quadruples, 2 suites & 2 apartments.
Price: Doubles 500-1500 Frs (€ 76.22-228.67); suites 1500 Frs; apartments & quadruples 2200 Frs.
Breakfast: 75 Frs.
Meals: Lunch & dinner 165-245 Frs. Picnic 40-80 Frs.
Closed: Never.

From Bordeaux D936 dir. Bergerac for 12km. Right on D671 to Créon then D121 dir. Branne. Château signposted promenade à cheval, then pillared entrance to château.

　　　MMap 234-7　　　ASP Map No: 12

The Basque Country
The South-West
The Pyrenees

CDTL-32
The Snow-lit sharp annunciation of the Pyrenees.
Louis MacNeice

Château d'Agnos

64400 Agnos
Pyrénées-Atlantiques

Tel: (0)5 59 36 12 52
Fax: (0)5 59 36 12 52

Heather & Desmond Nears-Crouch

Originally an aristocratic hunting lodge, Agnos was a convent for 30 years until this exceptional couple converted it into a fabulous guest house. Heather, warmly communicative, and Desmond, a talented retired architect, both widely travelled and possessed of a great sense of fun, have done wonders with cells and refectory — and still do all the cooking. The black and white bathroom with the antique cast-iron bath and concave ceiling used to be the château's treasure room — it is now attached to the gilt-furnished *Henri IV* suite. The whole house left us agape: high ceilings framing remarkable mirrors, original paintings set into panelling, a cunning mixture of period and modern furniture and a panelled dining room with a superb floor of ancient yellow and stone-coloured tiles and a black marble fountain. Look out for the medieval kitchen: the old prison. Your hosts would be grateful if you could find the secret passage which King François I is said to have used (he is known to have stayed here and he had regular amorous escapades). A place of great style, much history and refined food.

Rooms: 5: 1 suite for four; 2 suites for three; 2 twins.
Price: 380-650 Frs (€ 57.93-99.09).
Extra bed 100 Frs.
Breakfast: Included
Meals: Dinner 100-120 Frs.
Closed: February.

From Pau N 134 for 35km to Oloron Ste Marie; through town and S on N134 dir. Zaragoza for 1km. In Bidos right for Agnos.

180

Hôtel Bidegain

13 rue de La Navarre
64130 Mauléon
Pyrénées-Atlantiques

Tel: (0)5 59 28 16 05
Fax: (0)5 59 19 10 26

Pierre & Martine Chilo

Time has stood still for this extraordinary hotel on the border between the Pays Basque and the Béarn, and it has done so at several different moments: when *diligences* trundled under the archway into the courtyard; in the 1930s when the 'Adams family' *salon* (so named by the Chilo's 14-year-old daughter) was decorated; and when, in the '60s, the orange, green and yellow wallpaper flowered in one of the bedrooms. The charm of the place is in the décor of the bedrooms' bees-waxed furniture, high ceilings and Basque prints as much as in the welcome offered by the Chilos — who clearly enjoy their job. There's a shaded terrace where you can eat outside and *petits salons feutrés* for cosy winter suppers. Pierre Chilo is a chef who likes to use the local game, fruit and vegetables sold every morning in the market under the windows of the hotel. Imagine waking and leaning out of your window to see your meal being chosen and bought right under your nose. Of course if you feel like sleeping late the double-glazing should allow you to, but what a waste of an opportunity.

Rooms: 25 doubles/twins.
Price: 190-330 Frs (€ 28.97-50.31).
Breakfast: 45 Frs.
Meals: Lunch, including carafe of wine & coffee, 70 Frs. Dinner à la carte.
Closed: Saturdays & Sundays except in summer.

From A64 exit Salies de Béarn onto D933 to Sauveterre de Béarn. D23 to Mauléon dir. St Jean Pied de Port. Hotel just beside Château d'Andurain.

Maison Garnier

29 rue Gambetta
64200 Biarritz
Pyrénées-Atlantiques

Tel: (0)5 59 01 60 70
Fax: (0)5 59 01 60 80
E-mail: maison.garnier@wanadoo.fr
web:
perso.wanadoo.fr/maison.garnier/

Jean-Christophe Garnier

In glamorous Biarritz, playground of royalty and stars, here is a jewel of sophisticated simplicity. Pristine-white bathrooms have 10-inch-diameter showerheads. Bedrooms are done in subtle mixtures of white, eggshell, dark chocolate and soft coffee with the occasional splash of brilliant colour. The bright breakfast room has Basque floorboards setting off the pale walls, white linen as a foil for lovely tableware, light pouring in from great windows. Guests are enchanted by hotel and owner: both have real charm and radiate renewal. Monsieur Garnier was in tourism and fashion. Then, in 1999, having fallen in love with Biarritz, he decided to turn this old boarding house into a smart little hotel where people would nevertheless feel at home. So no hall counter, just a gorgeous wrought-iron stair-rail, a 1930s-feel *salon* with a deep sofa, an old fireplace and a magnificent oriental carpet: the tone is set right here, as you come in. And you will soon be at ease with your delightful, engaging host. On a quiet side street, five minutes walk from that fabulous surfing beach, this is remarkable value.

Rooms: 7: 5 doubles & 2 twins.
Price: 390-580 Frs (€ 59.46-88.42).
Breakfast: 40 Frs.
Meals: Available locally.
Closed: Telephone ahead.

From A63 exit Biarritz La Négresse dir. Centre Ville, Place Clémenceau. Straight ahead toward large white building Bank Inchauspé; left there onto Rue Gambetta. Free parking on street by hotel.

Le Saint Charles

47 avenue Reine Victoria
64200 Biarritz
Pyrénées-Atlantiques

Tel: (0)5 59 24 10 54
Fax: (0)5 59 24 56 74

Annie Faget-Marc

'Two steps', as the guide books say, from the sophisticated centre of Biarritz, you find yourself in this astonishingly secluded and quiet house, surrounded by greenery, set in an imaginatively designed and carefully-planted garden. Once owned by the Prince of Romania, the 1930's building has been a hotel for 60 years — hard to believe when you take in the countrified atmosphere, the *familiale et généreuse* cooking, and the relaxed feel which Annie has created. She and niece Pascal will take every care to make you want to return year after year. The bedrooms vary from very small to very big, with lots of old lace at the windows, good antiques and the faintly shabby charm of a well-loved family home. They all overlook the garden, and the creepers curling around the windows are a perfect backdrop to the arrangements of fresh and dried flowers in the rooms. Take a book and relax in the garden, try the excitement of the casinos of Biarritz, the fun of the Atlantic rollers on the Grande Plage, or sample the serious French approach to well-being in the *thalassotherapie* centre. You need never use your car.

Rooms: 13: 9 doubles/twins, 3 triples & 1 quadruple.
Price: Doubles 270-450 Frs (€ 41.16-68.6); triples 380-420 Frs; quadruple 350-390 Frs.
Breakfast: 38 Frs.
Meals: Many fine restaurants in town. Picnic lunch on request.
Closed: Never.

A63 exit 4 La Négresse dir. Biarritz Centre Ville. Av du Prés Kennedy joins Av du M'al Foch and ends at Place Clémenceau. Straight across onto Av Edouard VII; right on Av de la Marne. Hotel signposted.

Hôtel Laminak

Route de Saint Pée
64210 Arbonne (Biarritz)
Pyrénées-Atlantiques

Tel: (0)5 59 41 95 40
Fax: (0)5 59 41 87 65
web: www.touradour.com/laminak.htm

M & Mme Proux

The style is country cottage, with all the floral designs, stripes and neatly controlled flourishes that one might expect... almost English. The setting is gorgeous, with all the lush greenery of the Basque countryside at your feet and views up to the mountains. The hotel is on a quiet road outside the village of Arbonne, with a few discreetly screened neighbours and a big, handsome garden filled with mature shrubs and trees. In summer it is a delight to eat breakfast on the terrace. Inside it is neat and attractive, carpeted, wallpapered and with antique pine furniture. You will sleep well here, and be looked after with a quiet and warm efficiency by the new owner; this place has been a long-cherished dream of theirs. You can, too, settle round the open fire in the evenings, warmed by the easy comfort of the place and the satisfying sag of the leather furniture. It is but an easy hop from here to the coast and the throbbing vitality of Biarritz. And those mountains are worth a week's effort in themselves. Come and eat peaches; the trees are heavy with them.

Rooms: 10 doubles/twins.
Price: Doubles 350-590 Frs
(€ 53.36-89.94). Extra bed 100 Frs.
Children up to 10 free.
Breakfast: 55 Frs.
Meals: Dinner 50-100 Frs, by reservation.
Closed: Mid-November-end December.

A63 exit 4 La Négresse and follow signs to Arbonne where hotel is signposted.

Hôtel La Devinière

5 rue Loquin
64500 Saint Jean de Luz
Pyrénées-Atlantiques

Tel: (0)5 59 26 05 51
Fax: (0)5 59 51 26 38

M Bernard Carrère

Louis XIV married the Spanish Infanta here and the church door was walled up for ever! In the middle of this historic border town, Bernard first renovated his fine old mansion as a private home and then decided to "let outsiders in too": become an insider and feel welcomed. In the *salon* with its lamps, sumptuous antique books, grand piano and lovely old French armchairs, you will want to curl up with a book, peeking through the richly-draped curtains at the little green haven of a garden, so unexpected in the city centre. You can sit and read there too, in summer, after breakfast among the flowers. Your room has the same atmosphere: fine fabrics and antique furniture, wrought iron, brass or beautifully-renovated wooden Basque beds, co-ordinated bathrooms, excellent sound insulation, attention to detail. The Carrères are a generous, artistic family; Bernard's daughter's paintings enhance *salon* and staircase, he's passionate about his region, writes about the Basque Country and will entrance you with his tales.

Rooms: 8 doubles/twins.
Price: 650-850 Frs (€ 99.09-129.58).
Breakfast: 55 Frs.
Meals: Many fine restaurants in town.
Closed: Never.

From A63 exit St Jean de Luz Nord dir. town centre. Hotel signposted. As you have to drive into pedestrian areas, telephone ahead for exact directions.

Lehen Tokia

Chemin Achotarreta
64500 Ciboure
Pyrénées-Atlantiques

Tel: (0)5 59 47 18 16
Fax: (0)5 59 47 38 04
E-mail: info@lehen-tokia.com
web: lehen-tokia.com

Yan Personnaz

The extraordinary name of this house means 'The First Place' in Basque, and the place is as extraordinary as its name implies. Built in the 1920s by the Basque architect Hiriart, for a British 'gentleman' and his Mexican-Basque wife, it is a monument to Art Deco. Indeed, Hiriart himself invented the expression to describe the style the house epitomises. With stained glass by Gruber, marble and parquet floors, furnishings, carpets and pictures made for the house, it feels as if, the owner suggests, it has been preserved, *dans son jus* like *confit* of goose. And here it is now for us to enjoy. The bedrooms, like the rest of the house, make you feel as if you are in a luxurious private house. The panelling, furnishings and luxurious bathrooms have tremendous style. As if the architecture wasn't enough, the house also has the most stunning views over the bay of St Jean de Luz, a rose garden and sumptuous breakfasts. This is the perfect haven for those who appreciate true style.

Rooms: 7: 6 doubles/twins & 1 suite.
Price: Doubles 500-950 Frs
(€ 76.22-144.83), suite 1200-1400 Frs.
Breakfast: 60 Frs.
Meals: Dinner 150-280 Frs.
Closed: Mid-November-mid-December.

From A63 exit St Jean de Luz Sud dir. Ciboure. After a sign reading 'Kechiloa' take a left; signposted.

La Maison Tamarin

Chemin de la Ferme de Kokotia
64500 Saint Jean de Luz
Pyrénées-Atlantiques

Tel: (0)5 59 47 59 60
Fax: (0)5 59 47 59 69
E-mail: enquiries@lamaisontamarin
web: lamaisontamarin.com

Nicole Barclay

You could sit all morning watching the mountains change colour endlessly and the sea shift tirelessly before you as the old timbers of this neo-Basque house creak in the wind. All rooms let you in on these two sides of the Basque Country. Built with fine old materials by Nicola's Scottish father, the house has nothing Scottish about it save deep sofas, floral fabrics and no shutters: perhaps the electronic entrance gates stand in their stead? Nicola, elegant, well-educated and quietly spoken, gained her experience, including cooking, in Alpine chalets but plans to organise golfing rather than skiing holidays here. Bedrooms, some small, some big (the quadruple is 48m^2), are all top quality, a mixture of posh and cosy, with luxury fabrics, soft duvets in crisp embroidered or lacey covers, fresh flowers and good use of colour. The terracotta tiles from the Spanish Basque country bring a warm glow to the lovely yellow breakfast/reception room. The enormous garden is very new but the big hedge keeps neighbours distant. And Nicola is so welcoming. *No smoking in bedrooms.*

Rooms: 7: 6 doubles/twins & 1 quadruple.
Price: 500-1000 Frs (€ 76.22-152.45).
Breakfast: 50 Frs.
Meals: Picnic lunch 80-200 Frs.
Closed: Never, but phone ahead.

A63 exit St Jean de Luz Nord onto N10 dir. Biarrritz 1km; exit Jean Vier Museum. Follow lane 500m. Only house with stone wall on right.

Grand Hôtel Vignemale

Chemin du Cirque
65120 Gavarnie
Hautes-Pyrénées

Tel: (0)5 62 92 40 00
Fax: (0)5 62 92 40 08
E-mail: hotelvignemale@gavarnie.com
web: www.gavarnie.com/grand-hotel-vignemale

Danielle & Christian Marchand

The site is outstanding, smack bang in the middle of the glacial Cirque de Gavarnie. It is the Mont Blanc of the Pyrénées. Surrounded by horse pastures, granite, snow and ice, there's not even a souvenir shop to spoil the view. Danielle and Christian chanced upon the place a decade ago, when the building was on its last legs — an eccentric edifice built by an Anglo-Irish count in 1903. For the local pair it was love at first sight; not only were they overwhelmed by the surroundings, they loved all the place has to offer: horses, wild animals, hiking. The residence, in spite of its grand name, has not quite recovered its former glory: more Vegas motel than four-star hotel. But rooms are perfectly adequate and the bedrooms carpeted and comfortable, with modern floral bedcovers, drapes and beige-flocked walls. A few have balconies. Your hosts are relaxed and easy, forever running after horses and resident dogs and cats; it's a great spot for a young family. Lots of horseback riding round the Cirque on the famous Meres horses — a species that thrives in high altitude — and truly wonderful walks.

Rooms: 24: 18 doubles, 4 triples &
2 quadruples.
Price: 690-890 Frs (€ 105.19-135.68).
Breakfast: Included.
Meals: Picnic lunch on request.
Closed: October-end April.

*From A64 exit Soumoulou or Tarbes Ouest
dir. Lourdes; N21 dir. Argelès Gazost; D921
dir. Luz. 49km from Lourdes.*

Domaine de Cantecor

La Madeleine
82270 Montpezat de Quercy
Tarn-et-Garonne

Tel: (0)5 65 21 87 44
Fax: (0)5 65 21 87 44

Joël & Chrystel Bazeille

Whether you are in the main house or one of the three converted stone outbuildings with their garden-level patios, all the colour-co-ordinated rooms are bright and cheerful. Bottled water, tissues and plenty of towels are a nice touch. The property has masses of character and the owners make it clear that they want you to feel at home; nowhere seems off-limits. At a very reasonable price (which includes wine), dinners cooked by Chrystel on her original stone stove — regional delicacies, flavours from Normandy where she and Joël were born, vegetarian dishes on request — are shared in an informal atmosphere on the terrace or in the dining room. On summer nights, the floodlit pool is simply enchanting and during the day you may well be unable to resist a game of *boules* on the lawn or the delights of a never-to-be-forgotten village fete. Comfortable sofas around an open fireplace, bookshelves stacked with paperbacks, a billiard table in the oak-timbered gallery, a country kitchen (the central meeting place) and samples of wine bought from local growers complete this charming picture.

Rooms: 5 doubles/twins & 1 studio for 3.
Price: 250-300 Frs (€ 38.11-45.73).
Breakfast: Included.
Meals: Table d'hôtes menu, including aperitif, wine & coffee, 110 Frs.
Closed: Never.

From Cahors N20 dir. Montauban for 20km; La Madeleine on left. Signposted.

L'Arbre d'Or

16 rue Despeyrous
82500 Beaumont de Lomagne
Tarn-et-Garonne

Tel: (0)5 63 65 32 34
Fax: (0)5 63 65 29 85

Peggy & Tony Ellard

The 'golden tree' is Chinese and turn of the century (the last one); it's a Ginkgo Biloba, and probably the finest in France. Tony will tell you its story and will explain why he believes Beaumont de Lomagne is the finest example of a bastide town in south-west France; it's certainly very handsome. He and Peggy came here 10 years ago, obviously love the place, and take great care of their guests; they've given thought to disabled access, are happy to look after cyclists and walkers and actively host their evening meals. Peggy's a keen cook and has adopted traditional, regional recipes and food which you can eat outside in the shaded garden or in the dining room with its tiled floor, open fire and exposed beams. There's a comfortably old-fashioned, lived-in, atmosphere in the sitting room — large sofas, books (and TV) — and in the bedrooms too, which are mostly large-windowed; some overlook the garden, some the street and have marble fireplaces, interesting old furniture and pretty decorative touches. A 17th-century gentleman's residence-turned-hotel with plenty of character.

Rooms: 6: 5 doubles/twins & 1 double/twin with private shower in hallway.
Price: 260-290 Frs (€ 39.64-44.21) (reduction for 3 nights or more).
Breakfast: Included.
Meals: Dinner, including aperitif, wine & coffee, 100-120 Frs.
Closed: January 1-15.

From A62 exit Castel Sarrasin. From A20 exit Montauban. D928 dir. Auch. Once in Beaumont, L'Arbre d'Or is opposite post office.

La Maison des Consuls

6 place Maréchal Leclerc
09500 Mirepoix
Ariège

Tel: (0)5 61 68 81 81
Fax: (0)5 61 68 81 15
E-mail: pyrene@afatvoyages.fr

Bernard Garcia

The medieval main square of Mirepoix, almost entirely surrounded by 16th-century carved and timbered arcades, has been miraculously preserved. Underneath the arches, beside the shops and cafés, is the entrance to *La Maison des Consuls*, a supremely elegant renovation of an old period piece (it was the gaol in the 1400s). All that could be saved has been saved, all that could be shown is shown and no expense has been spared on décor or bathrooms. Each room is different: '*Marquess*' is elaborately regal, '*Bishop*' is richly sober, '*Dame Louise*' has Renaissance stripes and a high beamed ceiling, others, including '*Travelling Salesmen*', are more modern; the ultra-modern '*Astronomer*' suite is splendiferous with its terrace and telescope. The bathrooms are almost the best part: new marble and old mahogany, fluffy towels and etched glass doors. Some rooms give onto the magnificent square and all its activity; others look over the sweet little courtyard where breakfast is served in good weather. Otherwise, the old kitchen serves as a small, cosy breakfast room

Rooms: 8: 7 doubles & 1 suite.
Price: Doubles 420-500 Frs (€ 64.03-76.22);
suite 605-695 Frs.
Breakfast: 40 Frs, regional 65 Frs.
Meals: Many fine restaurants in town.
Closed: Never.

*From Toulouse N20 (soon to be new A66) south to
Pamiers/Lavelanet exit. Then east on D119 to Mirepoix.
Hotel in centre of Mirepoix.*

Languedoc-Roussillon

The fruit market, in particular, is superior to everything of
the kind; but I will not tantalize you by saying any more
on that subject, unless you were near enough to eat a
bottle of champagne in the way that God gives it.
Philip Thicknesse

Auberge L'Atalaya

66800 Llo
Pyrénées-Orientales

Tel: (0)4 68 04 70 04
Fax: (0)4 68 04 01 29

Ghilaine Toussaint

A place of majestic beauty and wild poetry; a timeless Catalan farmhouse clinging to a rocky hillside; an owner of rare taste and talent — poet, philospher, musician and lover of beauty. Such is l'Atalaya: a house that captures the imagination and promises riches earthly and spiritual. Family antiques are in all rooms, fine fabrics dress lovely old beds, bathrooms are deluxe, stained-glass windows illuminate corridors, fresh figs may grace the tables in the intimate little breakfast room and in the big, light-filled dining room, mouth-watering meals are served before that boggling view, while the grand piano awaits its pianist. Your hostess has put her heart into renovating the house she bought as a ruin and it has a quiet, cosy, hide-away atmosphere that is also very elegant: the architecture and décor are in harmony and people of sensitive taste feel utterly at home here. The wonderful little village has hot springs, the river gorges are home to rare butterflies, the hills have sheep and Romanesque churches, there are innumerable activities. What a place!

Rooms: 13: 5 twins/triples, 7 doubles & 1 suite.
Price: Doubles 510-790 Frs (€ 77.75-120.43).
Breakfast: 67 Frs.
Meals: Lunch/dinner 168-268 Frs.
Closed: November & January 20-Easter.

From Perpignan N116 W through Prades to Saillagouse. Left for Llo, then left for Eyne. Hotel 1km on right.

La Terrasse au Soleil
Route de Fontfrède
66400 Céret
Pyrénées-Orientales

Tel: (0)4 68 87 01 94
Fax: (0)4 68 87 39 24
E-mail: terrasse-au-
soleil.hotel@wanadoo.fr
web: www.la-terrasse-au-soleil.com

M Leveillé Nizerolles

Take at least a weekend, for a splurge of activity and delicious indulgence. It has space: a four-hectare garden, a terrace with olive and mimosa trees, a vineyard; and sports: a big pool and a tiny golf course, a tennis court and three jogging circuits, and deep green views over the hills to Mont Canigou. It's a self-contained retreat of "luxurious simplicity" (the owner's expression) in four connecting villas where the yellow, blue and green colour schemes bring a fresh, casual atmosphere — what one might call Southern California in French Catalonia. Rooms are big and airy, done in excellent fabrics with custom-made wooden furniture, but not over-filled; suites have terraces and two bathrooms. Food counts a lot and delicious meals are served on china made to order in Italy; there's a warm, inviting bar between the indoor and outdoor dining rooms, the sitting area is restfully cool — all designed for guests to feel pampered but not softened. A path has even been cut to Céret so that you don't have to walk along the road. Monsieur Leveillé is very present and very attentive — you will like him.

Rooms: 21: 14 doubles & 7 suites.
Price: Doubles 840-1500 Frs
(€ 128.06-228.67); suites 1040-1700 Frs.
Breakfast: Included.
Meals: Lunch 160 Frs; dinner 240 Frs.
Picnic lunches available.
Closed: Never. Restaurant closed for lunch weekdays.

From Perpignan A9 S to Le Boulou then D115 SW to Céret. Hotel is 4km beyond Céret on road to Fontfrède.

193   MMap 235-56   **ASP Map No: 18**

La Belle Demeure

Auberge du Roua
Chemin du Roua
66700 Argelès sur Mer
Pyrénées-Orientales

Tel: (0)4 68 95 85 85
Fax: (0)4 68 95 83 50
E-mail: belle.demeure@little-france.com
web: www.little-france.com/demeure

Ricardo Danesi

Hard to guess that this small hotel was once an 18th-century mill: only the old stone walls and the odd beam remain. But this is the south, where life is lived *en plein air*. And outdoors at the Auberge is special: you could happily spend all day on the elegant terrace by the pool, surrounded by tropical plants. Tables and chairs are wooden-slatted, modern; parasols stylish. There is ample opportunity to escape the sun's dazzle without retreating indoors, and the views of the Pyrénées are splendid. Inside, all is spic-and-span. Bedrooms are anonymous but comfortable; bathrooms are attractive, some of marble, all a good size. This is a family-run hotel, a labour of love for the young Italian who first set eyes on it four years ago. The atmosphere is relaxed but the dining room, with its white napery and crystal, is formal and rightly so: Ricardo and his young chef have brought new life to the restaurant which has a terrific reputation. Impossible to stay here without sampling the mushroom ravioli with white truffles and similar delights. People travel from miles around to enjoy them.

Rooms: 14: 13 doubles & 1 triple.
Price: 300-650 Frs (€ 45.73-99.09).
Breakfast: 50 Frs.
Meals: Dinner 95-295 Frs.
Closed: November-February.

From Perpignan N114 south for 20km, exit 10 for Argelès sur Mer. In town, right at lights and follow signs for Auberge du Roua/La Belle Demeure.

Le Relais de Saint Dominique

Prouilhe
11270 Fanjeaux
Aude

Tel: (0)4 68 24 68 17
Fax: (0)4 68 24 68 18

Nadine Micouleau

In the 1800s, this coaching-inn was the last stop for a quick mug of ale and change of horse before heading up into the Pyrenees. Today, you won't want to go on. Nadine's cheerful greeting is as genuine as her wanting you to feel utterly pampered while free to come and go as you please. No expense or energy (hers is endless!) has been spared: crisp linens and thick towels in gleaming bathrooms, good beds and plenty of hanging space, sponge-painted walls with a good mix of antique and modern furniture. Unique touches here and there will have you silently wondering why *you'd* never thought of using Grandma's embroidered tablecloth as a simple cushion cover. American buffet breakfasts in the shaded courtyard in summer are a feast, and the 13th-century former monastery next door ideal for a delicious evening meal. Nothing's too much trouble for Nadine, and coming 'home' to sit by the pool is the perfect way to end a busy day. From Roman times onwards, Fanjeau has survived war and peace in one of France's strategic historical spots. Some of the regional wines, by the way, are an absolute 'must'.

Rooms: 6: 4 doubles/twins & 2 suites.
Price: Doubles 250-300 Frs
(€ 38.11-45.73); suites 500 Frs.
Breakfast: Buffet included.
Meals: Dinner next door.
Closed: Never.

*From A61 exit Bram D4 dir.
Fanjeaux/Mirepoix. After 5km left at
roundabout onto D119 dir. Montréal —
entrance to Le Relais is immediately on left.*

Château de Garrevaques

81700 Garrevaques
Tarn

Tel: (0)5 63 75 04 54
Fax: (0)5 63 70 26 44
E-mail: m.c.combes@wanadoo.fr
web: www.chateauandcountry.com/chateaux/garrevaques/

Marie-Christine & Claude Combes

'The walls were breached under fire of bombards and culverins'. Then came the Revolution, and more fire, then the German occupation; but the family is adept at rising from the ashes and the 15th generation of Ginestes is now in charge. Marie-Christine has all the charm and passion to make a go of such a splendid place — slightly faded in parts, stuffed with interest. There are huge reception rooms, magnificent antiques, some original 18th-century wallpaper by Zuber, wood-block floors, a dining room with wood-panelled ceiling. Up the spiral stone stairs there is a games room, with billiards, cards, easy chairs and antiques pieces. The Blue Room next door is blue throughout; in such a vast room the effect is stunning. Bathrooms are modern if not luxurious, perhaps a necessary afterthought. All the bedrooms on this floor are charming, one with a four-poster. Upstairs again the rooms are smaller, but equally colourful and stylish. The pool is less remarkable, and the Orangerie is for group receptions. But the garden is a good place to be, studded with old trees as grand as the chateau.

Rooms: 8: 7 doubles & 1 suite for 3/4.
Price: Doubles 650-700 Frs
(€ 99.09-106.71); suites 1200 Frs.
Breakfast: Included.
Meals: Buffet lunch 60-80 Frs;
dinner 150-170 Frs including aperitif,
local wine & coffee.
Closed: Never.

*From Revel D1 dir. Caraman. Opposite
gendarmerie in Revel, D79F to Garrevaques
for 5km. Château at end of village on right.*

Le Du Dropin

Route des Paumés
54321 Scorchières

Tel: (0)5 54 32 10 12
E-mail: reception@stargazy.fr
web: www.stargazy.fr

M & Mme de Mented

If you are one of those who think global warming is a good thing, come to enjoy the carefully crafted open roof and the sense of freedom that this unusual house 'offers' (as estate agents will have it). What is most remarkable is the way in which that one tiny, perfect, monastic bedroom — our editor's idea of a special place — has been fitted into a house that apparently has no sheltered space. We salute the designer. Whether you need fresh air or a clear view of the stars, the design is a clever solution to what is now a major problem — polluted air in sealed hotel rooms. The colour scheme upstairs is perhaps a little dark, with randomly placed 'scorch' marks on walls that have been (bravely?) left in a 'raw' state. Space has been allowed for you to choose your own sleeping rhythm, and your cooking needs are cleverly met by bringing nature, so to speak, into the house. The dialogue between the simple, square, open fenestration and the cracked white surface reveals an understanding of the vocabulary of southern French modern architecture. The owners may not put in an appearance, but are easy-going about the way you treat the place.

Rooms: Rooms: 1 twin.
Price: Twin 50 Frs
(€ 152.4490176478234).
Breakfast: Buffet 75F (in bedroom).
Meals: Available locally.
Closed: Impossible.

Domaine de Rasigous

81290 Saint Affrique les Montagnes **Tel:** (0)5 63 73 30 50
Tarn   **Fax:** (0)5 63 73 30 51

Fons Pessers & Ben Wilke

The drawing room is the magnet of this exceptional house: gentle colours, fabulous furnishings and, in winter, log fire in marble fireplace. The soft yellow and white dining room is full of modern art collected in Fons and Ben's native Holland. Never twee, the tables are beautifully decorated for good-looking, varied food and local wines (especially the delicious Gaillac). Natural light, bare floorboards with fine rugs or luxurious plain carpets give that country-house feel to the large, heavenly bedrooms, sensitively decorated with rich colours and interesting furniture. The three suites are elegantly unfrilly. Luxurious bathrooms have been ingeniously fitted into odd spaces — the freestanding bath is most handsome. Even the single room, with its *lit bateau*, lovely linen and bathroom in a walk-in cupboard, is on the 'noble' floor, not under the eaves. The courtyard is ideal for summer breakfasts and the park keeps the house safe from outside intrusions. A dream! The owners' artistic flair and hospitality make this a wonderful place to stay — try to give it at least two nights.

Rooms: 8: 5 rooms & 3 suites.
Price: Singles 225-325 Frs (€ 34.3-49.55);
doubles 400-500 Frs; suites 600-750 Frs.
Breakfast: 55 Frs.
Meals: Dinner, 3 courses, 140 Frs.
Closed: December 15-January 15.

From Mazamet D621 dir. Soual for 16km; left on D85 to St Affrique les Montagnes. 2km further on D85. Green sign on left.

Les Bergeries de Ponderach

Route de Narbonne
34220 Saint Pons de Thomières
Hérault

Tel: (0)4 67 97 02 57
Fax: (0)4 67 97 29 75

Gilles Lentin

Monsieur Lentin remembers this *bergerie* when it was full of sheep; he now fills it with contented guests. The whole place is an expression of his cultivated tastes in music, painting (he used to run a well-known art gallery in Montpellier), food and wine. You enter your room through its own little lobby, from the freize-painted corridor. Notice the attention to detail in the choice of fabrics and furnishings, take in the luxury of the bathroom, make your way to your own private balcony and take a deep breath; you've arrived in a sort of earthly paradise. M Lentin offers music — sometimes live, with quartets in the courtyard on summer evenings — to his guests, but also the most intriguing and carefully chosen regional cooking. Sculpting your own perfect holiday here is not difficult, given all that's here for you — maybe one third exercise in the Parc Regional with its wonderful walks, one third culture visiting the Cathedral and its pink marble choir and one third gastro-hedonism with your feet under M Lentin's beautifully laden table.

Rooms: 7: 6 doubles & 1 suite.
Price: 330-480 Frs (€ 50.31-73.18).
Breakfast: 48 Frs.
Meals: Dinner 98-230 Frs. Picnic lunches available.
Closed: December-February.

From Béziers N112 to St Pons de Thomières. There, left for Narbonne D907. Hotel is about 1km out, just after the local swimming pool on left.

La Cerisaie

1 avenue de Bédarieux
34220 Riols
Hérault

Tel: (0)4 67 97 03 87
Fax: (0)4 67 97 03 88
E-mail: cerisaie@wanadoo.fr

Monique & Reinoud Weggelaar

It's easy to see why La Cerisaie seduced this charming Dutch couple into leaving the busy world of advertising: secreted away behind tall walls and high trees, the grand white façade of this *hotel de charme* is softened by pale blue shutters and a rampant wisteria. Beyond the black and white tiled hallway with old glass doors, all is spaciousness and elegance. Light pours into beautiful and perfectly proportioned rooms. A fine old staircase sweeps up to the bedrooms, calming and uncluttered, with original wooden floors, good pieces of furniture, warm rugs and big windows that overlook the garden (the garden is heavenly, filled with trees and scents and flowers, and a beautiful pool). One bedroom has its own little kitchen — perfect for a couple with a child. Monique has discovered the joys of cooking and does wonderful things with fresh fish, vegetables and herbs — 'those who dine here once dine every evening thereafter.' Reinoud is an expert on local wine. Retire with your coffee to the sitting room with its red ochre walls, ethnic rugs and fire. A gracious yet homely retreat.

Rooms: 6: 2 doubles, 3 twins & 1 suite for 2 with kitchenette.
Price: 380-460 Frs (€ 57.93-70.13).
Breakfast: Included.
Meals: Dinner 130 Frs; picnic lunches available.
Closed: November-end February. Restaurant closed Wednesdays.

From Béziers N112 dir. Castres/Mazamet/St Pons. 1km before St Pons right on D908 dir. Riols/Bédarieux. 3km to Riols. House signposted on left leaving Riols, through gates and park.

Domaine de Rieumège

Route de Saint Pons
34390 Olargues
Hérault

Tel: (0)4 67 97 73 99
Fax: (0)4 67 97 78 52

Hubert Henrotte

The truly beautiful dining room — giant beam, old mangers, lovely terraces — is the centre of Rieumège, honoured by gourmet cooking and very good wines. The owner fell in love with this fascinating group of old, many-levelled stone buildings, left Paris and aims to improve an already delightful place, renovating rooms and employing professional and charming staff. There is space for all to find privacy and peace in the luscious garden under the palms, oaks or pines, and the round pool and the tennis court are set properly apart. Big, traditional bedrooms and pretty suites in various buildings have good rugs on the floors and antiques — but not too many. Two suites even share a terrace and a private pool. People like the real but unlavish comfort — some stay three weeks for the fabulous Orb Country hiking and climbing, all come back in the evening for the excellent meat, fish and real vegetarian dishes. Monsieur Henriotte loves giving guests the warm welcome, comfortable rooms, good food and, above all, the simplicity he knows they want. And it's a magnificent part of the Languedoc.

Rooms: 12: 10 rooms & 2 suites.
Price: Doubles 430-925 Frs
(€ 65.55-141.02); suites 700-1200 Frs.
Breakfast: 65 Frs.
Meals: Lunch 120 Frs; dinner 190 Frs.
Closed: January-end March.

On D908 2.5 km after Olargues dir. Saint Pons. Signposted on big blue panel. About 55 km north of Béziers.

Hostellerie de Saint Alban

31 route d'Agde
Nézignan l'Evêque
34120 Pézenas
Hérault

Tel: (0)4 67 98 11 38
Fax: (0)4 67 98 91 63

Christophe & Monique Gugelmann

In an enchanting Languedocian village with alleys and archways to be explored, this is a beautifully proportioned, honey-coloured old mansion. The monumental pine tree must have been here before the house; its great twisting branches now hang over the gate. The superbly lush garden surrounds an attractive pool where you can have lunch in summer — fresh local melon, delicious salads — and the lovely old barn is being restored to house all proper pool-side comforts. Indoors, the charming young Swiss owners have gone for less luxuriance: the décor is charmingly plain, the feel is elegant, airy, well-kept. The biggish, light bedrooms have good pastel carpeting, white bedcovers, translucent curtains and sober colour schemes in beiges, greys and soft pinks. Furniture is modern minimal with moulded chairs and laminated headboards — no drowning in flounces here! There are always fresh flowers on the tables in the dining room and food is good. The Saint Alban is ideally placed for seaside and inland visits and many guests cycle out through the vines to the Canal du Midi.

Rooms: 14: 10 doubles, 3 triples & 1 quadruple.
Price: Doubles 390-530 Frs (€ 59.46-80.8); triples 550-630 Frs; quadruple 730 Frs.
Breakfast: 60 Frs.
Meals: Lunch & dinner 125-295 Frs. Picnic lunch 75 Frs.
Closed: December-January.

A9 exit 34 dir. Pézenas/Millau. Take D13 for 16km to Nézignan l'Evêque. Hotel on right as you enter village.

La Calade
Place de l'Eglise
34800 Octon
Hérault

Tel: (0)4 67 96 19 21
Fax: (0)4 67 96 19 21

Gilles & Sophie Schmitt

Octon is an unspoilt little village, typical of the flavour and architecture so informed by the Languedoc sun. Right under the old church, Sophie and Gilles Schmitt have created a colourful atmosphere within the white stone walls of the former presbytery. Don't expect great luxury: the setting is perfectly simple but the rooms and bathrooms are definitely adequate. New parquet floors add to the freshness of the place when it's hot, and the beds are comfortable. The terrace, shaded by acacia trees, is very appealing both at breakfast time and in the evenings — it also serves as the sitting area. The overall feel is bright and clean and the owners couldn't be more friendly and helpful. They, like their young son, particularly enjoy welcoming families with children. The La Calade restaurant is becoming quite popular, and there are plenty of places to visit, good paths for hikers, excellent local wines and the fabulous Lake Salagou for swimming and sailing. In short, a great base for daily excursions, where the warm welcome and the authentic atmosphere easily make up for somewhat basic comforts.

Rooms: 7: 3 doubles, 1 triple, & 3 quadruples.
Price: 245 Frs (€ 37.35).
Extra bed 90 Frs.
Breakfast: 35 Frs.
Meals: Dinner 104-190 Frs.
Closed: December-end February.

Leave A75 exit 54 or 55 — Lake Salagou. Dir. Octon on D148. Hotel in village centre next to church. Stone steps lead up to entrance.

Le Sanglier

Domaine de Cambourras
34700 Saint Jean de la Blaquière
Hérault

Tel: (0)4 67 44 70 51
Fax: (0)4 67 44 72 33
web: www.logassist.fr/sanglier

Monique Lormier

"One of France's most secret places". Madame, a *Maître Rotisseur,* cares for her menus (including wild boar and local fish), while Monsieur cares for his very good wine cellar in their deeply renovated sheepfold (just one stone wall survives from before). In the setting of vineyards and evergreen-clad hills, white outcrops, bright red earth and dense Mediterranean vegetation — strongly beautiful, even starkly wild — the Sanglier's rambling garden is welcoming with its terraces and masses of shade for eating and sitting outside. You can follow a generous breakfast of fresh cheese, cake and *fougace* with a delicious summer lunch and finish with dinner centred on Madame's wild boar speciality or steak grilled on vine stems. But there's lots to do here: exhibitions in Lodève, medieval St Guilhem, watery delights on Lake Salagou. Bedrooms are comfortable, unremarkably decorated, with mottled beige carpets and pastel bathroom suites. There are some lovely black and white photographs of local people, but come not for décor — the scenery is sublime and food is king here.

Rooms: 10: 7 doubles & 3 triples.
Price: Doubles 380-440 Frs
(€ 57.93-67.08); triples 500 Frs.
Breakfast: 52 Frs.
Meals: Lunch & dinner 100-230 Frs.
Picnic lunch from 40 Frs.
Closed: November 25-March 25.
Restaurant closed Wednesday lunchtimes
(low season).

From Montpellier N109 through St. Félix de Lodez dir. Rabieux, then D144 dir. St Jean de la Blaquière.

L'Auberge du Cèdre

Domaine de Cazeneuve
34270 Lauret
Hérault

Tel: (0)4 67 59 02 02
Fax: (0)4 67 59 03 44
E-mail: welcome@auberge-du-cedre.com
web: www.auberge-du-cedre.com

Françoise Antonin & Lutz Engelmann

No wonder guests return to this big, bustling house. Run by the robust and charming Françoise, the place is utterly relaxing. She and her multi-lingual husband Lutz love welcoming walkers, climbers, cyclists and families. Workshop groups are welcome too; a special space, separate from the big and comfy sitting room. The mellow-stoned auberge, adorned by green shutters, iron balustrades and *orangerie* windows at the rear, has been carefully restored. Bedrooms are plain, beamy, white, with the odd splash of ethnic colour and terracotta floors that gleam. Bathrooms are shared — there are eight in all; this is not the place for those looking for luxury rooms 'en suite'. But sharing keeps the prices down and there have been no complaints. On the contrary, the atmosphere is one of fun and shared laughter. Meals, chosen from a blackboard menu, are served in the *orangerie* or on the terrace. A great place for a family to stay: a swimming pool, with toddler pool, at the back, lots of space to run around in, and *boules* under the chestnut trees before you turn in for the night.

Rooms: 19 doubles/twins.
Price: 75-300 Frs p.p. (€ 11.43-45.73): this range is with or without full-board.
Breakfast: 35 Frs.
Meals: Lunch 135 Frs & dinner 150 Frs.
Closed: January — mid-March.

D17 from Montpellier N dir. Quissac. About 6km north of St Mathieu de Tréviers, left to Lauret — 1km. Through village follow signs for Cazeneuve & Auberge du Cèdre.

Atelier de Calvisson

48 Grand'Rue
30420 Calvisson
Gard

Tel: (0)4 66 01 23 91
Fax: (0)4 66 01 42 19

Régis & Corrine Burckel de Tell

There's a secret to this old townhouse in the little market town: from the narrow street it looks pretty dull, but enter their private courtyard — and another world. The courtyard, a wonderful source of light and greenery to the various rooms, is used for art exhibitions and Monsieur gives art lessons: drawing, painting and the *Gobelins* tapestry techniques. There's a biggish living area for guests and a wonderful vaulted dining room for candlelit dinners in a womb-like atmosphere of warm colours and stone walls. Summer breakfast is in the courtyard. Up a spiral staircase, the tempting rooms fan off at different levels (lovely smell of wax polish on the old tiled floor). Most beautifully restored with old doors and good windows that seem to frame pictures, it is all in honest good taste, with simple, solid antique furniture that's genuinely part of the house, and your charming young hostess is eager to help her guests. Lots of things to do here so close to Nîmes, Montpellier and the Camargue and in summer the house is a blessedly cool relief from the scorching sun outside. *Weekly rentals only mid-July to mid-September.*

Rooms: 6: 1 single, 3 doubles & 2 suites.
Price: Single 230 Frs (€ 35.06);
doubles 280 Frs; suites 350 Frs (for 3).
Breakfast: Included.
Meals: Dinner 90 Frs.
Closed: Never.

A9 exit Gallargues. Then N113 dir. Nîmes.
Just after Bas Rhône Canal D1 to Calvisson.
In village, up main street, two doors from
Town Hall.

L'Hacienda

Mas de Brignon
30320 Marguerittes
Gard

Tel: (0)4 66 75 02 25
Fax: (0)4 66 75 45 58
E-mail: hacienda@altavista.net

Jean-Jacques & Dominique Chauvin

A wonderfully warm welcome from your gentle hosts, so proud of their Spanish-style hotel-restaurant, so pleased to be able to share its comforts with you. Russet-shuttered and terracotta-tiled, this two-storey farmhouse has been transformed into a handsomely decorated five-bedroom hotel in stylish grounds with restaurant, sauna and pool. Flop onto a sun-lounger in the shade of a pink parasol (nothing to distract, only the chattering of the cicadas); breathe in the sweet scent of lavender — there are fields of it, as far as the eye can see — and take a dip in the heavenly pool. The bedrooms are furnished country style, very charming, with white walls, polished beams and delicate Provençal prints; most open onto a private terrace. The sitting-room too is flounce-free — tiled floors, white walls, floral sofas and chairs. But if you like good food and wine you're more likely to spend your evenings in the stylish, candle-lit dining-room seduced by the flavours of Provence: turbot and mullet, vegetables and herbs from the local markets and mouth-watering sweet creams flavoured with lavender and thyme. *A No Smoking hotel.*

Rooms: 12: 7 doubles/twins & 5 triples.
Price: Half-board 440-680 Frs p.p.
(June-September) (€ 67.08-103.67),
350-790 Frs p.p. low season.
Extra bed 130 Frs.
Breakfast: Buffet 70-85 Frs.
Meals: Dinner 195-315 Frs.
Closed: November-December.

A9 exit Nîmes Est/Uzès dir. Marguerittes.
In Marguerittes follow red signs.

Hostellerie Le Castellas

Grand'Rue **Tel:** (0)4 66 22 88 88
30210 Collias **Fax:** (0)4 66 22 84 28
Gard

Chantal Aparis

Oodles of style at this fabulously restored country house in the centre of a Provençal village. The main house, sturdy, green-shuttered, stone-built, acts as centre-piece to other ancient stone buildings, all of which are linked by gardens, arbours and outdoor pool. Every bedroom is different — one Egyptian in flavour, another Art Deco, a third Provençal — but share terracotta floors, white-washed walls and pale, polished beams. Luxury without clutter. The place is full of surprises: one bathroom, painted pale ochre, has a floor made entirely of pebbles, a local artist's fantasy. A bedroom has a terrace on its roof. Bathrooms have fluffy towels and impressive toiletries. The treats continue at table, where meals are taken in a simple, stone-vaulted dining-room. Our inspector loved the "delicate flavours and perfect service" (yet decided to forego the *foie gras* and champagne at breakfast!) All the staff are solicitous, discreet, full of smiles. They go out of their way to help — in particular Madame, who is gracious and charming, a perfectionist in everything she does.

Rooms: 17: 12 doubles/twins, 2 triples, 1 quadruple & 2 suites.
Price: Doubles 600-1100 Frs (€ 91.47-167.69); Extra bed 100 Frs.
Breakfast: 85 Frs.
Meals: Lunch & dinner 188-380. Frs. & à la carte menu also available.
Closed: Jan-end March. Restaurant closed Mon & Wed lunchtimes & Mon & Wed evenings June-end Sept.

A9 exit Remoulins/Pont du Gard dir. Uzès; left on D3 to Collias. Signposted in village.

ASP Map No: 14   MMap 240-16   **208**

Hôtel d'Entraigues

Place de l'Evêché
30700 Uzès
Gard

Tel: (0)4 66 22 32 68
Fax: (0)4 66 22 57 01
web: www.lcm.fr/savry
E-mail: hotels.entraigues-agoult@wanadoo.fr

Vincent Savry

When you sit on the wide terrace or swim in the mosaic-lined pool you feel some glorious monument might fall into your lap: Uzès is a perfect little Provençal town and Entraigues, in the shadow of Bishop's and Duke's Palaces, is at the heart of it. The hotel is in fact five cleverly connected 15th and 17th-century houses: an old building with a fascinating history and lots of stairs and corridors leading off the very French lobby where chairs invite you to sit and breathe in the old soul of stones and antiques. Each bedroom is an individual discovery, here a private terrace, there an eminently paintable rooftop view, wonderful furniture with personality and interest. The décor is exposed stone and white render, good fabrics and no clutter. We thought the family rooms were terrific, there's outdoor space and a simple buffet/family restaurant as well as the splendid 'Jardins de Castille' for gourmets. Vincent Savry, the younger generation of this great hotelier family, is quite delightful: cheerful and efficient, unflappable and proud of his hotel.

Rooms: 36 doubles/twins.
Price: 395-700 Frs (€ 60.22-106.71).
Breakfast: Buffet 60 Frs.
Meals: Lunch 80 Frs; dinner 135-280 Frs.
Closed: Never.

A9 exit Pont du Gard on D981 to Uzès.
Follow one-way system round towards
cathedral. Park in car park in front of
cathedral. Hotel opposite, across road.

Château d'Arpaillargues/Hôtel Marie d'Agoult

30700 Arpaillargues
Gard

Tel: (0)4 66 22 14 48
Fax: (0)4 66 22 56 10
web: www.lcm.fr/savry

Isabelle & Gérard Savry

This noble house, its 15th-century sternness transformed with gracious 18th-century windows, balconies and décor, is now an hotel that pampers but does not intimidate. Thick stone walls keep summer scorch at bay, balmy evenings are spent at table in the tree-studded courtyard, refined *salons*, vaulted dining rooms and a superb staircase are reminders of a more elegant age. History, aristocratic and literary, hangs in the air: the heroine of *Les Liaisons Dangereuses* was an Agoult; so was Liszt's mistress, mother of Cosima Wagner, who left her husband here for the composer and Paris. Rooms are big (slightly smaller in the outbuilding), very comfortable, with fascinating antiques and features (double doors, fireplaces and mouldings), interesting smallish but mosaic-decorated bathrooms and occasional private terraces. Back through those great iron gates and across the little road are the secluded garden and swimming pool. This is a deeply serene place of ancient atmosphere and modern, not over-luxurious, comfort where the welcome is relaxed yet efficient.

Rooms: 29: 27 doubles/twins & 2 suites.
Price: 500-1200 Frs (€ 109.76-163.12).
Breakfast: Buffet 70 Frs.
Meals: Lunch & dinner 160-250 Frs.
Closed: November 2-March 30.

Uzès D982 to Arpaillargues (4km). Château on left as you enter the village. Well signposted.

The Auvergne

CDT Cantal

We are never so happy or so unhappy as we suppose.

La Rochfoucauld

La Lozerette

Cocurès
48400 Florac
Lozère

Tel: (0)4 66 45 06 04
Fax: (0)4 66 45 12 93

Pierrette Agulhon

In September 1878, the young Robert Louis Stevenson set off from Le Monastier with his donkey Modestine to walk south the 220km to St Jean du Gard. Towards the end of his journey he stopped in the Cevennes village of Cocurès, on the river Tarn, just above the National Park. Here Pierrette runs the country inn started by her grandmother and passed on to her by her parents. Her father is still around to advise on the best walks. The staff are especially warm and friendly and cope smilingly with a totally packed restaurant and hotel. Pierrette is very much a hands-on owner, running the reception, taking orders in the restaurant and managing the wine cellar: she is a trained *sommelier* and will pick you out just the right bottle. Bedrooms are fairly large, with wood floors and headboards and are done in stripes, checks or flowers: colour co-ordinated but not twee. All have balconies with flower boxes. The whole hotel is spotless without looking clinical. You can play boules in the garden, walk in the National Park or follow Stevenson's trail, either on foot, on a donkey or on horseback.

Rooms: 21 doubles.
Price: 290-490 frs (€ 44.21-74.7).
Breakfast: 42 Frs.
Meals: Lunch & dinner 88-240 Frs. Dinner for hotel residents only.
Closed: November-Easter. Restaurant closed Tuesdays & Wednesday lunchtimes in low season.

From Florac on N106 dir. Mende. Right on D998 dir. Le Pont de Montvert. After 4km Cocurès village. La Lozerette is on left. Well signposted.

Hostellerie du Levézou

Rue du Chienne
12410 Salles Curan
Aveyron

Tel: (0)5 65 46 34 16
Fax: (0)5 65 46 01 19

Christine Michel

A sturdy, Virginia-Creeper-clad 14th-century château — a marvellous old place that's been in the family for four generations. Christine is engaging and loves looking after her guests. Her father, David, is the chef, and specializes in country cooking with a modern twist. Step back in time as you enter the reception area with its high vaulted ceiling, oak panelling and stone walls lined with settles. The dining room is equally grand, all upholstered chairs, crisp linen, candles and gleaming silver — but again, there's a charmingly old-fashioned feel to it. The courtyard is reached through yet another fine stone archway, this one dominated by a carved oak door. Shaded by an enormous vine, the *cour* is a delightful, sunlight-dappled arbour in which to enjoy breakfast or lunch — very French, all bright geraniums in pots and graceful, white, metalwork chairs. Bedrooms, reached by a wide, spiral, wooden stairway, are plain but spotlessly clean; bathrooms are well-mirrored and well-lit. Ask for a room with a view because the views are special — the château stands at the top of the village.

Rooms: 18 doubles/twins.
Price: 230-450 Frs (€ 35.06-68.6).
Breakfast: 45 Frs.
Meals: Dinner 99-50 Frs;
children 75 Frs.
Closed: November-Easter.

From Rodez N88 + D911 dir. Millau for 26km; 2.5km after Pont Salars, right on D993 to Salles Curan.

Auberge Arborie

Domaine du Bois
98765 Trie sur Ment

Tel: (0)7 65 43 21 00
E-mail: edforeitz@ease.fr
web: www.aubarb.fr

Edouard Foreitz

'Perched' is one of the words that we try to avoid in these books, but it is wholly suitable here. The owner is, it must be admitted, a cantankerous soul who refuses political correctness: only the very nimble can make it as far as the sitting room. And when you do get there, there are more steps to climb to get into your bunk. Hard to know where tree ends and house begins, really. Lavatorial arrangements are ingenious, if mediæval. (Further explanation is unnecessary.) Cooking is for the brave: this is the third house on the spot, for the surroundings are, shall we say, somewhat combustible. But that is a matter for the timid only, for the house is defiantly unusual, special in a dozen ways. All the material is recycled, including the food — an ingenious way of expressing a new millenial, environmental awareness. (You may hope for gourmands preceding you.) The views are peerless; squirrels are your table companions and your peace is guaranteed, for few of our readers manage to find it, usually, we imagine, passing underneath. But do try. It is a marvellous place for hanging out and letting go.

Rooms: Rooms: 2 Bunks. Extra hammock available.
Price: 2000 Frs (less is more).
Breakfast: 50 Frs Vegan/Continental.
Meals: Freely picked from surroundings.
Closed: Ladder removed at midnight.

L'Oustal del Barry

Place du Faubourg
12270 Najac
Aveyron

Tel: (0)5 65 29 74 32
Fax: (0)5 65 29 75 32
E-mail: oustal@caramail.com
web: www.oustaldelbarry.com

Catherine Miquel

Madame Miquel takes food and wine seriously. The kitchen and cellar are the first priority in her 18th-century town house in the centre of one of France's most picturesque and popular hill villages. At the top of the hill, and surrounded by shaded gardens, the house also provides the peace and quiet one longs for after a hard day's sight-seeing. 'Quiet, agreeable rooms' have deep views of the château and the dramatic countryside which surrounds it. But it is for the food, the wine and the welcome that many people travel long distances to get here. Madame is the fifth generation of her family to live in this house. Her chef makes all his own jams and patisserie; he grows his own vegetables and fruit and buys locally what he does not grow. The cuisine, therefore, is seasonal and very regional but he tries to add that *'petit grain de folie'* which gives the menus their originality. As one of their guests has said, Madame Miquel and her staff epitomise the saying of Brillat Savarin: 'True hospitality takes complete responsibility for a guest's happiness throughout the time he is under your roof'. It sounds better in French... so go and find out.

Rooms: 20: 17 doubles/twins & 3 triples.
Price: Doubles 210-450 Frs
(€ 32.01-68.6); triples 420 Frs.
Breakfast: 50 Frs.
Meals: Lunch & dinner 120-260 Frs;
children 65 Frs. Picnic 50 Frs.
Closed: Mid-November-end March.

20km S of Villefranche de Rouergue on
D922. Right dir. Najac on D39 for 5km.

Hostellerie de la Maronne

Le Theil
15140 Saint Martin Valmeroux (Salers)
Cantal

Tel: (0)4 71 69 20 33
Fax: (0)4 71 69 28 22
E-mail: hotelmaronne@cfi15.fr
web: www.cfi15.fr/hotelmaronne

M & Mme Decock

Silence! Rolling green space! In glorious unsung country where the little Maronne hurtles towards its gorge and brown cows echo the russet of autumn, this 1800s manor looks out to wooded hills and dark mountains. You will meet its charming, subtly humorous owner and be well fed by his Malgache wife in a dining room with soft quiet colours and pretty rugs. The lovely double drawing room has deep sofas, two fireplaces, more rugs, some intriguing Malgache furniture. Bedrooms, all with excellent bedding, scattered on different levels in a small warren of buildings, past flowering terraces and an indoor flowerbed, vary in size. Nearly all have the sweeping valley view (two rooms at the back are up against the hillside); the best are the terrace rooms. Sober décor is enlivened by exotic pieces (a Japanese dressing table, an inlaid coffee table); good but old-fashioned bathrooms are due for renovation. The pool is ideal for landscape-gazing, there's fabulous walking, saunas, too, and you will be made to feel very welcome in this house of silence: no seminars, no piped music, headphones for telly — bliss.

Rooms: 21: 18 doubles/twins & 3 suites.
Price: Doubles 520-680 Frs
(€ 79.27-103.67), suites 690-790 Frs.
Breakfast: 60 Frs.
Meals: 150-280 Frs & à la carte.
Closed: November-end March. Restaurant open evenings all year.

From Aurillac D922 N for 33km to Saint Martin Valmeroux, then D37 dir. Fontanges.

Château de Maulmont

Saint Priest Bramefant.
63310 Randan
Puy-de-Dôme

Tel: (0)4 70 59 03 45
Fax: (0)4 70 59 11 88
E-mail: hotel.chateau-maulmont@wanadoo.fr

Mary & Théo Bosman & Marianne Strach

This extraordinary place, built in 1830 by Louis Philippe for his sister Adélaïde, has long views and Architecture: medieval crenellations, 16th-century brick patterning, Loire-Valley slate roofs, neo-Gothic windows, even real Templar ruins — a cornucopia of character. The Dutch owners provide endless activities (golf driving range, riding, swimming, rowing on the pond) and cultivate a certain "formal informality". They have preserved original features — carved inside shutters, the old spit, the astounding banqueting hall with its stained-glass portraits of Adélaïde in various moods — and collected some stunning furniture. Bedrooms go from small to very big, from plain honest comfortable with simple shower room to draped and four-postered château-romantic with marble bathroom (the *Luxe* rooms are worth the difference). And do visit the *'King's Room'*, a round blue and white (original paint!) 'tent' in a tower, for a brilliant whisper-to-shout effect. Dining rooms are tempting, there are evening entertainments — wine-tasting, music, spit-roast dinner — and staff are alert and eager.

Rooms: 25: 22 doubles/twins & 3 apartments.
Price: Standard 375-450 Frs (€ 57.17-68.6), luxe 650-725 Frs.
Breakfast: 45 Frs.
Meals: Lunch & dinner 75-220 Frs.
Closed: January-mid-March.

From A71 exit 12 A719 then N209 dir. Vichy to Bellerive. Continue dir. Vichy then Hauterive & St Yorre. On leaving Hauterive on D131, D55 to St Priest Bramefant-Les Graveyrons (not on map but signposted) — right on D59 to château.

Le Pré Bossu

43150 Moudeyres   **Tel:** (0)4 71 05 10 70
Haute-Loire   **Fax:** (0)4 71 05 10 21

M & Mme Grootaert

The silence is part and parcel of this fabulous setting in the depths of the countryside. A hotel for the past 30 years, Le Pré Bossu oozes warmth and solidity. Bedrooms are fairly basic but each has at least one piece of fine furniture. Its Belgian owners are passionate about the environment so there's strictly no smoking, and they organise mushroom-hunting weekends in the spring and autumn. M Grootaert handles the cooking, inspired by his own vegetable garden or the fresh produce he brings back from his regular trips to Lyon. Specialities include a vegetable menu (not called 'vegetarian' since he doesn't consider it a philosophy) as well as fish. 'Well-behaved' children are welcome and it's an ideal spot for either a quiet stay or an adventure holiday taking in canoeing, ballooning and lots of country hikes. At an altitude of 1,300m, it can get chilly at any time of the year so there's always a huge fire lit every morning in the library/breakfast room where you are served freshly-squeezed orange juice and a choice of home-made jams.

Rooms: 11: 10 doubles/twins &
1 suite for 4.
Price: Doubles 425-495 Frs
(€ 64.79-75.46); suite 760 Frs.
Extra bed 100 Frs.
Breakfast: Buffet 65 Frs.
Meals: Dinner from 185 Frs.
Picnic lunch on request.
Closed: November-Easter.

From Le Puy en Velay D15 dir. Valence for
15km. At Les Pandraux D36 dir. Laussonne for 6km; left dir. Moudeyres. Hotel at
entrance of village.

The Rhône Valley

CDT Dauphine

The delta of the Rhône is something quite different from
the rest of France. It is a wedge of Greece and
of the East thrust into the Gauls.

Hilaire Belloc

Le Clair de la Plume

Place de Mail
26230 Grignan
Drôme

Tel: (0)4 75 91 81 30
Fax: (0)4 75 91 81 31
E-mail: plume2@wanadoo.fr

Jean Luc Valadeau

Famous for its old-fashioned and English roses spilling into winding streets, Grignan is a paradise for rose-lovers in summer. Yet pushing open the courtyard gate of this pink-façaded guest house brings you to something new. Jean-Luc Valadeau has created such a feeling of warmth and hospitality — as he puts it, 'a home with all the comforts of a hotel'. His bustling staff are equally welcoming, leading you off through elegant, cosy rooms, antique pieces catching your eye on the way. The small terraced garden adds to the feeling of privacy, light floods in over the original staircase and the bedrooms are very quiet. Beautifully decorated — Louis Philippe wardrobes in some, country-style wicker chairs in others — all have luxurious bathrooms. Stencilled walls, ragged walls, original floor tiles or shining oak planks — a great combination of good taste and authenticity. After an excellent breakfast, the *Salon de Thé* is open from 10am to 10pm for exotic selections of tea, sandwiches, mouth-watering pâtisseries and locally-made traditional ice-cream. There are also lots of restaurants nearby.

Rooms: 10 doubles/twins.
Price: Doubles/twins 490-880 Frs
(€ 74.7-134.16). Extra bed 185 Frs;
baby bed 60 Frs.
Breakfast: Included.
Meals: Available locally.
Closed: Never

20km from Montélimar. A7 exit Montélimar
Sud dir. Bollène/Nyons/Gap then Grignan.
Signposted in town.

Manoir d'Ile à Pidais

Nulle Part sur Terre
36912

Tel: (0)0 00 00 01
Fax: (0)0 00 00 02
E-mail: araignee@cob.web
web: www.cob.web

N. Importe-qui

The photo below shows you what to expect: a gentle informality of style, efficiency without effort. The house is reached after a brief, three-hour drive along charmingly rustic tracks, bumps and pot-holes all authentically of their time. You may get the impression that you are the only person to have been along here for many years, a trick that many a better resourced hotel has failed to pull off. The informality is further revealed in the welcoming way that not just some, but all, of the windows have been left open for you. The open-door approach, too, is taken to new levels of welcome: it is not even on its hinges. While there is clearly much restoration yet to be done, the basic structure of this fine old building is still there, integrity intact — for there are no additions or ugly modern 'reforms'. The lean-to to the right of the house is true to itself, a refreshingly old-fashioned retreat for the viscerally challenged. The chimneys reveal the presence of two great open fireplaces. Your source of fire-wood is close at hand, an unusual convenience. Just help yourself to the panelling, if previous guests have — in their delight at finding it — left any.

Rooms: "Open plan" — bring a bed.
Price: Unspeakable.
Breakfast: Fresh eggs laid in rafters.
Meals: Truly organic, totally wild.
Closed: Check padlock on nearby gate.

Follow garden path...

Auberge du Vieux Village d'Aubres

Route de Gap
26110 Nyons
Drôme

Tel: (0)4 75 26 12 89
Fax: (0)4 75 26 38 10
web: web provence

Mireille Demangel-Colombe

The setting is spectacular, the views pure Cézanne. The swimming pool must have one of the finest settings in all France. Built by the Colombe family on the former site of the medieval château of Aubres, this modern auberge is run by the gently attentive and efficient Madame Colombe and her charming staff. The food is excellent, regional cooking at its best, with an unusual flexibility when faced with unusual diets. The breakfast and dining rooms are light, attractive and feminine with pretty, rush-seated country chairs, rugs on floors and good quality napery and china. More of the feminine touch on the terrace, a symphony of white and cérise. Bedrooms, which are scattered in separate, terracotta-roofed buildings, are furnished in a straightforward, '70s style, televisions taking pride of place. But you'll love the private terraces — those heavenly views! Nyons is famous for its microclimate: no mistral, no fog, no severe frosts. Lavender, oleander and other Mediterranean plants abound; the lovely old village of Aubres is surrounded by olive trees, for which the area is also renowned.

Rooms: 20: 16 doubles/twins & 4 apartments.
Price: Doubles 300-780 Frs (€ 45.73-118.91); apartments 1100 Frs.
Breakfast: 52 Frs.
Meals: Lunch & dinner 80-178 Frs; children 45 Frs.
Closed: Never. Restaurant closed Wednesdays & Thursday lunchtimes.

From Nyons D94 to Aubres (3km). At traffic lights left up steep hill. Well signposted.

Château de la Commanderie

17 avenue d'Echirolles
38230 Eybens
Isère

Tel: (0)4 76 25 34 58
Fax: (0)4 76 24 07 31
E-mail: chateau.commanderie@wanadoo.fr

M de Beaumont

Grand it is, and some of the makers of that grandeur — Knights Templar and Maltese, princes and prime ministers, presidents and financiers — look down upon you as you eat in the magnificent dining room (illustrated), a favourite restaurant for the discerning palates of Grenoble. But the atmosphere is of an intimate family-run hotel. The whole place is awash with family antiques and heirlooms, unquestionable good taste prevails in every room and fresh flowers add that touch of life and genuine attention. Bedrooms are divided among four separate buildings, adding to the sense of intimacy. Rooms in *Château* and *Chalet* are the more traditional with carved wooden beds and gilt-framed mirrors, though some of them give onto a small road. The *Orangerie* has rooms that, once you have negotiated the rather plain corridors, look out over fine parkland and are deliciously peaceful. The least expensive rooms are in the *Petit Pavilion*, on the road side. But whichever you choose, you will feel thoroughly welcome and pampered, and it's excellent value for families.

Rooms: 25 doubles/twins.
Price: 485-720 Frs (€ 73.94-109.76).
Breakfast: Buffet 62 Frs.
Meals: Lunch & dinner 169-310 Frs.
Closed: December 20-January 3.
Restaurant closed Mondays, Saturday lunchtimes & Sunday nights.

From Grenoble exit 5 Rocade Sud dir. Eybens; right after Esso garage. Entrance to hotel is 300m on left at turning in road.

Auberge des Chasseurs

Naz Dessus
01170 Echenevex
Ain

Tel: (0)4 50 41 54 07
Fax: (0)4 50 41 90 61

Dominique Lamy

Dominique is a jolly man who is very proud of the Auberge, which his grandparents built as a farm in 1860, and its fantastic sweeping view of the Jura Mountains and Mont Blanc. You might be a bit surprised by the African theme in the reception area, but don't let it put you off. Most of the hotel looks more Swedish and this does have an explanation. A Swedish woman who lives nearby was employed 10 years ago to decorate the hotel. She spent two years meticulously painting the panelled walls and decorating the ceilings and beams in a typically Swedish style which blends in well with the mountain views. The bedrooms are all individually decorated: many once again with panelled and painted ceilings and colour-washed walls, some pale, some in fairly strong colours. The big dining room is panelled in yellow with intricately patterned beams, matching country style yellow chairs and crisp white cloths. The food is a big reason for staying here and Dominique is a prize-winning expert on Burgundy wines. And — rare find — his list is both knowledgeable and suited to any budget.

Rooms: 15 singles & doubles.
Price: 400-800 Frs (€ 68.6-121.96).
Extra bed 150 Frs.
Breakfast: 58 Frs.
Meals: Lunch 75-100 Frs; dinner
175-205 Frs. Half-board arrangements for
3 days or more.
Closed: Mid-November-mid-April.

*Exit A40 at Bellegarde dir. Gex. 2km before
Gex follow signs to Echenevex. Hotel
signposted.*

The Alps

Mont Blanc is the monarch of mountains;
They crown'd him long ago
On a throne of rocks, in a robe of clouds,
With a diadem of snow.
Lord Byron

L'Ancolie

Lac des Dronières
74350 Cruseilles
Haute-Savoie

Tel: (0)4 50 44 28 98
Fax: (0)4 50 44 09 73
E-mail: ancolie-hotel@wanadoo.fr

Yves Lefebvre

L'Ancolie is exceptionally welcoming and so are the staff, reflecting the owner's cheerful efficiency. In a well-kept garden with woods at its back and a lake lapping at its feet, it was custom-designed in 1993 to replace the family's original hotel: they wanted modern comfort in traditional style. So there are wooden balconies and fitted carpets, great log fires in the stone fireplace and a picture window for guests to watch the chefs preparing rich traditional Savoyard specialities in the kitchen. In summer, the big restaurant opens onto a terrace where you are served before the supremely tranquil lake view. Big bedrooms have lots of wood, of course, and clean-cut modern furniture; some have balconies; luxury bed linen adds a touch of class and bathrooms are as up-to-date as you could wish. As well as fishing in the lake and great walks from the door, there's a good golf course nearby plus delightful little Annecy and cosmopolitan Geneva to be visited (each 20km away). L'Ancolie is ideal for families (small children need supervising near the lake) and excellent value.

Rooms: 10 doubles.
Price: 350-520 Frs (€ 53.36-79.27).
Extra bed 50 Frs.
Breakfast: 55 Frs.
Meals: Lunch & dinner 125-250 Frs.
Closed: Two weeks in February (French school holidays).

From Annecy RN 201 dir. Cruseilles. In village take D15 — hotel immediately after Institut Aéronautique.

Hôtel Auberge Camelia

74570 Aviernoz
Haute-Savoie

Tel: (0)4 50 22 44 24
Fax: (0)4 50 22 43 25
E-mail: info@hotelcamelia.com
web: www.hotelcamelia.com

Suzanne & Roger Farrell-Cook

Roger loves to talk about local history, including stories about the Resistance: the woman who owned the Camelia during the war had strong connections with the *clandestines*. But the inn was thoroughly modernised by Roger and Sue ten years ago and now the breakfast buffet is laid out in the old dining room, there's a small, intimate restaurant in the old kitchen, and the bedrooms, carpeted and larger than average, are straightforwardly comfortable with white walls, unfussy furnishings and good big bathrooms. The delicious, open garden has a spring-fed fountain and a sunny terrace where meals are served whenever possible in the sight of impressive hills. Your happy hosts have apparently boundless energy and will take you off in their red minibus or direct you to walks. See the spectacular flower meadows, taste wine, ski at all levels — you can even watch the Alpine cattle stroll past your window, their great bells ringing. A very welcoming inn with delightful owners and friendly staff who make sure your every need is met, including the need for good food.

Rooms: 12: 5 doubles, 6 triples &
1 quadruple.
Price: Doubles 390-510 Frs
(€ 59.46-77.75); triples 485 Frs.
Breakfast: 35 Frs.
Meals: Lunch & dinner from 98 Frs.
Picnic lunch on request 43 Frs.
Closed: Never.

From Annecy D5 dir.Villaz; through Villaz dir. La Roche sur Foron. Auberge on left at Aviernoz.

Hôtel Le Cottage Fernand Bise

Au Bord du Lac
74290 Talloires
Haute-Savoie

Tel: (0)4 50 60 71 10
Fax: (0)4 50 60 77 51
E-mail: cottagebise@wanadoo.fr
web: www.cottagebise.com

Jean-Claude & Christine Bise

Not many cottages have 35 bedrooms; not many have this fabulous setting, either — you might be in a Wagner opera as you gaze at the sun setting over the 'Roc de Chère' across the Lac d'Annecy from the terrace. The three buildings which make up the hotel look, unsurprisingly, like Alpine chalets and are set in pretty, well-planted gardens in which you can wander on your way to meet one of the local millionaires. M and Mme Bise run this welcoming, relaxed establishment with a quiet Savoyard efficiency. *'Douillette'*, that lovely word which is the French equivalent of 'cosy', perfectly describes the atmosphere in the bedrooms, with their floral chintz fabrics and comfortable furniture. Well away from the bustle of Annecy itself, but close enough to everything it offers, this is a wonderfully adult holiday centre, offering activities for the sporty and inspiration for the arty who wish to follow in the footsteps of Cézanne or Lamartine. Comfort *and* culture.

Rooms: 35 doubles/twins.
Price: 450-1200 Frs (€ 68.6-182.94).
Extra bed 160 Frs (book ahead).
Breakfast: 75 Frs.
Meals: Lunch & dinner 180-270 Frs.
Closed: October 10-April 20.

In Annecy follow signs Bord du Lac dir. Thônes D909. At Veyrier du Lac follow D909A to Talloires. Well signposted in Talloires.

La Villa des Fleurs

Route du Port
74290 Talloires
Haute-Savoie

Tel: (0)4 50 60 71 14
Fax: (0)4 50 60 74 06
web: www.oda.fr/aa/la-villa-des-fleurs

Charles & Marie-France Jeagler

Such a pretty village, on what is reputed to be the cleanest lake in Europe. The Villa des Fleurs was converted into an hotel in 1923 and Charles and Marie-France have owned it since 1973: Charles and their son Sébastien are the chefs. A big bonus is that they belong to a local scheme which will allow you free access to tennis courts, bikes, kayaks, pedal boats and golf (for a small fee in July and August) and reduced rates for water skiing and catamaran hire. This is probably not the best hotel for young children but the sporty will enjoy all the acitivity on offer. The dining room is light and airy but painted in a surprising shade of pink. In summer you can eat on a very pleasant terrace at the top of the pretty garden where loungers are provided to sleep off your lunch. Bedrooms are very French with lots of flowery wallpaper and curtains and most overlook the lake. This is a family hotel, but they do also cater for smallish seminars and conferences.

Rooms: 8 doubles/twins.
Price: 490-610 Frs (€ 74.70-92.99).
Extra bed 90 Frs.
Breakfast: Included.
Meals: Half-board 495-590 Frs p.p.
(2 nights minimum).
Closed: Mid-November-mid-December.

From Annecy D909 along lake to Talloires dir. Albertville. Signposted in Talloires.

Chalet Hôtel de La Croix-Fry

Manigod   **Tel:** (0)4 50 44 90 16
74230 Thônes   **Fax:** (0)4 50 44 94 87
Haute-Savoie   **web:** www.oda.fr/aa/croixfry

Marie Ange Guelpa-Veyrat

Swim under the pure blue sky with the snowy summits watching over you. Even much-travelled guests are dazzled by this spot. Snuggle into super-soft sheepskin-covered sofas and be spoiled by discreet and smiling staff, mostly members of the extended family who practise the sort of charm that Swiss hotel schools cannot teach. Built 20 years ago by great-grandmother as a summer farm for family and animals, this friendly house has become a superb example of the dream chalet hotel — with a string of independent chalets for families who may use the hotel facilities. A flower-filled copper cheese cauldron greets you at the door of the sitting area and in winter a big open fire makes the ubiquitous wood glow. Next door, where the dining-room windows frame mountains, pastures and valley, the pretty furniture and pottery are local. Bedrooms have more wood, soft carpeting, pleasing fabrics, antique bits and excellent bathrooms (half have whirlpool baths). Great value in summer or winter, when there's even a minibus to shuttle guests to ski slopes.

Rooms: 10: 6 doubles & 4 suites.
Price: 950-2000 Frs (€ 144.83-304.9).
Breakfast: 100 Frs.
Meals: Lunch & dinner 150-430 Frs.
Closed: April 15-June 15 & September-mid December. Restaurant closed Monday & Tuesday lunchtimes.

*From Annecy D909 dir. Thônes. D12
towards Serraval & Manigod. Shortly after,
take D16 to Manigod — through village,
hotel on right before ski area.*

Chalet l'Isella

Les Murailles
74230 Manigod
Haute-Savoie

Tel: (0)4 50 44 97 35
Fax: (0)4 50 44 97 35

Bruno & Angela Marconnet

Walk through the chalet onto the wooden deck and you walk into the view —
swathes of Alpine pastures roll away from your feet, great rocky, snowy peaks rise
mightily to left and right and the clear, clean air sings. The new building is a
perfectly traditional Alpine chalet with extra-big windows in the communal rooms
so that the space outside can rush in. The sitting room is big, soft and comfortable
with massive beams and a local stone fireplace; there's a separate television and
music room and the airy dining room, laid with local pottery on close-knit tables, is
all clad, naturally, in pine and thick fabrics. More alpinism in the pretty, pale, pine-
furnished bedrooms. It is a wonderful, quietly welcoming mountain retreat. You can
sit in deep sofas indoors or lounge on the deck, walk straight out into those pastures
or drive up to the plateau in ten minutes; skiing is also on the doorstep; there's
fascinating old Annecy with wonderful restaurants and shops just down the road,
and the lake (said to be the cleanest in Europe) with all sorts of water sports and
tempting restaurants.

Rooms: 10: 4 doubles, 1 studio, 1 triple &
4 quadruples.
Price: Doubles 160-300 Frs
(€ 24.39-45.73); studio & triple 300 Frs;
quadruples 280 Frs per person.
Breakfast: 30 Frs.
Meals: Table d'hôtes 110 Frs.
Closed: Never.

*From Annecy D909 to Thônes then D12 dir.
Serraval & Manigod. Shortly after, D16 to
Manigod. After village follow signs for
Chalet l'Isella.*

Le Fer à Cheval

36 route du Crêt d'Arbois
74120 Megève
Haute-Savoie

Tel: (0)4 50 21 30 39
Fax: (0)4 50 93 07 60

Isabelle & Marc Sibuet

Why Fer à Cherval (horseshoe)? Because the original chalet was once a flourishing smithy. Horseshoes went out and it became an hotel, adding those wooden balconies, gable ends and typically elaborate Megève carvings. Inside, it's all warmth, timbered cosiness and a sense of luxury. Antiques — a grandfather clock, a fine old chest of drawers — and personal *objets* remove any taint of expensive blandness. The suites are superb: two double bedrooms plus sitting room with functioning log fire in each, such a treat (book well ahead); other rooms, just as well designed and decorated with pretty co-ordinated fabrics, are good value; bathrooms are excellent. The delightful, energetic young owners, proud of what they and earlier generations have achieved and keen to move with the times while keeping to tradition, cultivate an atmosphere of relaxed comfort and good taste — deep sofas, candlelit dinners, good French cuisine. A dream place for a mountain holiday — probably overfull in winter so why not try it in summer when this is idyllic walking country. *Half-board only.*

Rooms: 47: 39 doubles/twins & 8 suites each with double bedroom, lounge & log fire.
Price: Doubles 600-940 Frs p.p. (half-board) (€ 91.47-143.3); prices for suites on request. Extra bed 250 Frs.
Breakfast: Included.
Meals: Half-board only.
Closed: Easter-June & mid-September-mid-December.

From A40 exit Sallanches. N212 dir. Albertville. After 12km left dir. centre ville. Hotel signposted on left.

Le Mont Blanc

Place de l'Eglise
Rue Ambroise Martin
74120 Megève
Haute-Savoie

Tel: (0)4 50 21 20 02
Fax: (0)4 50 21 45 28
E-mail: contact@hotelmontblanc.com
web: www.hotelmontblanc.com

Marie Geneviève Socquet

Cocteau came to the Mont Blanc, with other great names (his drawings are all over the ground floor) and its popularity is waxing again. It is a superbly warm and atmospheric hotel where pine is king: panelled walls, coffered ceilings, carved cornices, chairs and bedheads — Megève woodworkers vying with each other in originality. The foyer, where staff seem as happy as their guests, is a remarkably deep and tempting sitting area — soft sofas and carved chests, pictures and gentle lights — that becomes home the moment you arrive; easy to imagine the wild 'celebrity' parties of the fifties. Rooms are magnificent in their warm pine. As owner and decorator, Jocelyne Sibuet's choice of wallpapers and fabrics blend subtly with the rustic wood, a perfect foil for her antiques, paintings and copies of traditional Savoyard furniture. Your quilted, much-pillowed bed may shelter in a frill-decked alcove, the heavy curtains in contrasting pattern. It seems expensive but it's a real treat to stay here, at the summit of style, with all the restaurants of the village on your doorstep. And they are such nice people.

Rooms: 51: 40 doubles/twins, 11 suites.
Price: Club 790-1170 Frs
(€ 120.43-178.27), prestige
1120-1420 Frs, suites 1490-1700 Frs.
Breakfast: 80 Frs.
Meals: Home-made hot chocolate, tea and blueberry tarts in lounge.
Closed: Never.

Exit A40 Sallanches then N212 dir.
Albertville. Megève is 13km. Follow hotel
signs to centre of village.

Au Coin du Feu

Route de Rochebrune
74120 Megève
Haute-Savoie

Tel: (0)4 50 21 04 94
Fax: (0)4 50 21 20 15
E-mail: contact@coindufeu.com
web: www.coindufeu.com

Mireille Baud

Outside the bustle of 'central Megève', here is another house converted by Jocelyne and Jean-Louis Sibuet into a delicious and intimate place to stay, just a short walk from the village and the ski lift. It feels more like sharing a big chalet with friends than being in a normal hotel and the décor makes the whole place hum warmly. In the sitting room, a log fire burns in the sculpted fireplace, a chessboard awaits its players by the tartan-covered sofa, the floor glows with burnished old tiles and most things are made of wood. There are thick curtains, mountain antiques and dried flowers, naive paintings and hunting memorabilia, and tea by the fire with a huge choice of teas and comforting blueberry tart has become a ritual. Bedrooms are in cosy chalet style, their beds are in alcoves or under little canopies, their duvets are fluffy, their fabrics flowery, their pictures interesting. Finally, the Restaurant Saint Nicolas is one of Megève's favourite eating houses where tradition and invention join hands with all the local tastes and specialities.

Rooms: 23 rooms: "club" for one/ two; large for two/ three; suites for two to four.
Price: Club 660-810 Frs (€ 100.62-123.48), large 920-1020 Frs, suites 1020-1290 Frs. Extra bed 180 Frs. Baby bed 130 Frs. Half board in winter.
Breakfast: Included.
Meals: Dinner 250 Frs.
Closed: April-July 22 & late August-mid-September. Restaurant closed during summer.

Exit A40 Sallanches then the N212 dir. Albertville. Megève is 13km. Follow hotel signs to centre of village, direction 'Rochebrune Téléphérique'. Signposted.

ASP Map No: 10   MMap 244-20   **231**

Hostellerie Les Châtaigniers

Rue Maurice Frank
73110 La Rochette
Savoie

Tel: (0)4 79 25 50 21
Fax: (0)4 79 25 79 97
E-mail: Leschataigniers@wanadoo.fr

Anne-Charlotte Rey & Philippe Roman

A fun, off-beat atmosphere reigns in this Hitchcock-lookalike house and the unconventional revel in it. Philippe Roman, chef, poet and entertainer, invites you to his Poet's Table: he does all the cooking (of superb dishes, we are told — he has cooked in many places, including Kenya), has written a book of rhyming recipes and may sing them to you after dinner, or improvise one of his *théâtre-cuisine* sketches (all in French, of course). Anne-Charlotte appreciates the comic ironies of life: her family used to own the fine château you see over the way. Together they are a remarkable team of lively, intelligent hosts. Their elegant dining room is small enough to cultivate an intimate private house feel despite the separate tables. Their big antique-furnished bedrooms, called *Romantique* or *Courtisane* or *Candide*, are fabulous, a couple even have 'perfect' bathrooms. Beyond the swimming pool (for residents only) and the monkey-puzzle trees in the garden, the mountains tower, the snow still clings in June. Unforgettable.

Rooms: 5: 1 twin, 2 doubles, 1 suite & 1 studio for 2/4.
Price: Doubles 1070 Frs (€ 163.12); suites 1770 Frs, half board for two.
Breakfast: Included.
Meals: Full board available for minimum 3 days.
Closed: January 2-15.

From A41 exit Pontcharra; D925 dir. Albertville. At La Rochette dir. Hôtel de Ville then Arvillard. Châtaigniers 200m on left.

Provence-Riviera

Provence… the land where the silver-grey earth
is impregnated with the light of the sky.
Henry James

Auberge de Reillanne

04110 Reillanne
Alpes-de-Haute-Provence

Tel: (0)4 92 76 45 95
Fax: (0)4 92 76 45 95

Monique Balmand

The solid squareness of this lovely old 18th-century house, so typical of the area, reassures you, invites you in. And you are not disappointed: you'll feel good here, even if you can't quite define the source of the positive energy. Madame Balmand clearly has a connection to the spirit of the place and has used all her flair and good taste, making all the curtains and bedcovers herself, to transform the old inn into a very special place to stay. Bedrooms are large and airy, done in cool, restful colours with big cupboards and rattan furniture. There are beams, properly white-washed walls and books. Bathrooms are big and simple too. Downstairs, the sitting and dining areas are decorated in warm, embracing colours with terracotta tiles, white tablecloths and flame-coloured curtains. This would be a place for a restful holiday with long meditative walks in the hills, a place to come and write that novel or simply to get to know the gentle, delicate, smiling owner who loves nothing better than to receive people in her magical house. She organises painting exhibitions, about three times a year. *No smoking in some rooms.*

Rooms: 6: 3 doubles & 3 triples.
Price: Doubles 280-420 Frs (€ 42.69-64.03), triples 530 Frs. Extra bed 150 Frs.
Breakfast: 45 Frs.
Meals: Dinner 140 Frs for half-board guests. Non-residents 380 Frs.
Closed: November-mid-December & January.

From Avignon N100 through Apt and Céreste. About 8km after Céreste left on D214 to Reillanne. Hotel on right (80km from Avignon).

Mas de Grateloup

Route de la Coopérative de Villedieu
84110 Buisson
Vaucluse

Tel: (0)4 90 28 97 34
Fax: (0)4 90 28 97 37
E-mail: masgrateloup@aol.com
web: www.mas-grateloup.com

Gérard Poron & Nadège Moutard

Getting there is a triumph in itself. The reward, however, is a delightfully attractive little house, Provençal to its roots, with views for miles and miles across wild and lush low-lying hills. The swimming pool is one of those which seem to bring the countryside into the pool. It is dangerously seductive so you may forget to do all that sight-seeing. Each room has its own entrance and you could easily settle in. Nadège is young, her husband an architect, hence the intelligent use of space. The dining room is in the very attractively converted old wine cellar, though you are more likely to be out under the moonlight, on the terrace, white china on blue tablecloth, bottoms on comfortable, slatted wooden teak chairs. There are two living rooms, a fireplace, everything for young children and babies. Breakfast is typically generous and hard to leave, probably in the delectable courtyard, elegant round blue tables and delicate iron chairs against fading ochre plasterwork. The bedrooms are simple, easy on the eye, perhaps with white bedcovers and beige walls. Or blue-and-white covers and blue furniture. Charming.

Rooms: 5 including 3 suites.
Price: 350-550 Frs (€ 53.36-83.85).
Breakfast: Buffet included.
Meals: Table d'hôtes, including aperitif, wine, coffee, 130 Frs.
Closed: Never, but phone ahead.

From A7 exit Bollène dir. Nyons/Vaison la Romaine; 1.5km after Suze la Rousse and Tulette, right dir. Buisson/Vaison la Romaine; left at first crossroads dir. Villedieu. Mas 800m on right.

Château Talaud

84870 Loriol du Comtat
Vaucluse

Tel: (0)4 90 65 71 00
Fax: (0)4 90 65 77 93
E-mail: chateautalaud@infonie.fr
web: www.avignon-et-provence.com/chateautalau

Conny & Hein Deiters-Kommer

Lavish and elegant — a stunning place and lovely people. Hein has a wine export business, Conny gives her whole self to her house and her guests. Among ancient vineyards, the ineffably gracious 18th-century château speaks of a long-gone southern way of life. Enter, and see it has not all vanished. Restored by the owners to a very high standard, the finely-proportioned rooms have been furnished with antiques, many of them family pieces, and thick, luxurious fabrics. The big bedrooms mix old and new, *Directoire* armchairs and featherweight duvets, with consummate taste; bathrooms are old-style hymns to modernity. But the high point must be the exquisite swimming pool, an adapted 17th-century irrigation tank: through an arch to the first, shallow cistern, leading to a deeper pool beyond — incredibly beautiful. Guests may laze in the lovely gardens but Conny is happy to help you plan visits in this fascinating area. Then return to one of her delicious meals where guests all sit together: An exceptionally fine, well-kept guesthouse.

Rooms: 7: 5 doubles, 1 suite & 1 apartment.
Price: Doubles 750-950 Frs
(€ 114.34-144.83); suite 1000 Frs; apartment 5500 Frs (rented weekly).
Breakfast: Included.
Meals: Dinner, twice a week, 4 courses including wine, 250 Frs.
Closed: February.

Leave N7 on D950 dir. Carpentras. Exit D107 at Loriol du Comtat/Monteux Est. On r'about left dir. Loriol. After 1km château on left, signposted Propriété Privée.

Hostellerie de Crillon le Brave

Place de l'Eglise
84410 Crillon le Brave
Vaucluse

Tel: (0)4 90 65 61 61
Fax: (0)4 90 65 62 86
E-mail: crillonbrave@relaischateaux.fr
web: www.crillonlebrave.com

Peter Chittick & Craig Miller

Not just an hotel in Provence, a gateway to Provençal *art de vivre*. In a medieval hill-top village facing legendary Mont Ventoux, it is four old stone houses — the presbytery, the grocery — snuggled round the church, saved from ruin and turned into a most civilised hostelry. You may simply delight in being in fascinating Provence, in the old village, in a beautifully-furnished light-flooded room — beams, glowing Soleidado fabrics, view of hills, village or valley, super bathroom — with a delectable terraced garden of rocks, moss, fountain and cypress. Or you may join one of Craig's Provence discovery weeks — the biscuit craftswoman, the Soleidado designers, the herb growers, the potters — or one of the chef's cookery courses, or their Wine Experience. There are markets and festivals, walks and ruins — the ever-helpful staff know it all and "Nothing is impossible for our clients". Rooms vary in size, all are lush and cheerful. The restaurant, formerly the village cattle shed, has a high stone vault with a fireplace big enough to sleep in and, of course, gourmet food on the tables.

Rooms: 23: 16 doubles, 5 suites &
1 2-bedroom house.
Price: 900-1650 Frs (€ 137.2-251.54);
extra person 190 Frs. House: 1 room
1600 Frs, 2 rooms 2000 Frs.
Breakfast: 90-150 Frs.
Meals: Picnic lunch 95 & 150 Frs.
Simple lunches served by the pool.
Dinner 240-390 Frs.
Closed: January 3-March 11.

From A7 exit Avignon; D942 to Carpentas (16km) then D974 to Crillon le Brave (14km).

Hostellerie du Val de Sault

Route de Saint-Trinit
Ancien chemin d'Aurel
84390 Sault
Vaucluse

Tel: (0)4 90 64 01 41
Fax: (0)4 90 64 12 74

Yves Gattechaut & Ildiko de Hanny

Jean Giono calls this landscape "a sea of corn gold and lavender blue": from your terrace here you can contemplate the poet's waves and the familiar shape of Mont Ventoux, the painter's peak, beyond. The charming, communicative couple of owners — she with an artistic background, he a passionate cook — have gathered all possible information, know everyone there is to know on the Provence scene; they also provide imaginative food, in the informal atmosphere of their light, airy restaurant. And... children can eat earlier. Perched just above the woods in a big garden, this is a modern building with lots of space inside and out; wooden floors and pine-slatted walls bring live warmth, colour schemes are vibrant, storage is excellent; baths in the suites have Jacuzzi jets. Each room feels like a very private space with its terrace (the suites have room for loungers on theirs); the pool, bar and restaurant are there for conviviality, the fitness room, tennis court and *boules* pitch for exercise.

Rooms: 17: 12 doubles/twins & 5 suites.
Price: 480-590 Frs (€ 73.18-89.94);
suites 640-830 Frs. (Prices per person for half-board).
Breakfast: 72 Frs if not included in half-board.
Meals: Lunch from 129 Frs. Dinner included in half-board.
Closed: November-end March.

A7 exit Avignon Nord/Le Pontet dir.
Carpentras (20km). Follow signs Sault/Villes sur Auzon. D1 Col des Abeilles dir.
Sault (30km); dir. Saint Trinit/Fourcalquier. After big turn, left between Fire
Department and supermarket, 1km to hostellerie in heart of forest.

237   MMap 245-18   **ASP Map No: 14**

Hôtel la Gacholle

Route de Murs   **Tel:** (0)4 90 72 01 36
84220 Gordes   **Fax:** (0)4 90 72 01 81
Vaucluse

Eric Bongert & Hervé Sabat

These two young men are artistic and naturally welcoming. They left their arty but unpretentious café in Paris for La Gacholle two years ago. And what a spot it is: look over the shoulders of the evergreen oaks and melt before the splendid tapestry of the valley below and the Luberon beyond: all bedrooms have this view, three have private terraces, and breakfasting as the sun rises leaves a deep memory. The hotel is 25 years old but built with local stone and style and covered in greenery so it blends perfectly into the 'beautiful French village' scene. Eric and Hervé have a sober and original approach to décor based on natural colours and materials, textured finishes to set off beautiful linens, cottons, hemp, wax-painted walls in corridors — a natural but sophisticated atmosphere with a glance at Provençal style. The same softness clothes the restaurant: old wooden furniture, sand-coloured hand-textured walls, filtering curtains and an aphorism for hedonists: "The only way to get rid of temptation is to yield to it" (Oscar Wilde, of course). Take the time to enjoy it all.

Rooms: 12 doubles/twins.
Price: Price: 450-750 Frs (€ 68.6-114.34).
Breakfast: 65 Frs.
Meals: Picnic lunch available. Weekday lunch 85 Frs. Weekend lunch & dinner 195 Frs. 'A la carte' choices for residents.
Closed: January-mid March.

From Avignon N100 dir Apt; left on D2 to Gordes; just before village, left to Murs then La Gacholle.

Hôtel Les Romarins

Route de l'Abbaye de Sénanque
84220 Gordes
Vaucluse

Tel: (0)4 90 72 12 13
Fax: (0)4 90 72 13 13

Anny Charles

Anny Charles has been running this three-star hotel overlooking one of France's most beautiful villages for ten years. Forget the buildings on either side: the secluded pool and garden give you a real feeling of getting away from it all and the hotel even has its own private path into town. The fabulous hilltop view of Gordes makes you want to linger as long as possible over a delicious buffet breakfast, usually taken on the terrace. Inside, the sitting room is comfortable without being over-lavish and the warmth of the open fire is always welcome on days when the chilly *mistral* wind gets up. The white-walled bedrooms are cool and comfortable, if a little sombre, but quiet. Anny doesn't serve evening meals, but she'll gladly book a restaurant for you or let you explore the local culinary scene on your own. Vivacious, always busy and particularly welcoming, she takes a lot of pleasure in making you feel at home. A happy spot, easy living, great walking.

Rooms: 10 doubles/triples.
Price: 500-800 Frs (€ 76.22-121.96).
Breakfast: 60 Frs.
Meals: Restaurants nearby.
Closed: December 15-February 15.

From Avignon E on N7 then left onto N100 dir. Apt; left to Gordes. Route de Sénanque is on left on entering Gordes. Hotel 200m on right, well signposted.

239 MMap 245-80 **ASP Map No: 14**

Auberge du Presbytère

Place de la Fontaine
84400 Saignon
Vaucluse

Tel: (0)4 90 74 11 50
Fax: (0)4 90 04 68 51
E-mail:
auberge.presbytere@wanadoo.fr
web: www.provence-
luberon.com/auberge1_fr.html

Jean-Pierre de Lutz

'When the wind blows at Saignon, tiles fly off in Avignon', is a local saying about the mistral, the fierce wind that howls down from mountains to Mediterranean. This 11th-century village of only 100 inhabitants is in the heart of the Luberon hills and lavender fields; the Auberge du Presbytère is in the heart of Saignon, half hidden behind an old tree near the village's statue-topped fountain. You can have lunch under this tree, or in a pretty terraced garden. Each of the bedrooms — Blue, Pink, Flower, Grape, Fountain — are striking, although the latter two lack the spartan charm of the others. The Blue Room with its stone terrace looks out onto the hills and the simplest of all the rooms, the little Pink one, has sleigh beds. Jean-Pierre, the owner's quietly charming son, will make you feel at home and, though this is perhaps not an obvious choice with children, provides early supper specially for them.

Rooms: 10: 9 doubles/twins & 1 suite. 2 third-floor rooms with terrace.
Price: 290-580 Frs (€ 44.21-88.42).
Breakfast: 50 Frs.
Meals: Lunch 125 Frs; dinner 175 Frs. Menus change daily with 3-4 choices.
Closed: Mid-November-mid-December & January. Restaurant closed Wednesday & Thursday lunchtimes.

From Apt N100. At roundabout with 1 olive and 3 cyprus trees dir. Saignon to beginning of village. Left on lane for 'riverains' (residents) to Place de la Fontaine.

ASP Map No: 14   MMap 245-31   **240**

Le Relais du Procureur

Rue Basse
84710 Lacoste
Vaucluse

Tel: (0)4 90 75 82 28
Fax: (0)4 90 75 86 94
E-mail:
relaisprocureur@luberon.org
web: www.luberon.org

Antoine Court de Gebelin

The inner courtyard garden around a pretty pool is a measure of the peace you'll find in this 17th-century dwelling, even when the village streets are thronging with visitors in the summer. Respect for his guests' tranquillity is among the owner's priorities, his professional eye as a photographer ensuring more than simple attention to detail in the authentic renovations he embarked on over a decade ago. White stone walls resplendent with old prints and paintings reflect both natural light and the soft hues of stylised lamps, in an overall tableau dominated by refinement and comfort. The seven bedrooms, some with views over the Luberon hills, are all big (the largest is 39m²) and most enable children and parents to share the same room. The hotel is not really suitable for small children, though, partly due to the stone staircases and elegant furniture. But also due to the gentle quietness so appreciated by guests all year round. A far cry from what life might have been like at the enigmatic Marquis de Sade's château overlooking the village!

Rooms: 7 including 1 triple & 1 quadruple.
Price: Doubles & triples 500-750 Frs
(€ 76.22-114.34); quadruple 750-800 Frs.
Breakfast: Included.
Meals: Lunch & dinner 119-289 Frs.
À la carte also available.
Closed: Occasionally January-April. Restaurant closed November-March.

From Avignon N100 E to Lumières; right to Lacoste; in village keep right following signs to Mairie/Poste to one-way main street — hotel next to bakery.

Mas des Capelans

84580 Oppède
Vaucluse

Tel: (0)4 90 76 99 04
Fax: (0)4 90 76 90 29

Jacqueline & Philippe Poiri

Why buy a house in Provence and have to do all the work? Here, you will feel at home but be free to lounge all day by the pool, having a leisurely lunch between dips and wandering in to change before an aperitif as you watch the sun go down behind the hills. Jacqueline and Philippe have been running the Mas des Capelans, the 18th-century home of a silkworm breeder set among the vineyards and fields, for 13 years now and their personal touch comes through both in the relaxed atmosphere and the house itself. The furniture and bits and pieces in the bedrooms have been collected over the years and not simply bought to give the place the right look. The rooms are largish and simply decorated, with plenty of cushions and flowers. A great place for children; one room has an adjoining room for them and a private terrace while another has children's beds on a split-level. Dinner is under the mulberry trees unless the mistral is blowing. If you feel like a drink later, simply help yourself from the outside bar and settle up when you pay your bill.

Rooms: 9: 5 doubles/twins, 2 family suites & 2 triples.
Price: Doubles 600-1500 Frs (€ 91.47-228.67);
triples 1100 Frs; suites 1100-1500 Frs.
Breakfast: Buffet included.
Meals: Dinner 160 Frs (by reservation).
Poolside lunch 110 Frs.
Closed: November-end February.

From Avignon S D22 onto N100 dir. Oppède. Signposted.

La Bastide de Voulonne

84220 Cabrières d'Avignon
Vaucluse

Tel: (0)4 90 76 77 55
Fax: (0)4 90 76 77 56
E-mail: bastide-voulonne@avignon-et-provence.com
web: www.avignon-et-provence.com/bastide-voulonn

Sophie & Alain Rebourg

This bastide sits in splendid isolation in the lavender fields stretching beneath the ancient hilltop villages perched on the Luberon Mountains. The heart of this 18th-century farm is an inner courtyard where you can breakfast to the soothing sound of the fountain. Sophie and Alain have been open for guests here for three years after rescuing the Bastide from years of neglect. They have done a fantastic job, sticking to natural, local colours, with tiled floors. The bedrooms are huge. The garden — more like a park really — is vast, with a big pool not far from the house. It's a fantastic place for children; Sophie and Alain have young twins. They plan to grow vegetables in the garden and menus already centre round local food. Breakfast is a buffet, in an airy, tiled breakfast room if it's too chilly for the courtyard: this shouldn't happen very often, except in winter. Dinner is served at one long table in a big dining hall where the centrepiece is the carefully restored old bread oven. There are loads of places around for lunch, or Sophie will do you a picnic.

Rooms: 6: 5 doubles & 1 suite.
Price: Doubles 600-800 Frs
(€ 91.47-121.96); suite 1000-1300 Frs.
Breakfast: 55 Frs.
Meals: Dinner 150 Frs.
Closed: Never (reservation only January &
February). Restaurant closed Tuesdays.

*After Avignon leave A7 on N100 dir. Apt.
At Coustellet crossroads take dir.
Gordes/Cabrières; at roundabout (Collège de
Calavon) dir. Gordes/Les Imberts. After 1km turn right — bastide is 600m on left.*

Hôtel d'Europe

12 place Crillon
84000 Avignon
Vaucluse

Tel: (0)4 90 14 76 76
Fax: (0)4 90 14 76 71
E-mail:
reservations@hotel-d-europe.fr
web: www.hotel-d-europe.fr

M Daudège

Built in 1580 for the Marquis de Graveson, this mansion, a mitre's throw from the Papal Palace, was taken from its noble owner by the Revolution and turned into an hotel. When you stay here, you will be following in the steps of great writers (Victor Hugo, Tennessee Williams), painters (Dali, Picasso), even Napoleon, though in earlier times people arrived by boat. Since this is no longer possible, the hotel has a car park. Owner René Daire has run the Europe for 20 years with his impeccable, perfectionist touch — and pretty perfect it is, with the help of his superbly cultivated manager: it is one of our larger hotels but it is still small enough for them to take personal care of each guest. This is traditional French hospitality in all its splendour. Bedrooms vary from large to huge, from simply elegant to sumptuous; many have crisp white cotton bedcovers that give a fresh touch among the moulded, mirrored walls, the antiques and the plush-covered chairs. Meals are served at fine tables in the tapestry-hung dining room or, better still, on the terrace where the fountain sings.

Rooms: 45 including 4 triples & 3 suites.
Price: Doubles/triples 660-2200 Frs
(€ 100.62-335.39); suites 3000-3300 Frs.
Breakfast: 98 Frs.
Meals: Lunch & dinner 180-285 Frs.
Closed: Never.

Exit Avignon dir. Centre Ville.From ring
road around the ramparts, turn on Porte de
L'Oulle dir. Place Crillon. Hotel and Place
de Crillon signposted.

Mas du Clarousset

La Roubine du Joly
Route de Cacherel
13460 Saintes Maries de la Mer
Bouches-du-Rhône

Tel: (0)4 90 97 81 66
Fax: (0)4 90 97 88 59

Mme Eyssette

The Mas du Clarousset, once a hunting lodge, is deep in the Camargue, in the heart of the National Park, up a little road lined with oleanders. Lying by the pool, or sitting on the terrace behind your room, you smell wild grassland only feet away. Mme Eyssette, who was born round here and has worked in the hotel 'industry' for over 40 years, thinks of the Mas as "more like home than a hotel". She knows the area like the back of her hand and will be a great help, whether you want to go bird-watching, riding — with a wild west-style old Camargue saddle on an agile white pony — canoeing or simply to the beach. This is a great place for children since, apart from all the activities nearby, there is so much room for them to roam and play. The 10 Provençal-style rooms are really small bungalows, set in a staggered line, each with a car space at the front and a terrace at the back. The heart of the hotel is a big whitewashed dining room where meals are eaten at two long tables. Mme Eyssette will bend over backwards to make you welcome — even bringing tea or coffee to your room before breakfast.

Rooms: 10 doubles/twins.
Price: 780-970 Frs (€ 118.91-147.88).
Children under 3 free.
Extra bed 170 Frs.
Breakfast: Continental included. Other choices on request.
Meals: Lunch: picnic on request or served by the pool.
Closed: Mid-November-mid-December.

N570 from Arles to Stes Maries de la Mer. There left on D85A. Mas on right.

Grand Hôtel Nord Pinus

Place du Forum
13200 Arles
Bouches-du-Rhône

Tel: (0)4 90 93 44 44
Fax: (0)4 90 93 34 00
E-mail: info@nord-pinus.com
web: www.nord-pinus.com

Mme Igou

There is no other like it — an Arlesian legend, where Spain meets France, ancient Rome meets the 20th century. Built in 1865 on Roman vaults, it came to fame in the '50s when a clown and a cabaret singer owned it: famous bullfighters dressed here before entering the arena and the arty crowd flocked (Cocteau, Picasso, Hemingway etc). Anne Igou keeps the magic alive today with her strong personality and cinema, fashion and photography folk — and bullfighters still have 'their' superb Spanish Rococo room. The style is vibrant and alive at this display of Art Deco furniture and fittings, great corrida posters and toreador costumes, North African carpets and artefacts, fabulous Provençal colours and ironwork. Colour and light are deftly used to create a soft, nostalgic atmosphere where you feel both warm and cool, smart and artistic — where each guest is an individual, each room is differently interesting. And breakfast is a festival of real French tastes — more magic, more nostalgia. As Cocteau said: "An hotel with a soul". Though the tourist invasion may make it noisy during the summer.

Rooms: 25: 20 doubles/twins & 5 suites.
Price: Doubles 840 Frs (€ 128.06); twins 990 Frs; suites 1700 Frs. Extra bed 150 Frs.
Breakfast: 75 Frs.
Meals: Lunch 98 Frs; dinner 180 Frs & à la carte. Half board 150 Frs; full board 300 Frs.
Closed: Never.

From A54 exit Arles Centre dir. Centre Ancien. Take Blvd des Lices at main post office; left on Rue Jaurès; then left on Rue Cloître, left again to Place du Forum.

Auberge La Régalido
Rue Frédéric Mistral
13990 Fontvieille
Bouches-du-Rhône

Tel: (0)4 90 54 60 22
Fax: (0)4 90 54 64 29
E-mail:
regalido@relaischateaux.fr
web:
www.relaischateaux.fr/regalido

M Michel

Have you heard of the Mitifiot olive-oil press? If so you will be doubly pleased at having read *Lettres de mon Moulin*, for it features. Alphonse Daudet lived in the village. Somehow the transition from literary press to modern hotel has been seamless, for you have all the charm you could want in Provence. There are blue shutters invaded by creeper, terracotta tiles and parasols, pergolas and flowers, shrubs and wrought-iron lampstands on the terrace, and an amazing garden that seems to invade every corner. The atmosphere is classy yet 'family', formal but easygoing. The food does justice to the hotel, with a Michelin rosette and presentation to match. Father and son both cook, and are now into the fourth generation of chefs. What else? A beautifully converted stone vaulted dining room, tapestry on the wall, elegant with white table cloths and high-backed cane chairs. Bedrooms are fresh, light and airy, named and coloured after flowers. They are well-designed, yet traditional, with good views too. Huge care has been taken over everything, so expect to be treated royally, and to wallow in good living.

Rooms: 15: 10 doubles, 3 family &
2 junior suites.
Price: Doubles 710-2050 Frs
(€ 108.24-312.52); triples 1550-2460 Frs;
suites 1640-2440 Frs.
Breakfast: 42-105 Frs.
Meals: 260-410 Frs.
Closed: January 4-mid-February.
Restaurant closed Mondays & Tuesday
lunchtimes.

From the A8 and A9 exit 7 at Arles dir.
Tarascon for first three roundabouts.
At fourth, dir. Fontvieille.

Mas de l'Oulivié

Les Arcoules
13520 Les Baux de Provence
Bouches-du-Rhône

Tel: (0)4 90 54 35 78
Fax: (0)4 90 54 44 31
E-mail: contact@masdeloulivie.com
web: www.masdeloulivie.com

Emmanuel Achard

Refreshing to find a modern hotel that brings together old and new so harmoniously and with such impeccable taste. Having fallen in love with the olive groves, lavender fields and chalky white hillsides of Les Baux-de-Provence, the family built ten years ago the hotel of their dreams: a creamy fronted, almond-green shuttered, Provence-style structure, roofed with lovingly reclaimed terracotta tiles, landscaped with cypress and oleander. Every last detail has been carefully crafted, from the locally made oak furniture to the handmade tiles round the pool. And what a pool! Temptingly curvaceous, with a Jacuzzi and pebble beach for children. Furnishings are fresh, local, designed for deep comfort. Bedrooms are creamy coloured, country-style with an elegant twist. The bar/living-room has a rustic fireplace; filled with flowers in the summer. The young Archards love to provide guests with the very best and that includes lunches served by the pool (they also sell their own lavender and oil). Mas de l'Oulivie joins the *crème de la crème* of Provence's small country hotels — a stylish retreat.

Rooms: 23 including 1 suite & 6 triples.
Price: Doubles/triples 620-1400 Frs
(€ 94.52-213.43); suite 1840-2300 Frs.
Extra bed 160 Frs.
Breakfast: 60-80 Frs.
Meals: Poolside lunches à la carte.
Closed: Mid-November-mid-March.

A7 exit Avignon Sud dir. Noves/St Rémy/Les Baux. A54 exit St Martin de Crau dir. Les Baux or Arles-Fourchon.

Mas de Cornud

Petite Route des Baux
13210 Saint Rémy de Provence
Bouches-du-Rhône

Tel: (0)4 90 92 39 32
Fax: (0)4 90 92 55 99
E-mail: mascornud@compuserve.com
web: www.mascornud.com

David & Nitockrees Tadros Carpita

Guest house and cookery school are combined in a typical farmhouse where two majestic plane trees stand guard and the scents and light of Provence hover. Nito, a nature-lover, cares about how colour creates feeling, how fabrics comfort: she and David, willing American 'exiles', have done a superb restoration where every object is clearly the best (hangings from Kashmir, old French tiles). Bedrooms are big and varied, all beautifully decorated yet warmly simple. The atmosphere is convivial and open: you are a member of a family here, so join the others at the bar, choose a book in the library, have a swim in the big pool then a drink from the honesty bar. The kitchen is the vital centre of Cornud: here you eat if the weather is inclement — otherwise the garden has some lovely eating spots — and learn if you have come for cookery lessons (many stay without following a course). A traditional country kitchen, with cast-iron range, long wooden table, baskets and dried herbs, it also has a non-slip floor and granite worktops — homely but professional. Come and be part of Provence for a week.

Rooms: 6: 5 doubles/twins & 1 suite.
Price: Doubles 750-1150 Frs
(€ 114.34-175.32); suite 1150 Frs.
Extra beds 140-230 Frs.
Breakfast: Included.
Meals: Lunch 150 Frs; hosted dinner 300 Frs. Picnic lunch available.
Closed: January-February.

3 km W of St Rémy de Provence on D99 dir. Tarascon. Left on D27 dir. Les Baux; after 1km turn left at sign Château des Alpilles onto D31; Mas is 200m on left.

La Maison

Domaine de Bournissac
Montée d'Eyragues
13550 Paluds de Noves
Bouches-du-Rhône

Tel: (0)4 90 90 25 25
Fax: (0)4 90 90 25 26
E-mail: annie@lamaison-a-bournissac.com
web: www.lamaison-a-bournissac.com

Alain & Annie Zéau

This huge noble house with its beautiful stone buildings laid out round a courtyard has been converted and decorated with gusto and unfaltering taste — understandably, since the Zéaus are an energetic, artistic couple who also run a restaurant-art gallery; and Annie painted lots of the pictures here. There is a wonderful soft beige Provençal finish on the walls, a fine patina on the furniture, a different beautiful bedcover in each room. It feels like a sophisticated private house, with cosy corners — the lovely *salon* with fireplace and books, another sitting area in a wide, sea-grass-floored corridor — pretty objects everywhere, lovely old fireplaces, beams and elegant linens. The big shady terrace outside the dining room is the place to eat in summer, gazing down into the valley and across to the Alpilles (the pool lies discreetly in the lower garden). The owners care about guests' comfort and pleasure: bedrooms are big, bathrooms deluxe, tables most beautifully decorated, meals inventive and refined. Although it only opened in July 1999 it already feels loved and lived-in.

Rooms: 13: 6 doubles, 1 triple & 3 suites (1 for 4).
Price: 600-1200 Frs (€ 91.47-182.94).
Children under 10 free.
Breakfast: 60 Frs.
Meals: Lunch & dinner 240 Frs.
Half-board 260 Frs.
Closed: January-March. Restaurant closed Mondays.

From A7 exit Avignon Sud to Noves then dir.
St Rémy on D30 for 4km. Right on D29 dir. Eyragues. Left at top of hill. Signposted
Domaine de Bournissac.

Domaine de Valmouriane

Petite Route des Baux
D 27
13210 Saint Rémy de Provence
Bouches-du-Rhône

Tel: (0)4 90 92 44 62
Fax: (0)4 90 92 37 32
E-mail: domdeval@wanadoo.fr
web: www.valmouriane.com

Judith & Brian MacHugo

The house is a mere 200 years old but the Gallo-Roman remains in the grounds date from the fourth century and out in the bosky flowering garden, where the very modern landscaped pool and the Jacuzzi lie, you feel anciently rooted. Yet the atmosphere is casual and friendly: it could be an English club in a Provençal setting and people who come here feel they are among old friends. The old stone buildings are typical Provence and so is the Mediterranean herb garden. A mixture of English and French furniture warms the space round the original carved stone fireplace in the *grand salon*; you can play billiards or tennis or walk out of the six-hectare estate straight into the wild countryside. Most bedrooms are big and airy, all are extremely comfortable, some have private terraces (rooms at the back with a poorer view are the cheaper). Imaginative meals are served in the big-windowed dining room or on the terrace. A place of peace and relaxation that is close to all the natural cultural delights of Provence.

Rooms: 14, some with private terraces:
12 doubles/twins, 1 family room & 1 suite.
Price: 590-1190 Frs (€ 89.94-181.41);
family room 1160 Frs; suite 1240-1550 Frs.
Extra bed 100 Frs.
Breakfast: 75 Frs.
Meals: Lunch & dinner 175-290 Frs.
Closed: Never.

From St Rémy D99 W dir. Tarascon for 3.5km; left on D27 dir. Les Baux for 2km — Domaine on right.

Le Provençal

Place Saint Pierre
83400 Giens
Var

Tel: (0)4 98 04 54 54
Fax: (0)4 98 04 54 40
E-mail: leprovencal@wanadoo.fr

Mme Michel

Perched on a cliff with a dazzling view of coast and islands, Le Provençal has large luxuriant grounds across the little road just below the hotel and a superb sea-water pool a short walk through the tall pines to where the sea leaps over the rocks. On the way down, you notice the well-integrated self-catering complex among the trees (available all year round). The hotel, built in the 1960s, is classically, florally comfortable: fitted carpets, good bathrooms, many balconies. But come for remarkable-value food in the dining room where red-clothed tables carrying monogrammed china flow onto the terrace and out to that staggering seascape. Choose your lobster or trout from the great tank, relax and enjoy the professional yet friendly service of Madame Michel's excellent staff. The area is fascinating: from the tiny harbour of La Tour Fondue you can take a splendid wooden boat across to magical Porquerolles or the National Park on Port Cros, visit Babar's town of Hyères with its wide palm-lined avenues or walk round pretty Giens itself. Pure Provence.

Rooms: 41: 31 doubles/twins &
10 triples. Self-catering apartments.
Price: Doubles 345-680 Frs
(€ 52.59-103.67). Extra bed 150 Frs.
Breakfast: Buffet 65 Frs.
Meals: Lunch & dinner 130 Frs. Picnic
lunch 80 Frs.
Closed: November-early March.

From Hyères dir. Presqu'Ile de Giens/Ile de Porquerolles. At end of long straight road and several r'bouts, Giens signposted right (about 1.5km before La Tour Fondue). Hotel on left at beginning of village.

Le Manoir

Ile de Port Cros
83400 Hyères
Var

Tel: (0)4 94 05 90 52
Fax: (0)4 94 05 90 89

Pierre Buffet

Circles of bliss: tables beneath fragrant eucalyptus and canvas parasols; this magical dining terrace enfolded in the greenly wooded National Park of Port Cros; the island ringed by a translucid sea whence rises a light breeze. No cars, no mobiles, only one hotel. The lordly family who built the manor in 1835 sold it, and symbolically the title, to the Buffets in 1920. Your aristocratically affable host runs it as a classy country house bathed in peace and trust: the pool, hidden in a meadow a short walk away, has an honesty bar; you may borrow a motor dinghy to visit the rocky coves (and take a picnic hamper) — it is a privilege to experience this attitude from a gentler age. The interior smacks of just that: a large lobby crowded with 'cocktail' tables and old low chairs, proper, strait-laced dining room — neither used very often, of course — and some gloriously old-fashioned bathrooms (most have been modernised, nostalgics would say unfortunately). Rooms, however, are done in smart fabrics with fine, plain furniture and good lamps. Not just special — unique. *Half-board only.*

Rooms: 23: 5 doubles/twins,
15 triples/quadruples & 3 suites.
Price: 990-3080 Frs p.p., half-board only
(€ 150.92-469.54).
Breakfast: Included.
Meals: Lunch 265 Frs. Dinner included.
Closed: October 4-mid-April.

From Hyères, Le Lavandou or Cavalaire take steamer to Port Cros island. Le Manoir's mini-moke will greet you and take your luggage — you may prefer the 5-minute stroll to hotel.

La Grande Maison

Domaine de Campaux   **Tel:** (0)4 94 49 55 40
98 route du Dom   **Fax:** (0)4 94 49 55 23
83230 Bormes les Mimosas
Var

Laurence Lépinay

The approach to the Domaine, through vineyards and wineries, prepares you for the charm of the house itself. The friendly, 300 year-old façade is shaded by equally ancient plain trees and an ancient tractor collection. This very French atmosphere extends to the interior of the house, where crumbling plaster in the hall and missing *nid d'abeille* tiles might offend British notions of tidiness. Inside the bedrooms, however, the breath-taking scale of the rooms, their delightful country-style decoration and spotlessness would satisfy the sternest of Anglo-Saxon critics. Each suite or bedroom has its own charm and its own equally beautifully decorated bathroom (if the children have never bathed in a kidney-shaped bath, ask for *La Bleue*). Downstairs, there is a choice of three delightful places to eat — outside on the terrace under the trees, in the formal dining area of the salon, or at the oval oak table of the vast, comforting kitchen. If you are looking for a retreat to which you can take the children and still enjoy the luxuries of Provençal life, come.

Rooms: 5: 3 doubles & 2 suites.
Price: 500-800 Frs (€ 76.22-121.96).
Breakfast: 45 Frs.
Meals: Dinner 160 Frs.
Closed: January or February.

From edge of Cogolin take N98 (Toulon Nord) through village La Môle. After approximately 5km Domaine de Campaux signposted on right.

La Croisette

2 boulevard des Romarins
B.P. 27
83120 Sainte Maxime
Var

Tel: (0)4 94 96 17 75
Fax: (0)4 94 96 52 40
E-mail: contact@hotel-la-croisette.com
web: www.hotel-la-croisette.com

M & Mme Patrick Vastesaeger

The charming young Belgian owner of this pretty, pink and blue Riviera hotel threw in his job in the Middle East for a new life as hotelier. A year on, he is thoroughly enjoying his new role. His enthusiasm for the place is contagious: new curtains, pictures and cushions are planned for the bar-cum-wet-weather breakfast room, white edges round the shutters will lend a 'Venetian' air to the front. But much will remain, including the attractive old floor tiles inside and out. Cane furniture graces the cool country-style bedrooms, where the walls are painted white and the fabrics reflect the colours of the *Midi*. A few have balconies with views of the yacht-studded sea; others their own terraces. As rooms are not large, these are a plus. Bathrooms are sparklingly clean. Breakfast is nearly always served on the terrace, on white china at white-clothed tables under wide parasols. No swimming pool, no noise, no fuss — just a lovely quiet garden with a fountain that's prettily lit at night. A stone's throw from the beaches and the centre of Ste Maxime, La Croisette is an oasis of greenery and peace.

Rooms: 17: 14 doubles/twins & 3 triples.
Price: 490-980 Frs (€ 74.7-149.4). Extra bed 150 Frs.
Breakfast: 50 Frs.
Meals: Available locally.
Closed: November-end February

From Port Grimaud coast road dir. Ste. Maxime. At entrance to town follow blue sign to m'way A8; turn <u>left</u> at first r'bout and almost imm'ly left again to arrive in hotel's private road.

Le Logis du Guetteur

Place du Château
83460 Les Arcs sur Argens
Var

Tel: (0)4 94 99 51 10
Fax: (0)4 94 99 51 29
E-mail: le.logis.du.guetteur@wanadoo.fr

Max Callegari

We couldn't fault this place: 11th-century décor, 19th-century service, 21st-century comfort. A vertical rabbit warren of brilliantly renovated old stones round a cobbled courtyard at the top of a medieval village beneath the castle keep, the 'Watchman's House' has romance, intimacy, good taste and devastatingly attractive and welcoming owners. Below the courtyard, the summer dining room is one of the most beautiful, wide, stone-flagged terraces we know — flowers, wonderful food on perfectly-dressed tables and incomparable panoramic view. Along a 'secret' passage, the winter restaurant in the stone-walled, carefully-lit, medieval-furnished vaults is just as cosy as you'd wish in a snowstorm — and the food as delicious as in summer. Bedrooms are not large but classically chic, extremely comfortable and have perfect little bathrooms. The pool almost makes the cup overflow. Astoundingly, 35 years ago this beautiful little village was a heap of red-grey stones, about to be bulldozed to make way for skyline blocks, when just saved by a group of caring Parisians. Come and give thanks!

Rooms: 10: 8 doubles/twins & 2 suites.
Price: Doubles 550-650 Frs
(€ 83.85-99.09); suites 800 Frs.
Breakfast: 60 Frs.
Meals: Lunch & dinner 155-50 Frs.
Closed: Mid-January-February.

From A8 exit 36 Le Muy. N7 dir. Le Luc 3km; right into Les Arcs. Le Logis and Vieille Ville signposted at far end of Les Arcs. (Five minutes by taxi from Les Arcs railway station.)

Hôtel Le San Pedro

Avenue du Colonel Brooke Valescure
83700 Saint Raphaël
Var

Tel: (0)4 94 19 90 20
Fax: (0)4 94 19 90 21
E-mail: info@hotel-sanpedro.com
web: www.hotel-sanpedro.com

Alain Donat

Getting here requires faith in the local road maps, but the hotel will send navigation details if you ask. Hidden away in a residential district between Saint Tropez and Cannes, this hacienda-style dwelling was built 20 years ago by an unknown architect of aristocratic Spanish origin. Monsieur Donat runs his Armada ship with enthusiasm, constantly upgrading its image. The staff couldn't be more friendly and efficient. Wall tapestries and woven rugs in the vaulted reception room are comfortably, charmingly done, and there seems no better place to enjoy summer eating *à la carte* or from a choice of evening menus than on the pool-side terrace. If you're not on one of the nearby golf courses or out exploring the Côte d'Azur on a rented bike, you could treat yourself to a sauna at the hotel or nip down to the beach at Saint Raphael. But the secluded setting of parasol pines and gardens brimming with tropical vegetation is a tempting place to spend all day. The car park is locked at night, and the cheerful family spaniel abolishes anyone's stuffiness.

Rooms: 28: 27 doubles & 1 suite.
Price: Doubles 490-850 Frs
(€ 74.7-129.58); suite 750-1700 Frs.
Breakfast: Buffet 60 Frs.
Meals: Lunch & dinner 120-280 Frs.
Closed: 2 weeks in November.

A8 exit Fréjus/St Raphaël, through approx. 6 roundabouts then 2 roundabouts signposted Agay. At roundabout Le Rond Point des Anglais take avenue Colonel Brooke. Hotel 800m on right.

Centre International Marie Eugénie Milleret (CIMEM)

37 avenue du Commandant Bret
06400 Cannes
Alpes-Maritimes

Tel: (0)4 97 06 66 70
Fax: (0)4 97 06 66 76
E-mail: assomption.cannes@wanadoo.fr
web: perso.wanadoo.fr/cimem/

Sœur Anne-Pierre

A convent in Cannes! This unlikely establishment offers the best of two totally different worlds: the peace and quiet of a secluded retreat and, minutes away, the worldly sophistication of Cannes. It is run with the dedication and warmth one would expect from 'the best kind of nuns' who, without promoting their faith, simply allow it to inform everything they do. The rooms, once the cells of the 60-odd nuns who lived here before France became a secular state, are plain but perfectly comfortable, many with views over to the sea. The breakfast, which you can have in the somewhat austere dining room or take out to the rather more *sympathique* terrace, is both copious and delicious. Lunch (which can be a picnic if you order in advance) and dinner are unfussy, homely affairs, but at this price you could offer yourself the occasional blow-out in Cannes. This is a place for refreshment of the soul, whether you find it lying in the sun on the beach, under the trees in the garden, or in the chapel accompanied by Soeur Marie-Claude's soaring soprano at Mass.

Rooms: 65 doubles/ twins.
Price: Half-board 360-470 Frs (€ 54.88-76.22). Full-board 460-570 Frs.
Breakfast: Buffet included.
Meals: Lunch included in full-board (can be picnic). Dinner included in half-board.
Closed: Never.

A8 exit Cannes dir. Centre Ville. At top of Bd Carnot left (after lycée & opp. Hôtel Amarante) into Bd des Anglais. At bottom right into Bd de la République. Second T left Av du Commandant Bret. CIMEM 500 yds up hill on left.

Imperial Garoupe

770 chemin de la Garoupe
06600 Cap d'Antibes
Alpes-Maritimes

Tel: (0)4 92 93 31 61
Fax: (0)4 92 93 31 62
E-mail: hotel-imp@webstore.fr
web: www.imperial-garoupe.com

Gilbert Irondelle

A spot of luxury on the Cap d'Antibes — the sort of place where towels are laid out for guests by the (heated) pool and waiters regularly check on thirst levels. The building is low, modern, pink and white Italianate. Your car will be parked for you and any jangling nerves soothed by classical music playing in the entrance hall. M Irondelle is a highly professional hotelier and his multilingual staff reflect his standards. Chef Christophe Turquier has an impressive background too, having presided over smart hotel kitchens in Asia and the Caribbean as well as in his native France. Lunch by the pool, dine in the light-filled dining room with its elegant cane chairs, a touch of Provence and of North Africa in the décor. Bedrooms, with either terrace or balcony looking over the groomed Mediterranean garden, are large; classically comfortable with pale carpets, subtly floral fabrics and fabulous marbled bathrooms of the 'two basin, separate loo' variety. Wander down to the private beach or stretch your legs on the Cap's coastal path, pop into Antibes or Juan les Pins — very Riviera.

Rooms: 30: 26 doubles & 4 apartments.
Price: Doubles 1600-1990 Frs (€ 243.92-303.37); apartments 2600-3400 Frs.
Breakfast: 110 Frs.
Meals: Lunch à la carte; dinner 280 Frs.
Closed: November-March.

From Antibes or Juan les Pins, direction Plages de la Garoupe. Signposted.

La Grande Bastide

Route de la Colle
06570 Saint Paul de Vence
Alpes-Maritimes

Tel: (0)4 93 32 50 30
Fax: (0)4 93 32 50 59
E-mail: stpaullgb@lemel.fr
web: www.la-grande-bastide.com

Brigitte Laloum

This 18th-century *bastide* has been turned into a country-house hotel which provides immense luxury, plus the most fantastic views of one of the jewels of Provence: St Paul de Vence. This is not simply an enchantingly 'typical' village, it is also an important artistic centre, still frequented by musicians, writers and painters following in the footsteps of Matisse, Daudet and Pagnol. From the welcoming entrance ("here, you feel good in the space," said one visitor), along the 'outside corridors' which look out over the gardens, to the rooms, decorated in Provençal style — painted furniture, pretty cotton prints, pastel painted walls — you feel the personal touch of the owners. 'Cascades' are a promised addition to the already luxurious pool which is set in beautifully planted gardens and overlooked by the terrace where you can enjoy a breakfast worthy of the setting. You may just want yoghurt and honey, or perhaps the full 'English', with a sophisticated French spin, appeals. Whatever you choose, peace and quiet, a warm welcome and a truly painstaking attention to your comfort, is guaranteed.

Rooms: 11: 8 doubles/twins & 3 suites.
Price: Doubles 850-1200 Frs
(€ 129.58-182.94); suites 1000-1800 Frs.
Breakfast: 70 Frs.
Meals: Informal lunch by the pool.
Closed: November 22-December 26 &
January 5-March 15.

From A8 exit 47 dir. Cagnes sur Mer, St. Paul de Vence. After La Colle sur Loup, hotel is signposted on left.

Hôtel Diana

Avenue des Poilus
06140 Vence
Alpes-Maritimes

Tel: (0)4 93 58 28 56
Fax: (0)4 93 24 64 06

J.J. Baly

A modern building of no great architectural interest but in a quiet street close to the old centre of Vence and with friendly and helpful staff. M Baly has a passion for contemporary art and is always keen to talk to other enthusiasts. With the Matisse Chapel and the Fondation Maeght so close by, not to mention the wider region's treasures, the area attracts them. The bedrooms are on five floors — those with kitchenettes tend to be booked early — and are perfectly, comfortably functional. Beds and lighting are good and there's space both to sit in an armchair and to write at the desk. Furniture is mostly repro and modern and windows are double-glazed both on the street and the courtyard side. You can breakfast in your room, in the pleasant small garden or on small wooden tables indoors — there's no fuss and the presentation is simple and attractive in white and blue. This is definitely good value for the area which should be visited out of season if possible. There is some wonderful countryside nearby. *Only for well behaved children.*

Rooms: 18: 10 doubles & 8 triples.
Price: 430-450 Frs (€ 65.55-68.6).
Breakfast: 40 Frs.
Meals: Picnic lunch 40 Frs. Snacks also available.
Closed: January.

From A8 exit Cagnes sur Mer dir. St. Paul de Vence or Vence, D36 or D336. In Vence direction centre, take second left. Hotel signposted just before entering old part of town.

Hôtel Windsor

11 rue Dalpozzo
06000 Nice
Alpes-Maritimes

Tel: (0)4 93 88 59 35
Fax: (0)4 93 88 94 57
E-mail: windsor@webstore.fr
web: www.webstore.fr/windsor

Bernard Redolfi-Strizzot

Another 1930s Riviera hotel with pool in palm grove and exotic birds in cages? All that... and much more. Bernard Redolfi has brought the '30s into the '90s by asking 20 contemporary artists to do a room each. 20 gifts of wit, provocation, flight of fancy, minimalist sobriety — and artistic creation: Joan Mas's *Cage à Mouches*, Jean le Gac's blue figures, cosmopolitan Ben's writing on the walls. The other rooms are far from plain, with Antoine Beaudoin's superb frescoes of Venice, Egypt, India — all our travel myths — and Tintin. Plain white beds have contrasting cushions or quilts; furniture is minimal and interesting; delightful little bathrooms, some directly off the room, are all individually treated. All is clear, pale colours, except in the richly exotic public areas: the much-travelled owners chose their exquisitely elaborate Chinese mandarin's bed for the bar, panelling and colourful plasterwork for the restaurant, a fine wire sculpture, stone and bamboo for the hall. Light filters gently through onto warmly smiling staff. And there's a stunning Turkish bath centre. Unbeatable. *No-smoking in some rooms.*

Rooms: 57 doubles/twins.
Price: Doubles 550-750 Frs (€ 83.85-114.34). Extra bed 100 Frs.
Breakfast: 50 Frs.
Meals: Lunch & dinner à la carte 150-250 Frs.
Closed: Never. Restaurant closed Saturday lunchtimes & Sundays.

In centre of Nice. A10 exit Promenade des Anglais. Left at museum on Rue Meyerbeer. Right on Rue de France and first left Rue Dalpozzo.

Hôtel Les Deux Frères

Place des Deux Frères
Roquebrune
06190 Cap Martin
Alpes-Maritimes

Tel: (0)4 93 28 99 00
Fax: (0)4 93 28 99 10
E-mail: 2freres@webstore.fr

Willem Bonnestroo

The oriental blue and gold ceiling of *1001 Nuits* will possibly lull you into one of the best night's sleep you've ever dreamed of. Or you may prefer the contrast of a vivid lime green decor, or the nautical hues of *Marine*. Fully renovated at the end of last year, most rooms are fairly small but have great views of the coastline, mountainside or the old village square. You'll get a smiling welcome from the young Dutch owner who combines Provençal comfort with an exotic flavour, even down to the seven languages he speaks and his restaurant's innovative fare. Long since abandoning suit and tie for less formal wear, Willem is full of ideas for catering to individual tastes, and children simply adore him! After parking in the village, you can either take advantage of the gaily-coloured 'taxi-train' which takes guests and luggage up and down the hill, or opt for the short, fairly steep path leading up to the hotel. Excellent value for money for the area, the place definitely has a lively air to it while remaining practical and professionally run. Ideal for the young at heart.

Rooms: 10 doubles/twins.
Price: 425-595 Frs (€ 64.79-90.71).
Breakfast: 60 Frs.
Meals: Lunch & dinner 120-245 Frs.
Closed: Never.

A10 exit 57 dir. Menton then Roquebrune. Left at Roquebrune/Vieux Village. Stop at municipal car park and walk 50m. Hotel electric train for clients and luggage.

Quick Reference Index

Quick Reference Index

Quick Reference Index

BIKE BIKE

These places wither are good bases
for cycling and may rent/lend bikes
too.

Quick Reference Index

SWIMMING POOL SWIM

These places have swimming pools in their grounds.

Additional Photo credits

Château de la Roque - J-B. Cauvin
Mas de l'Oulivié - G.M. Raget
Hôtel du Dragon - Nicolas Faur
Bon Labourer - P. Joly

French words and expressions

French words and expressions used in this book:

l'amuse-bouche - a 'little something' to nibble on while ordering a meal.

armoire à glace - a wardrobe with more or less elaborate regional-style carving and often a mirrored front. *Armoire à glace* is also used to describe a beefy rugby player.

la bastide - a stronghold, a small fortified village or, in Provence, it can simply be another word for farmhouse or mas (see below).

la Belle Epoque - 1901-1910.

la bergerie - a barn for sheep.

jouer aux boules, la pétanque - a "bowling" game played with metal balls on a dirt surface.

le chambre d'hôtes - a bed & breakfast.

le château - a mansion or stately home built for aristocrats between the 16th and 19th centuries.

château fort - a castle with defences and fortifications.

le chef de gare - station master.

la compôte - stewed fruit.

le confit - parts of goose or duck preserved in their own fat, then fried.

la Côte Sauvage - "Wild Coast" in Brittany.

les couchettes - beds on a train, sometimes bunkbeds.

la cour, la cour d'honneur - courtyard, a grand courtyard.

le cuir de Cordoue - tooled leather wallpaper from Cordoba, Spain.

déguster - to taste, sample or savour.

la dégustation - a tasting of wine, oysters, cheese NOT necessarily free.

la demi-lune - a decorative half or full-moon shaped canopy over a bed.

les deux chevaux - A type of car (2CV) with 2 fiscal horses in its engine.

Directoire (armchairs) - 1795-1799, Greek and Roman influences.

en plein air - outside.

l' Exposition Universelle - Universal Exhibition in Paris in 1890.

extra-muros - outside the walls (of a town or city).

la fougace - a flat plait-shaped bread sometimes studded with pieces of bacon, olives or nuts.

le grand hôtel de campagne - large country hotel.

le magret de canard en croûte - duck breast in a pastry shell.

la Mairie and l'Hôtel de Ville - town and city hall respectively. They are useful landmarks, easy to find in town centres.

la maison de maître (country) and *la maison bourgoise* (town) - both big, comfortable houses standing in quite, large grounds and built for well-to-do

French words and expressions

members of the liberal professions, captains of industry, trade, etc.

le manoir - manor house.

le Marais - marsh or marshland. *Marais Poitevin* near La Rochelle, with its miles of little waterways to be explored by boat. The 4th arrondissement of Paris, *Le Marais*, once a miserable, unhealthy low-lying slum and now entirely gentrified.

le mas Provençal - country house, usually long and low with old stone walls, a pan-tiled roof and painted shutters.

le métier - job or trade (also means loom).

le Midi - synonym of South; by extension, southern France.

la mille-feuille - layers of thin pastry separated by a butter cream, sprinkled with powdered sugar; anything baked in layers of flaky pastry.

le Mistral - the nerve-jangling wind that blows down the Rhône Valley.

le nid d'abeille - honeycomb.

l'œil de bœuf - round window.

le petit grain de folie - light touch of madness.

les petit salons feutrés - small cosy rooms.

piqué - textured cotton.

le pochoir - a method of decorative painting using stencils.

le potager - kitchen garden, whence the French word for everyday vegetable soup *le potage*.

pré salé - adjective used for lamb grazed on salted marshes.

le prix fixe - a two, three or four course meal at a set price.

Soléidado - Provençal patterned textiles.

le sommelier - the waiter in charge of your wine order.

son et lumière - an after dark, outdoor spectacle with lights and music.

la table d'hôtes - a three-course dinner with the owners of the house or château usually served at a long communal table.

du terroir - fashionabe term meaning rural, local, authentic; as coming from the untainted soil in a specific area, e.g. wines (*vin du terroir*), cheeses, foodstuffs, even people and political movements.

la thalassothérapie - a much in vogue health spa technique using sea water as the main ingredient.

la toile de Jouy - classic French fabrics and wallpapers depicting romantic scenes.

soigné - understated elegance.

le zinc - traditional surface for bar counter-tops.

False friends

A Few (*Faux Amis*) False Friends

Biologique (Bio) & Organique - Vegetables called 'organic' in English are known as *de culture biologique* in French, *bio* for short. If you talk about *organique* people will imagine you have trouble with your organs.

Biscuit & Gâteau - Biscuit literally means 'twice cooked' and properly applies to dehydrated army rations or the base for some sticky puddings. The usual words for sweet or savoury biscuits are *gâteaux secs* or *petits gâteaux*, also *gâteaux d'apéritif.*

Tourte - is the closest the French have to 'pie', i.e. with pastry above and below.

Tarte - is an open tart or flan.

Tartine & baguette - (usually) sliced in half and buttered, i.e. breakfast food.

Scotch - means adhesive tape or whisky - the context should help.

Soda - is a non-alcoholic, probably sweet, fizzy drink of some kind. If you want soda water you should ask for *eau gazeuse.*

Mousse - froth, foam, lather (beer, sea, soap) or foam rubber or moss.

Pomme de pin - is fircone. Pineapple is *ananas. Pamplemousse* is grapefruit.

Raisin - Is a fresh grape or grapes. Steinbeck's book is called *Les Raisins de la Colère*. Dried fruit is called: *Raisins de Corinthe* (currants - see the derivation?); ***Raisins de Smyrne*** (sultanas); *Raisins secs* (raisins!).

Grappe - is a bunch of grapes - *une grappe de raisins.*

Prune - is a fresh plum. A prune is *pruneau.*

Myrtille - is bilberry - they grow wild and delicious on the hills of southern France and make for a wonderful tart. Myrtle is *myrte.*

Verger - An orchard: many a greengrocer's shop is called *Aux Fruits du Verger.*

Marmelade - or **compote** means stewed fruit. Marmalade is called *confiture d'oranges amères.*

Cheminée - is French for fireplace, flue or chimney stack (the flue is also called *le conduit de cheminée*). *Un feu dans la cheminée* does not mean you need to call the fire brigade but *un feu de cheminée* does.

Une Commode - is a chest of drawers. A commode is *une chaise percée.*

Grange - simply means barn, not a big country house.

Actuel, Actuellement - A great pitfall this one - it means current, present - currently, presently, NOW and not As a Matter of Fact.

Eventuel - Eventuellement - Possible - should the occasion arise.

More tips for travel in France

Public Holidays

Be aware of public holidays; many national museums and galleries close on Tuesdays, others close on Mondays (e.g. Monet's garden in Giverny) as do many country restaurants, and opening times may be different on the following days:

New Year's Day (1 January)	**Bastille Day** (14 July)
May Day (1 May)	**Assumption** (15 August)
Liberation 1945 (8 May)	**All Saints** (1 November)
Armistice 1918 (11 November)	**Ascension** 1 June 24 May 9 May

Some moveable feasts	2000	2001	2002
Easter	23 April	5 April	31 March
Pentecost (Whit Sunday)	23 May	11 June	3 June

Beware also of the mass exodus over public holiday weekends and school holidays, both the first day - outward journey - and the last - return journey.

Roads and driving

Current speed limits are: Motorways 130 kph (80 mph), RN National trunk roads 110 kph (68 mph), other open roads 90 kph (56 mph), in towns 50 kph (30 mph). The road police are very active and can demand on-the-spot payment of fines.

One soon gets used to driving on the right but complacency leads to trouble; take special care coming out of car parks, private drives, narrow one-lane roads and coming onto roundabouts.

Many roads coming from the right still have priority - and drivers take it, come what may, so expect it always!

Directions

The French drive towards a destination and use road numbers far less than we do. Thus, to find your way *à la française,* know the general direction you want to go, i.e. the towns your route goes through, and when you see the signs marked *Autres Directions* or *Toutes Directions,* just follow towards the place name you're heading for or through - and have faith! Forget road numbers, they probably aren't marked anyway your heading.

Cultural confusions

En suite

En suite is not used in France to describe bathrooms off the bedroom and to do so can lead to terrible confusions. (To be clear, ask for a room *avec salle de bains et w.c.*). One booking for two 'en suites', became a disaster when the owners reserved a suite for these guests: the two adult couples were less than gruntled at having to fit into a double room leading to a 'children's' twin room leading to a shared bathroom. *Une suite* or *un appartement* means a large bedroom with a sitting area which is sometimes separate.

Greetings

We drop far more easily into first-name terms than the French. This reluctance on their part is not a sign of coldness, it's simply an Old National Habit, to be respected, we feel, like any other tribal ritual.
So it's advisable to wait for the signal from them as to when you have achieved more intimate status.

The French do not say *'Bonjour Madame Jones'* - this is considered rather familiar. They just say *'Bonjour Madame'* - which makes it easy to be lazy about remembering people's names.

At Table

(Don't be alarmed by all the etiquette below; making mistakes can be as much fun as getting it right!) A well-bred English lady would never dream of 'dunking' her croissant, toast or teacake in her cup - it is perfectly acceptable behaviour in French society.

Lunch/Dinner

1. Equipment

Glasses are centred at the top of the plate, not to the right, and you are expected to put your glass/glasses down in the same place each time and not allow them to wander back and forth, as the whim takes you.

Cutlery is laid concave face upwards in 'Anglo-Saxon' countries; in France it is proper to lay forks and spoons convex face upwards (crests are engraved accordingly). Do try and hold back your instinctive need to turn them over!

To the right of your plate, at the tip of the knife, you may find a knife-rest. This serves two purposes: to lay your knife on when you are not using it, rather than leaving it in your plate; to lay your knife AND fork on (points downwards) if you are asked to *'garder vos couverts'* (keep your knife and fork) while the plates are changed - e.g. between starter and main dish.

Cultural confusions

2. Food

Cheese comes BEFORE pudding in France - that's the way they do it!
The proper order is -

Entrée — starter rather than main dish à la Mrs Beeton

Plat principal — main dish of meat and vegetable(s)

Salade — usually just green leaves

Fromage — can be just one perfect Camembert or a vast tray with a dozen cheeses to choose from; in very smart places, there will be a second board for goat's cheese; the middle-of-the-road place has all cheeses on one board with one knife for cow and ewe and another for goat.

Dessert — ranging from plain fresh fruit to superbly complicated creamy structures.

Menus

The latest fashion is to offer a reasonably priced meal with a choice between either the main dish and dessert or the starter and the main dish. The only problem with this thrifty method is that it becomes a bit awkward if some start eating their first course before others who ordered a main course and dessert.

Cutting cheese

Cut a round cheese as you would cut a round cake - in triangular segments. When a ready-cut segment such as a piece of Brie is presented, the rule is to 'preserve the point', i.e. do not cut it straight across but take an angle which removes the existing point but makes another one. When slicing Roquefort take a bit of the crust; do not cut off the end of the wedge, everyone should get a bit of that.

The Company's History

In 1994, Alastair Sawday moved into publishing guides after ten years of running his own travel company, Alastair Sawday's Tours. This move was a direct result of personal frustration at the robotic nature of the write-ups in guides then on the market - their pre-occupation with trouser presses, coat hangers and 'all mod cons'. In rejecting what he saw as the 'clip-board' mentality, his start-up brief was straightforward: to select only those places to stay that were 'special'; and then to present the information in a way that was accessible, honest and, above all, fun to read.

"We are interested in meeting people, rather than counting appliances," explained Alastair Sawday, "for us, the warmth of welcome counts for more than gadgets in rooms, authentic atmosphere and charm more than fitness suites and jacuzzis. We aim to be selective on the basis of those indefinable qualities that make for a real holiday. You won't find sanitised hotel chains listed in our guides - commercial uniformity is not special...!"

The Books:

If you know Alastair Sawday's Guides, you will appreciate that the write-ups are vivid and honest - they can be trusted. Whether a place is grand or simple, perfect or flawed, it is included only if there is something special about it. These books offer a seductive range of places to stay. Colour photographs and maps, clear directions, easy-to-use symbols, including singing for wheelchair access, make the choosing easy, make it fun.

The Readers:

"... the most entertaining holiday for years; the most enchanting places."
"The book was a godsend and very easy to use."
"The best guide of its kind. It has opened a new world to us."

So now we have published guides to France, Italy, Ireland, Spain, Portugal and Britain. The leitmotif is always the same: we want to be trusted and to continue to make the most marvellous selections for people who, like us, are looking for a bit more LIFE in their travelling.

Alastair Sawday
Special Places to Stay Series

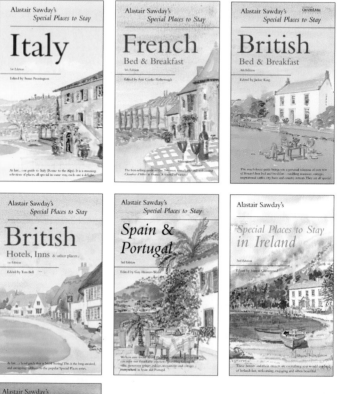

Join our Travel Club if you really want to get the best out of us!

Tel: 0117 929 9921 Fax: 0117 925 4712
www.sawdays.co.uk

Order Form UK

All these books are available in major bookshops or you may order them direct. Post and packaging are FREE.

	Price	No. copies
Special Places to Stay: **British Bed & Breakfast**		
Edition 4	£12.95	
Special Places to Stay: **British Hotels, Inns** and other places		
Edition 1	£10.95	
Special Places to Stay: **French Bed & Breakfast**		
Edition 5	£13.95	
Special Places to Stay: **French Hotels, Inns and Other Places**		
Edition 1	£11.95	
Special Places to Stay: **Paris Hotels**		
Edition 2	£8.95	
Special Places to Stay in Ireland		
Edition 2	£10.95	
Special Places to Stay in Spain & Portugal		
Edition 3	£11.95	
Special Places: **Italy**		
Edition 1	£9.95	

Please make cheques payable to: Alastair Sawday Publishing

Total [   ]

Please send cheques to: Alastair Sawday Publishing, 44 Ambra Vale East, Bristol BS8 4RE. **For credit card orders call 0117 929 9921 or order directly from our website www.sawdays.co.uk**

Name:

Address:

Postcode:

Tel: Fax:

If you do not wish to receive mail from other companies, please tick the box ❏

FH1

Order Form USA

All these books are available at your local bookstore, or you may order direct. Allow two to three weeks for delivery.

	Price	No. copies
***Special Places to Stay:* British Bed & Breakfast**		
Edition 4	$19.95	
***Special Places to Stay:* British Hotels, Inns** and other places		
Edition 1	$14.95	
***Special Places to Stay:* French Bed & Breakfast**		
Edition 5	$19.95	
***Special Places to Stay:* Paris Hotels**		
Edition 2	$14.95	
Special Places to Stay in Ireland		
Edition 2	$19.95	
Special Places to Stay in Spain & Portugal		
Edition 3	$14.95	
***Special Places to Stay:* Italy**		
Edition 1	$14.95	

Shipping in the continental USA: $3.95 for one book, $4.95 for two books, $5.95 for three or more books. Outside continental USA, call (800) 243-0495 for prices. For delivery to AK, CA, CO, CT, FL, GA, IL, IN, KS, MI, MN, MO, NE, NM, NC, OK, SC, TN, TX, VA, and WA, please add appropriate sales tax

Please make checks payable to: The Globe Pequot Press   **Total**

To order by phone with MasterCard or Visa: (800) 243-0495. 9 a.m. to 5 p.m. EST; by fax: (800) 820-2329, 24 hours; through our Website: www.globe-pequot.com; or by mail: The Globe Pequot Press, P.O. Box 480, Guilford, CT 06437.

Name: _____ Date: _____

Address: _____

Town: _____

State: _____ Zip code: _____

Tel: _____ Fax: _____

FH1

Bilingual booking form

A:

To: (hotel name)

Date:

Madame, Monsieur

Veuillez faire la réservation suivante au nome de:
Please make the following booking for (name):

Pour	*nuit(s)*	*Arriant le:*	*jour*	*mois*	*année*
For	night(s)	Arriving:	day	month	year
		Partant le:	*jour*	*mois*	*année*
		Leaving:	day	month	year

Si possible, nous aimerions   *chambres/suites/appartements,*
pour   *personnes disposées comme suit:*
We would like _____ room(s)/suite(s)/apartment(s)
for _____ people arranged as follows:

grand lit	*lits jumeaux*	*lit simple*
Double bed	Twin beds	Single bed

Nous aimerions également réserver le diner pour   *personnes le*
We would also like to book dinner for _____ people on _____ (date)

Veuillez nous envoyer la confirmation a l'adresse ci-dessous ainsi qu'une
brochure et un plan d'accès:
Please send confirmation to the following address together with a brochure
and map:

Name: Name:

Adresse: Address:

                    Pays: Country:

Fax:

E-mail:

FH1

Report Form

Comments on existing entries and new discoveries.

If you have any comments on entries in this guide, please let us have them. If you have a favourite house, hotel or inn or a new discovery, please let us know about it.

Report on:

Entry no: _____ Edition: _____

New Recommendation: _____

Date: _____

Name of hotel/B&B: _____

Address: _____

_____

_____ Postcode: _____

Tel: _____

My reasons are: _____

_____

_____

_____

_____

_____

_____

_____

_____

_____

_____

_____

_____

_____

FH1

Report Form

continued..

_____

_____

_____

_____

_____

_____

_____

_____

_____

_____

_____

_____

_____

_____

_____

My name and address:

Name: _____

Address: _____

_____ Postcode: _____

Tel: _____

Please send the completed form to:

Alastair Sawday Publishing, 44 Ambra Vale East, Bristol BS8 4RE, UK

Thank you so much for your help!

FH1

Index of Names

Index of Places